AN A–Z OF BEATRIX POTTER

AN A–Z OF BEATRIX POTTER

Penny Bradshaw

BLOOMSBURY ACADEMIC
LONDON • NEW YORK • OXFORD • NEW DELHI • SYDNEY

BLOOMSBURY ACADEMIC

Bloomsbury Publishing Plc, 50 Bedford Square, London, WC1B 3DP, UK
Bloomsbury Publishing Inc, 1359 Broadway, New York, NY 10018, USA
Bloomsbury Publishing Ireland, 29 Earlsfort Terrace, Dublin 2, D02 AY28, Ireland

BLOOMSBURY, BLOOMSBURY ACADEMIC and the Diana logo
are trademarks of Bloomsbury Publishing Plc

First published in Great Britain 2026

Copyright © Penny Bradshaw, 2026

Penny Bradshaw has asserted her right under the Copyright,
Designs and Patents Act, 1988, to be identified as Author of this work.

For legal purposes the Acknowledgements on p. ix constitute
an extension of this copyright page.

Cover design: Rebecca Heselton
Illustration © Rebecca Heselton

All rights reserved. No part of this publication may be: i) reproduced or transmitted in any form, electronic or mechanical, including photocopying, recording or by means of any information storage or retrieval system without prior permission in writing from the publishers; or ii) used or reproduced in any way for the training, development or operation of artificial intelligence (AI) technologies, including generative AI technologies. The rights holders expressly reserve this publication from the text and data mining exception as per Article 4(3) of the Digital Single Market Directive (EU) 2019/790.

Bloomsbury Publishing Plc does not have any control over, or responsibility for, any third-party websites referred to or in this book. All internet addresses given in this book were correct at the time of going to press. The author and publisher regret any inconvenience caused if addresses have changed or sites have ceased to exist, but can accept no responsibility for any such changes.

A catalogue record for this book is available from the British Library.
A catalog record for this book is available from the Library of Congress.

ISBN: HB: 978-1-3504-5335-7
PB: 978-1-3504-5334-0
ePDF: 978-1-3504-5336-4
eBook: 978-1-3504-5337-1

Typeset by Integra Software Services Pvt. Ltd.
Printed and bound in Great Britain

For product safety related questions contact productsafety@bloomsbury.com.

To find out more about our authors and books visit www.bloomsbury.com
and sign up for our newsletters.

CONTENTS

List of Illustrations	vii
Acknowledgements	ix
Texts and Abbreviations	x
Introduction	1
A is for Animal	7
B is for Beatrix	15
C is for Clothes	23
D is for Dancing	32
E is for Eating	40
F is for Fairy	48
G is for Ginnett's circus	54
H is for *Horn Book*	61
I is for Illness	68
J is for Journal	75
K is for Key	83
L is for Lake District	88
M is for Myriads of fairy fungi	95
N is for National Trust	103
O is for Over the hills and far away	112
P is for Peter Rabbit	120
Q is for Queerly	128
R is for Rabbit-tobacco	136
S is for Seasons	145
T is for Trees	152
U is for Uncanny	159

Contents

V is for Violence	166
W is for War	173
X is for Xarifa	179
Y is for Yellow	186
Z is for Zoo	193
Works Cited	201
Index	209

ILLUSTRATIONS

1 Beatrix Potter, drawing of a Common Bat/Pipistrelle, Bush Hall, Herts (dated 26 October 1884). Reproduced with permission of The Armitt Trust 9
2 Beatrix Potter, self-portrait sketch from autograph letter: London, to 'my dear Marjory' (Moore) 13 March 1900 (p. 2). Reproduced with permission of The Morgan Library & Museum. MA 2009.12. Gift of Colonel David McC. McKell, 1959 19
3 Illustration from *The Tailor of Gloucester* by Beatrix Potter © Frederick Warne & Co. Ltd., 1903, 2002 25
4 Head and shoulders close-up, from a photograph of 'Beatrix and her mother with relations and friends at Holehird' © 2024, The Beatrix Potter Society, https://beatrixpottersociety.org.uk/ 30
5 Illustration from *The Tale of Pigling Bland* by Beatrix Potter © Frederick Warne & Co. Ltd., 1913, 2002 33
6 Beatrix Potter's animal characters dancing round the Christmas tree (Christmas card design). Reproduced courtesy of Frederick Warne & Co. Ltd. 38
7 Watercolour by Beatrix Potter of *Cantharellus Umbonata*, collected at Dunkeld (19 November 1893). Reproduced with permission of The Armitt Trust 98
8 *Uncle Remus* illustration ('Brother Rabbit rescues Brother Terrapin') by Beatrix Potter dated 1895 © The Linder Collection, 1895, 2018 138
9 Illustration from *The Tale of Mr. Jeremy Fisher* by Beatrix Potter © Frederick Warne & Co. Ltd., 1906, 2002 161
10 Illustration from *The Tale of Johnny Town-Mouse* by Beatrix Potter © Frederick Warne & Co. Ltd., 1918, 2002 175
11 Photograph (taken by Rupert Potter) of Beatrix at the age of nineteen, with her pet mouse Xarifa. Lloyd E. Cotsen Collection of Potter Family Photographs, COTSEN5, Cotsen Children's Library, Department of Special Collections, Princeton University Library 183

Illustrations

12 Beatrix Potter, self-portrait sketches from autograph letter: London, to Noel Moore, 8 March 1895 (p. 4). Reproduced with permission of The Morgan Library & Museum. MA 2009.3. Gift of Colonel David McC. McKell, 1959   194

ACKNOWLEDGEMENTS

Much of the preliminary thinking about Beatrix Potter's work which underpins this book took place in seminars with students at the University of Cumbria over a period of more than twenty years, and I am grateful to all of the students with whom I have shared so many enriching conversations.

I would like to thank my friend and former colleague, Mike Greaney, whose own recent publication on Jane Austen inspired the A–Z format here, for his assistance during the project's early stages. I am very grateful also to both The Beatrix Potter Society and The Armitt Library & Museum for help offered at various points of the research process, and for allowing me to use images from their respective collections free of charge.

This project, like others before it, would not have come to fruition without my father's unwavering encouragement and support. As always, my deepest gratitude is to him, for once again 'holding my coat' while the book was being researched and written. My (now grown-up) sons also contributed to a reawakened love of Potter's work, brought about by their arrival in the world and by happy re-readings at their bedside. This book is dedicated to my wonderful family, with love.

TEXTS AND ABBREVIATIONS

Quotations from Potter's twenty-three tales, stories and nursery rhymes published as little books by Warne are taken from the 2002 edition in each case:

PR = *The Tale of Peter Rabbit* [1902]
TG = *The Tailor of Gloucester* [1903]
SN = *The Tale of Squirrel Nutkin* [1903]
BB = *The Tale of Benjamin Bunny* [1904]
TBM = *The Tale of Two Bad Mice* [1904]
TW = *The Tale of Mrs. Tiggy-Winkle* [1905]
PP = *The Tale of the Pie and the Patty-Pan* [1905]
FBR = *The Story of a Fierce Bad Rabbit* [1906]
M = *The Story of Miss Moppet* [1906]
JF = *The Tale of Mr. Jeremy Fisher* [1906]
TK = *The Tale of Tom Kitten* [1907]
JPD = *The Tale of Jemima Puddle-Duck* [1908]
SW = *The Tale of Samuel Whiskers* [1908]
FB = *The Tale of the Flopsy Bunnies* [1909]
GP = *The Tale of Ginger and Pickles* [1909]
TM = *The Tale of Mrs. Tittlemouse* [1910]
TT = *The Tale of Timmy Tiptoes* [1911]
T = *The Tale of Mr. Tod* [1912]
PB = *The Tale of Pigling Bland* [1913]
AD = *Appley Dapply's Nursery Rhymes* [1917]
JTM = *The Tale of Johnny Town-Mouse* [1918]
CP = *Cecily Parsley's Nursery Rhymes* [1922]
LPR = *The Tale of Little Pig Robinson* [1930]

The abbreviated initial form will be used to present page numbers in parenthesis. When the text is discussed, the title will be used but with '*The Tale of*' or '*The Story of*' omitted.

Other published books by Potter

PRA = *Peter Rabbit's Almanac for 1929*. Warne, 1929.
SA = *Sister Anne*. David McKay, 1932.
FC = *The Fairy Caravan* [1929]. Penguin, 2016.

Other works unpublished during Potter's lifetime

H = *A History of the Writings of Beatrix Potter, including unpublished work*, by Leslie Linder. Warne, 1971.
WBW = *Wag-by-Wall* [1944]. Warne, 1987.

Letters and other private writings

A = *Beatrix Potter's Americans: Selected Letters*, ed. Jane Crowell Morse. Horn Book, Inc., 1982.
J = *The Journal of Beatrix Potter 1881-1897*, ed. Leslie Linder. Warne, 1989.
L = *Beatrix Potter's Letters*, selected and introduced by Judy Taylor. Warne, 2001.
LC = *Letters to Children from Beatrix Potter*, collected and introduced by Judy Taylor. Warne, 2002.

Artwork (other than in the published books or where stated)

Art = *The Art of Beatrix Potter*, ed. Enid and Leslie Linder. Warne, 1972.

INTRODUCTION

The entry for **Beatrix** Potter (1866–1943) in the most recent edition of *The Oxford Companion to Children's Literature* is one of the longest single author entries in the book (Hahn 2015: 468–71), and Potter has been described as 'probably the single best-known writer for children in English (with the possible exception of J. K. Rowling)', author of the 'Harry Potter' books (Kutzer 2003: 33). As with Rowling, Potter's extraordinary success as a writer of books for children began almost immediately, following Warne's publication of **Peter Rabbit** in 1902. On the run up to the Second World **War**, Potter was herself describing 'Astronomical' sales figures for her little books, with more than 150,0000 being sold the previous year (*A*: 96). Potter's cultural influence is now vast and impossible to track, not least because it continues to grow globally via multiplications of her work through various channels and reworkings.

Whilst Potter's status as the creator of a set of beloved **animal** characters, who have appeared on British postage stamps and fifty pence coins as well as across multiple other mediums, is very well established, her reputation as a serious and influential writer tends to be acknowledged with more reluctance. An essay by the well-known children's literature critic, Humphrey Carpenter, records – with some incredulity – evidence of Potter's influence on twentieth-century writers. The essay opens with Carpenter's surprise at encountering a casual reference to Potter's work in a sonnet by the English poet, Blake Morrison, which was published in the *Times Literary Supplement* in April 1987. In the poem Morrison compares a couple of men, 'holed up in some bar', deep 'in their cups', to 'Chippy Hackee' and 'little Timmy Tiptoes hiding from their wives' (Carpenter 1989: 271). Carpenter observes that it is a 'bit of a jolt to find Beatrix Potter cited in such a context', going on to suggest that there would be no such surprise in finding a reference to Lewis Carroll since 'Carroll is respectable as a literary influence' (1989: 271). Despite Carpenter's apparent reluctance to see Potter herself in these terms and his assertion that chroniclers 'of the twentieth-century literary imagination are not likely to put Beatrix Potter on the map as a source for poets and novelists' (1989: 272), he goes on to point to some important writers who apparently found nothing problematic in making such an acknowledgement. These include the novelist Grahame Greene, who wrote that he had never lost his 'admiration for her books' and 'often reread her' (Greene [1971] 1999: 39), and the poet, W. H. Auden, who names Potter as a writer he admired in his 'Letter to Lord Byron' (1936):

> You must ask me who
> Have written just as I'd have liked to do.
> I stop and listen and the names I hear
> Are those of Firbank, Potter, Carroll, Lear.
>
> (Auden and MacNeice 1936: 202)

Such acknowledgements should be less surprising than they appear to be to Carpenter, since Potter took her own writing very seriously indeed, crafting and recrafting her words with great care. In one account of her writing process she said that her approach was to first 'scribble', then 'cut out, and write it again and again', adding that she would re-read the unrevised version of the Bible and the Old Testament if she felt that her 'style' wanted 'chastening' (*A*: 209). Throughout her life, Potter paid close attention to the rhythms and patterns of language, and to the possibility and power of words. It is these words which are the primary focus of this study.

Amongst the wealth of books written about Potter, two publications in particular represent important forerunners to my own broadly literary-critical approach to her work. One is *Beatrix Potter* (1986) by Ruth K. MacDonald, published as part of Twayne's English Authors series and the first book-length critical study of Potter which set out to analyse her 'books as literature' (Preface). A second crucial text in this respect is Daphne Kutzer's *Beatrix Potter: Writing in Code* (2003), which offers a detailed and contextualized analysis of Potter's writing in relation to 'the social and political events at the time' (2).

Whilst these two monographs constitute important milestones in Potter scholarship, attention in both cases is directed towards Potter's best-known *Tales*. MacDonald focuses exclusively on Potter's twenty-three little books and, though Kutzer does touch on Potter's later work, these texts are read as being outside the main Potter 'canon' and as constituting merely a 'coda' to her career (2003: 161, 153). Here, however, equal and due attention is given to Potter's wider body of writing, which is available in the public domain thanks to the impressive archival and editorial work of key Potter scholars

Introduction

such as Leslie Linder, Judy Taylor and Jane Crowell Morse. This more extensive oeuvre includes the **journal** Potter kept from 1881 to 1897, the two longer books she published in America in 1929 and 1932 respectively, as well as essays, articles, picture letters and stories which remained unpublished in her lifetime.

In moving between these various texts in relation to particular themes and topics, a much richer sense of Potter the writer emerges. Whilst she was first and foremost a children's author, Potter was also a writer in a broader sense, whose impulse to engage with the world through the written word began in her teens and remained with her to the end of her life. In reading across Potter's extensive body of writing in this way, we encounter her changing interests and a variety of styles but also, perhaps more importantly, points of continuity and coherent concerns, the most significant being her deep and abiding interest in the natural world.

As well as engaging with Potter's wider body of writing, what also makes the approach taken here unusual is the book's A–Z format. Analysis of Potter's work is arranged via twenty-six short, alphabetically ordered and interlinked essays. Each chapter takes as its starting point a word or phrase from Potter's published work or private writings. These words and phrases then become routes into an exploration of the current research landscape on Potter, a means of situating her work in relation to wider contexts and cultural frameworks, or opportunities for re-reading and reflecting on important aspects of her work. Some words or phrases have been chosen to provide a fresh angle on familiar Potter themes and topics (A is for **Animal**; O is for **Over the hills and far away**); others cast light on under-regarded corners of her imagination (D is for **Dancing**; G is for **Ginnett's circus**; U is for **Uncanny**); some consider the ways in which current critical debates are challenging or reshaping our understanding of her work (F is for **Fairy**; R is for **Rabbit-tobacco**); others explore aspects of Potter's legacies and impact (L is for **Lake District**; P is for **Peter Rabbit**; H is for *Horn Book*), including global reception, adaptations across various mediums and development of the Potter industry in relation to the **Lake District** as tourist destination. In many cases a deliberately surprising choice is made (e.g. K is for **Key** rather than Kitten and W is for **War** rather than Warne), to allow for relatively unexplored themes and topics in Potter's writing to be addressed. Attention to the wider range of Potter's writing in relation to these starting points opens up new perspectives on the achievement of one of Britain's best-known children's authors. This approach also reveals Potter's interconnected thinking and the way in which several crucial motifs within her work are intertwined. The titular 'A–Z' is therefore not intended to suggest a definitive guide to Potter and her work. Instead, the book offers a quirkier approach, using these words and phrases to suggest some new directions and thinking about Potter's writing and its legacies.

Beatrix Potter lived through a period of human history marked by a great deal of change and turbulence, from the last stages of the industrial revolution to the Second World **War**. She was born in London in 1866, just seven years after Charles Darwin published his evolutionary theories in *On the Origin of Species* and at a point at which pre-industrial patterns of life for most people in Britain had all but come to an end. She came of age during the *fin de siècle*, when the nineteenth century – which had seen Britain go through significant social changes and become one of the most wealthy and powerful countries in the world – reached its turbulent end and gave way to the twentieth century. Potter published her best-known children's books in the early years of that new century and during a period which came to be known (partly as a result of her own contributions) as the 'Golden Age' of children's literature. Potter's later books for children were published in a world which was still dealing with the impact of the First World **War**, alongside writers such as Virginia Woolf and T. S. Eliot, whose work reflected the fragmentary experiences of a new modern world. Potter's final years were informed by the rise of fascism in Europe and the horrors of the Second World **War**. She died in the **Lake District** in 1943, a place she had done much to shape and protect, and just eight years before that region was designated a National Park. In focusing on some of the central threads and ideas which are explored in Potter's work, this book attempts to resituate her writing within these changing contexts and to show how she engages in complex ways with one of the most transformatory seventy-year periods in human history.

In exploring Potter's wider body of work in relation to the contexts of her long writing life, one important cross-chapter thread which emerges is the way in which Potter brings an ecological awareness to the page via her words and her artwork. From her earliest writing to her last, Potter was attuned to the external natural world via **seasonal** patterns, nonhuman creatures, landscapes, flowers and **trees**. *The Fairy Caravan* (1929), which has been neglected by critics and is dismissed by Kutzer as 'unreadable' (2003: 150), is re-established here as a vital text and a culmination of Potter's environmental writing for children. Though beyond the scope of this book, there are suggestions here as to the potential influence (as well as the potential *for* influence) of Potter's work on the development of

Introduction

an environmental imagination in global cultural contexts and, on several occasions, connections are made between ideas expressed in her writing and more recent concerns or debates. It is perhaps worth mentioning in this respect that one of the many writers who identified Potter as an influence on their childhood imagination and were drawn to her work is American author, Rachel Carson (1907–64), whose book, *Silent Spring* (1962), is now recognized as one of the most important environmental texts of the twentieth century.

Not only is Potter's writing considered here as 'literature', but attention is given to the way in which she positions her own work in relation to wider literary contexts through quotations, allusions and other textual strategies. John Goldthwaite observes, 'how little has been made' of Potter's 'life in books' (1996: 287), and whilst he focuses his attention primarily on the influence of the *Uncle Remus* stories, the paucity of attention given to her 'life in books' in broader terms is addressed here. What emerges is a much richer sense of Potter's extensive imaginative repertoire. Potter was an avid and eclectic reader who ranged freely between poetry, novels, diaries, art catalogues, newspapers and scientific textbooks. It is clear both from references in her **journal** to book purchases made by her father, and the books bearing his book plate which were still at Castle Cottage at the point of her death, that the library at her London home was quite substantial. Potter also had access to libraries at the various private homes she visited, including Camfield Place – the home of her paternal grandparents – and the large furnished villas which the Potter family rented for their long summer holidays. When they were staying at Lennel House on the Scottish Borders in 1894, for example, Potter recalls reading 'sundry old novels, in good old calf binding contemporary with the house' (*J*: 364). Her literary fare that summer included Scott's *Heart of Midlothian* (1818) as well as epic poems from the Romantic period, Thomas Moore's *Lalla Rookh: An Oriental Romance* (1817) and Southey's *The Curse of Kehama* (1810). As a young woman she learned several of Shakespeare's plays by heart and later claimed to have memorized Walter Scott's long narrative poem, *The Lady of the Lake* (1810), at around the age of seven (*A*: 59). Literary references and allusions crop up regularly in Potter's writing, but the range of her reading can also be detected in other ways, not least in the unusual names she gave to her pets which, in several cases (such as **Xarifa** the dormouse), derive from literary sources.

Though Potter's artwork is discussed in several chapters, the primary focus of this study is Potter's writing, which has tended to receive rather less detailed attention as a wider body of work. As Potter wrote to one of her American correspondents in 1929, her English publishers 'consider the pictures first; and the words a poor second' (*A*: 31), and to some extent this is true also of many of her readers. Potter took great delight in the fact that in America, a new focus on children's literature via libraries and publications such as the **Horn Book** *Magazine* had caused her books to be discussed and read in a very different way. Here they were taken 'seriously' and viewed as 'literature' not as 'toy books' (*A*: 31). It is very much as 'literature' that Potter's extensive body of writing is reconsidered here.

A IS FOR ANIMAL

Towards the end of her life **Beatrix** Potter was approached by the daughter of her American publisher, who wanted to write an article for the ***Horn Book*** about the animals in her work. Potter's response was that she could not see 'what occasion or reason there is at the moment for referring to them' (*A*: 163). Since Potter expressed that view in 1942 there have been thousands of words written about her animal characters but, perhaps more importantly, the human relationship with nonhuman species has become ever more complicated, with human actions increasingly implicated in biodiversity loss and the acceleration of species extinction. As the Scottish poet and essayist, Kathleen Jamie, wrote in the early years of the twenty-first century, they 'say the day is coming – it might already be here – when no species on the planet will be able to further itself without reference or negotiation with us' and when 'our intervention or restraint will be a factor in their continued existence' (2005: 79). In our current moment, there is then perhaps more 'occasion' than ever to reflect on the ways in which Potter's stories about animals raise questions about how we perceive and respond to the other creatures with whom we share the planet, not least because the ideas we encounter in art and literature, especially at a formative age, may well play a crucial role in shaping future actions.

Potter's own personal interactions with animals are fascinating but far from unproblematic in relation to issues of animal welfare. Along with animals purchased from pet shops, she and her brother kept a wide range of wild creatures in the third-floor nursery of their London home. Though the Potter siblings spent a great deal of time and energy caring for their pets, it seems probable that, in some cases, separation from their natural habitat reduced the life expectancy and quality of life for these animals. Potter was herself aware of this possibility, writing of her pet hedgehog, 'Tiggy', 'I am a little afraid that the long course of unnatural diet & indoor life is beginning to tell on her', adding it is 'a wonder she has lasted so long' (*L*: 139). Nonetheless, it is Potter's almost obsessive fascination with animals and her desire to both study and interact with them, that sits at the heart of the legacy she left behind: a unique and important body of imaginative writing about animals for young readers.

Studies of those factors which shape human attitudes to animals have recently pointed to the role of 'nonhuman charisma' to account for the way in which some animal types tend to generate more positive human responses than others; these 'charismatic species' are usually those which exhibit some physical traits which resemble the appearance of human babies and display a sort of 'reciprocity to human action and concern' (Lorimer 2007: 919). For the most part, it is mammals which fit into this category and, by way of contrast, other animal species can produce a strongly negative response, including 'visceral feelings of disgust and even panic'; examples here might include arachnids, reptiles, any insects in large numbers and parasitic insects, all of which often fail to generate a positive reaction and can appear instead as 'other' or threatening to the human subject (Lorimer 2007: 919–20).

Potter's earliest writing on animals can be found in the private **journal** she kept from 1881 to 1897 and here it is notable that she herself evinces no obvious bias or increased preference towards creatures which display 'charismatic' traits. Along with rabbits, dogs, mice and a hedgehog, the Potter siblings also kept a range of other animals, including lizards, a frog, a toad, newts, a ring snake, a bat and snails. Potter writes about these various creatures in much the same way, offering a mixture of factual observations and personal responses which suggest a liking for them all. The ring-snake is 'pretty' and smells strongly but 'not unpleasantly' (*J*: 54). The toad is 'very tame', turning round for food when a hand is put near him (*J*: 362), and the bat is a 'charming little creature' who is very active on its legs (*J*: 106). Potter adds that most people are 'ignorant' about bats (*J*: 106), and a few weeks after recording these observations in her **journal**, she produced some beautifully observed pencil and ink drawings of the bat which reveal a detailed knowledge of its anatomy (see Figure 1).

Potter's response to the death of creatures in her care also suggests that she felt a strong emotional attachment to even those animals which do not typically elicit positive human responses. She describes the death of the pet snails as an 'awful tragedy', adding 'I am very much put out about the poor things', which had such a 'surprising difference of character' (*J*: 59) and, following the death of her lizard Judy, she writes, 'I have had a great deal of pleasure from that little creature' (*J*: 82).

Whilst these examples relate to individual creatures who were kept as pets, there is no evidence of revulsion in Potter's early writing towards other creatures encountered in life, including those which tend to incur the most

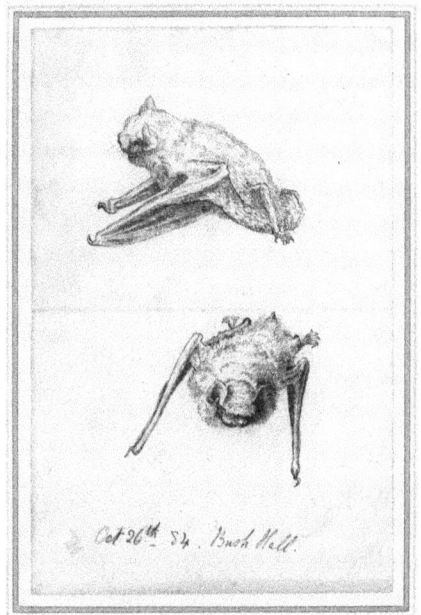

Figure 1 Common Bat/Pipistrelle by Beatrix Potter (1884).

negative socio-cultural responses. Even parasites such as fleas and bedbugs, which transgress bodily and domestic boundaries, generate little more than a humorous passing comment. On one occasion she records having slept soundly in spite of 'friends from the dog show' (*J*: 51) and, on finding bedbugs in a Torquay hotel, merely observes that it is possible to have 'too much Natural History in a bed' (*J*: 315).

This acceptance of the many and diverse living creatures with whom we share our world is almost certainly to do with Potter's strongly scientific leanings, which emerged in early studies of animals and plants before being channelled into more sustained work in the field of mycology. As Peter Hollindale argues, Potter was a 'meticulous student of natural history and natural science', and these qualities are crucial to understanding her subsequent imaginative handling of animals (1999: 6). We only have to look at some of her many detailed drawings of spiders as seen under a microscope – in which those elements which so often generate feelings of squeamishness and revulsion, such as claws, mouth and hairs on legs, are focused on and enlarged (Hobbs 1987: 76) – to understand that all living creatures were approached by Potter in a spirit of scientific interest as well as with a genuine fascination. It is of course this preliminary scientific approach and training which makes Potter's animal drawings so effective, since even when anthropomorphized, there is an anatomical truth to her handing of these creatures.

It is apparent from Potter's **journal** and letters that she enjoyed meeting new animals and took a great deal of pleasure in interacting with them. Along with spending time with the various household pets, Potter also took up opportunities to encounter other animal species via **circus** and **zoo** visits. Potter's early writings also sometimes reflect on animal behaviour in ways which acknowledge the limitations of our knowledge about other species, recognizing that nonhuman creatures work to rhythms and environmental patterns which humans cannot perceive or understand. The term 'more-than-human' is sometimes used by twenty-first-century environmental writers in preference to terms such as 'nonhuman' or 'animal', as a reminder that the rest of the living world has intrinsic causal powers of its own, and a sense of this emerges in Potter's writing. In one early **journal** passage she notes that the rooks left the old **trees** in Kensington a short time before they were felled, and left the rookery in Kensington Gardens the autumn before the **trees** there were cut down. In response to this phenomenon, she asks herself: 'I wonder how the rooks know'? (*J*: 48). Here Potter's close attention to bird behaviour leads first to an observation about their unusual movements and this, in turn, leads to a speculation that other species on the planet may well have different kinds of awareness to our own. Potter would later develop an idea of the nonhuman world existing beyond the knowledge of humans in her handling of the animal/human divide in *The Fairy Caravan*, her collection of stories based around a **circus** troupe of animals. Here animals are categorized as 'Little Folk' and humans as 'Big Folk', and the reader is given privileged access to the world of the 'Little Folk' which is usually hidden from human view. Not only does the animal world operate in ways which humans do not see or understand, but the book also intimates that the animals have access to special kinds of knowledge and insight, since it is they who 'can see things where the Big Folk can see nothing' (*FC*: 156).

Though Potter's early writings and artwork show her engaging with a diverse range of species, she was aware that certain animals lend themselves to anthropomorphization and recent scholarly work suggests that those animals which have come to be deemed 'charismatic' in our culture are also those which tend to be more 'readily anthropomorphized' (Coates 2015: 275). Potter herself found it easier to anthropomorphize some animals (most notably mice, rabbits, pigs and cats) more than others, including other mammals such as dogs, but her most famous and popular animal characters are those which conform to many of the traits often identified in 'charismatic' species. Though Potter was herself fascinated by insects, they play only minor supporting roles in her published *Tales* – appearing, for example, as pests (albeit beautifully drawn ones) who need to be removed from the domestic space in *Mrs. Tittlemouse*. Even so, there is a truth and accuracy to Potter's depiction of these creatures, which is sometimes used for humorous ends, such as the spider who critically examines the knots by which Tom Kitten has been tied up in *Samuel Whiskers*, because he was a good 'judge', having used them regularly to 'tie up unfortunate blue-bottles' (*SW*: 54).

This insistence on a truthfulness to both the appearance and nature of her animal characters is, as several critics have argued, a major factor in the success and appeal of Potter's fictional characters (Kerslake 2021: 71; Lane 1946: 118; Laws 2021: 117). Potter herself wrote very critically of what she perceived to be the failings of contemporary children's author, Kenneth Grahame, in this respect, observing that 'writers for children ought to have a sufficient recognition of what things look like' and pointing disparagingly to the fact that in *The Wind in the Willows* (1908) Grahame described his character Toad as 'combing his *hair*' (*L*: 450). Potter concludes that it is a 'mistake to fly in the face of nature' and, though a frog may 'wear galoshes', toads should not have beards or wigs (*L*: 450). Even when dressed in **clothes** or walking on hind legs, Potter's animal characters are not merely anatomically accurate, they also behave in fundamental ways like the animal they represent.

It is perhaps her interest in all species, even those creatures which have tended to generate negative responses, which makes Potter so vital in terms of the development of a literary genre which has the potential to evoke an early environmental awareness in young readers. Though the literary trope of animals who talk has ancient origins, talking-animal stories only developed as a distinctive genre for a child audience in the late eighteenth and early nineteenth centuries (Cosslett 2006: 1) and this genre has been identified as a crucial body of writing in the history of environmental literature for children. Lawrence Buell argues that writing which 'purports to imagine nonhuman life-worlds from the standpoint of the creatures themselves', implicitly 'chides' human indifference and 'cruelty towards other creatures', and lodges a 'claim that humans should take the interests and welfare of other creatures more greatly into account' (2014: 409). Indeed, Buell describes **Peter Rabbit** as an 'anticipatory response' to ideas put forward in the 1980s by the environmental writer, Barry Lopaz, in generating an early sense of the 'plurality of other life-worlds beyond just the human that coexist "as part of a coherent and shared landscape"' (Buell 2014: 412).

Talking-animal stories also though ask us to reflect on animal/human relations and in Potter the handling of such relations is always complex – not least because, as a result of her unusually nuanced acts of anthropomorphism, Potter's animal characters simultaneously reflect both the behaviour of particular animal species (with a cat behaving in fundamental ways like a cat, a fox like a fox, and so on) and that of humans (such as a disobedient child or a mother obsessed with social appearances). Nonetheless, as Tess Cosslett argues, these 'books insist, or at least take for granted that their stories are related to their readers' understanding and/or treatment of animals in the world beyond the book', and because of a child's tendency to identify with 'animal protagonists', the 'subversion of human dominance is always at least part of their effect' (2006: 182). Such an effect is reinforced by the ways in which adult humans are shown in some ways to be a threat to animals in many of Potter's stories, from Mr. McGregor's actions in Potter's first published *Tale*, to Captain Butcher's in *Pig Robinson*, her last.

In *The Fairy Caravan*, 'Big Folk' are actively feared and avoided by the animal **circus** troupe, who use the magical properties of a fern seed to render themselves invisible to humans. Animal encounters with humans in this book are rarely positive and even Potter herself (referred to by the animals as 'Mistress Heelis') is identified with the Big Folk, who have 'ruined the smithies and stolen the roads' (*FC*: 178). Here animals are closely connected to the natural environment, with humans positioned on the side of an encroaching and often destructive 'civilization'. Within the book, the negative impact of human behaviour on the natural environment is also shown in other ways, such as by the dumping of detritus, 'old pots and pans, fruit tins, jam pots, and broken bottles', close to where the **circus** animals camp (*FC*: 24–5).

Whilst the animal characters all escape their threatened fates at the hands of humans here and within Potter's well-known *Tales*, in a story written in 1911 but unpublished in her lifetime, the impact of humans on animals is explored rather differently. 'The Mole Catcher's Burying' is an unusual dark and Gothic short story in which Potter imagines a kind of animal revenge against human cruelty. The story is told from the perspective of moles who hear the news that the hated mole catcher, Jimmy Dacre – actually the name of a farmer who lived a few miles south of Potter's home in Sawrey (*H*: 376) – is dying. The news passes from mole to mole via their complex system of underground tunnels in a way that functions as a kind of metaphor for the animal lives, networks and modes of communication which remain, for the most part, invisible to humans. The moles 'clap and clash their shovels' at the news before sharing their harrowing litany of losses at Dacre's hands: 'My castle did he dig up in Hindsyke' and 'killed my children in the nest' says one, others he slew 'while they slept' (*H*: 379). Told from the perspective of the moles, in speech which is imbued with the language and syntax of the Old Testament, the death toll reads as a horrifying catalogue of destruction as well as a narrative of divine vengeance. Without waiting for Dacre to die, the moles make their way to the church graveyard like an avenging army: 'Hundreds of black velvet moles bearing shovels rustle over the road, through the dead leaves' and together they dig his grave. As they continue to recount instances of Dacre's **violence** and cruelty ('Eight of my sons hath he snared', 'Seven of my daughters'), the moles chant 'Dig brothers, dig', so that the digging of his grave becomes their assurance that no more 'shall the tally mount' (*H*: 380). Daybreak brings the news that the mole catcher is finally dead, but the sexton finds the grave already prepared. Though focused on the act of burying, this fascinating story brings to the surface the subtext of human **violence** and threat towards the creatures with whom we share the planet, which runs through Potter's better-known *Tales*.

Though Potter's writing often deals with the animal/human relationship in terms of the negative impact of humans on animal existence, her approach to anthropomorphism also enables us to make connections between humans and other living creatures. As Potter's first biographer, Margaret Lane, perceptively suggests, Potter recognized the 'invisible thread of sympathy which runs through the whole animal creation, including man' (1946: 119), and a posthumously published story, *Wag-by-Wall*, explores this idea, offering an uplifting narrative about what can happen when humans reconnect with nonhuman species.

Wag-by-Wall is the story of a poor lonely old woman named Sally Benson, whose husband is dead and whose only daughter has run off with a 'wastrel' (*WBW*: 46). Sally is left alone with the company of a clock (the 'wag-by-wall'), her singing kettle and a pair of white owls who live in the shed. Sally is 'very fond of the owls' and each year the little owlets, 'like balls of fluff', are born (*WBW*: 42 and 32). When the smallest owl falls out of the nest, Sally puts him back and at other times dries him by the fire (*WBW*: 20). Ultimately the love and care which Sally shows to the owls has a direct impact on her own future, via a magical occurrence which sits at the heart of the story.

Having received a letter telling her that her daughter and son-in-law are dead and that there is a grandchild with no-one to care for her, Sally is distraught as she has no money to pay for the child to be sent to her. While the old woman sits weeping, the owl who has been sitting on the chimney stack suddenly falls down the chimney. Sally rushes to help the owl and discovers an old stocking filled with gold which the owl has dislodged on its journey down the chimney. The ending of the story is one of continuity in terms of both human and animal/human relations: the granddaughter lives happily with her grandmother and every summer the 'white owls' nest in the woodshed (*WBW*: 64).

Though *Wag-by-Wall* was not published during Potter's lifetime, versions of the story were written around 1909, and it was paired in her imagination with one of her earliest *Tales*. She describes *Wag-by-Wall* as a 'pendant to *The Tailor of Gloucester*', one telling of a 'lonely old man' and the other of a 'lonely old woman' (*H*: 328). The term 'pendant' is used by Potter here to suggest that the two stories match or complement each other, and they do so in ways that go beyond her focus on two lonely human characters. A more significant parallel relates to the consequences of acts of spontaneous kindness on the part of humans towards animals – in the case of *Wag-by-Wall*, Sally's care of the owls and, in *The Tailor of Gloucester*, the old man freeing the mice caught by his cat. These acts result in a reversal of usual hierarchies, with the humans becoming in some way dependent on the animals, but also a change in the pattern of human fate. This central motif is slightly reminiscent of the crucial scene in Samuel Taylor Coleridge's poem 'The Rime of the Ancient Mariner' (1798), in which the sailor – having been cursed to wear the albatross he has killed around his neck – suddenly feels a 'spring of love' for the sea snakes he sees around the ship and he blesses them 'unaware' (Coleridge 1997: 176). At this moment the albatross falls off, the cursed ship begins to move and the mariner starts to come back to a fuller life. Although neither the Tailor nor Sally has personally committed any crime against the universe, they are nonetheless trapped in a pattern of human suffering from which there appears to be no escape and, in both cases, their spontaneous acts of kindness towards the animal kingdom result in the unleashing of some sort of inexplicable magical power which radically changes their lives for the good.

Always fascinated by the natural pattern of the **seasons**, it is significant that Potter turns to ancient folklore relating to hinge points of the year to frame these magical occurrences. Both stories are set on Christmas Eve and, as Potter writes in *The Tailor of Gloucester*, there is 'an old story that all the beasts can talk, in the night between Christmas Eve and Christmas day in the morning', though, she adds, 'there are very few folk that can hear them, or know what it is that they say' (*TG*: 36). Both of these *Tales* use this idea to depict a moment of folkloric reconnection between humans and animals and, in so doing, draw attention to the 'invisible thread' which exists between ourselves and the other creatures with whom we share the earth.

B IS FOR BEATRIX

Few writers have been subject to such extensive posthumous biographical scrutiny as Beatrix Potter. Authors, including writers of books for children, tend to receive at least as much critical interest in their published work as their life story but, in Potter's case, attention is significantly skewed towards the biographical. Such interest began during her lifetime and though Potter found requests for personal information 'perplexing', she provided the following potted biography in order to prevent any 'silly' sense of mystery:

> Beatrix Potter is Mrs. William Heelis. She lives in the north of England, her home is among the mountains and lakes that she has drawn in her picture books. Her husband is a lawyer. They have no family. Mrs. Heelis is in her 60th year. She leads a very busy contented life, living always in the country and managing a large sheep farm on her own land.
>
> (A: 8)

To this summary, which notably focuses entirely on her identity in later life as Mrs Heelis and gives no details at all about earlier biographical contexts, she adds, 'I don't think anybody requires to know more about me' (A: 8).

Despite Potter's own attempts to shut down public interest in her life story, the first Potter biography was published just three years after her death and, in some ways, set a precedent for much of what would follow. The dustjacket of Margaret Lane's *The Tale of Beatrix Potter: A Biography* (1946) features a photograph of a young Potter contained in an oval frame, positioned just where one of her eponymous **animal** characters would appear on one of the covers of her own little books, and thus Potter's own 'Tale' is framed as a narrative equal to one of her own charming fictions.

Fascination with Potter's life story shows no sign of waning in the twenty-first century. Despite the publication in 2007 of Linda Lear's meticulously researched (and probably definitive) biography, *Beatrix Potter: A Life in Nature*, there has been a marked increase in the publication of biographies – including ones by

Dennison (2017), Cohen (2020) and Gristwood (2021) – which suggests an ongoing desire to revisit and retell her story.

There have also been many other retellings of Potter's life story both on stage and screen from the late twentieth century onwards, such as: *Beatrix* (1998), a stage play starring Patricia Routledge; a television biopic called *The Tale of Beatrix Potter* (1983), directed by Bill Hays and starring Penelope Wilton, and another called *Beatrix: The Early Life of Beatrix Potter* (1990), directed by Mike Healey and starring Helena Bonham Carter. Most significant of all, in terms of reach and global reception, is Chris Noonan's major film biopic, *Miss Potter* (2006), with American actress Renée Zellweger in the lead role. Like the original Lane biography, this film uses the motif of Potter's own storytelling term, a 'Tale', to frame the on-screen treatment of her life, with its poster strapline: 'The Life of Beatrix Potter is the most enchanting tale of all.' This is accompanied by an image of Zellweger gazing into the camera and raising her finger to her lips, to indicate that she is about to share a secret and is swearing us to secrecy. The idea that we are being given access to some previously unknown information about Potter's deeply private life was also used in the marketing of the Lane biography, with the blurb claiming that few 'lives have been more jealously hidden from the public eye than Beatrix Potter's' and that when she died in December 1943 'no-one, not even her husband, knew the full story of her life' (Lane 1946). In both the first Potter biography and the most famous screen biopic of her life, a crucial aspect of the marketing strategy is to suggest that we are being given access, for the first time, to Potter's untold and secret life. Ironically, at the point at which Lane made this claim, a significant portion of that 'full story', in the form of Potter's coded private **journal**, was still gathering dust in the **Lake District** and had yet to be decoded.

Though this vital body of autobiographical writing does not inform the Lane biography, that book nonetheless establishes a number of motifs which would come to be seen as central to the story of Potter's life as it has been told and retold. Her 'Tale' has been reconstructed as featuring several fairy-tale ingredients: escape from loneliness and domestic oppression, the gaining of independence and fame, personal tragedy (with the death of her fiancé Norman Warne in 1905), then long-awaited happiness and fulfilment, through marriage to William Heelis and life as a landowner and countrywoman in the **Lake District**. The tendency to isolate and emphasize these elements has though resulted in a rather distorted understanding of Potter's life and the construction of a simplified and idealized popular image of 'Beatrix Potter'. *Miss Potter* foregrounds many of these ingredients and some of the negative reviews of the film pick up on issues relating to this handling of her life story. A *Guardian* review, for example, describes the film as 'cliche-ridden' and 'chocolate-boxy', criticizing the ways in which it 'distorts (actually flattens out) the facts' and turns an 'extraordinary life into an ordinary one' (French 2007). Though the film had considerable popular appeal and significantly increased Potter-related tourism to the **Lake District**, it is a long way from capturing the brilliant, complex, contradictory, hard-working, witty, 'obstinate', 'hard-headed' (*A*: 207), mercurial and astonishingly gifted woman who emerges from the pages of both her private and public writings. When interviewed about playing Beatrix Potter in the 2006 film, *Miss Potter*, Zellweger said that 'she continued to be a mystery to me; the more research I did, the less I thought I actually knew who she might be' (Riley 2006), and the final film does not really take us any further on that journey of understanding.

Alongside biographical constructions of Potter, we also have autobiographical ones, which occur in different textual contexts. These appear within her private coded diaries and letters, but also within the pages of her children's books. When considered together these constructions suggest that issues relating to identity and a quest for selfhood are perhaps more central to Potter's story than those various themes which regularly emerge in biographical accounts. The difficulties Potter experienced in her sense of who she was or wanted to be can be approached initially via the thorny matter of names. The woman the world would come to know as 'Beatrix Potter' was in fact named after her mother and born Helen Potter. To avoid confusion between the two Helens, she quickly came to be called by her middle name, Beatrix. During childhood she and her brother (who also used his middle name) were known in the inner family circle by the truncated nicknames: 'B' and 'Bertie' (Taylor 1986: 24). Early drawings by Potter show her experimenting with her name(s), often signing the work Helen Beatrix Potter or H. B. P. In two surviving letters from her early childhood, she signs herself H. B. Potter but by the age of sixteen she was beginning to sign off letters as 'Beatrix Potter' (*L*: 11–13; *Art*: 14–16). What we might think of as the first stage in her quest for selfhood had begun.

Somewhere in between these two points Potter began to keep a **journal**, written in a secret code of her own invention. The existence of this text and its content was certainly a significant 'secret' within Potter's story until Leslie Linder found the diaries and cracked her private code in the late-1950s. Though much of the day-to-day content is not such as would obviously demand secrecy, there are some passages in which Potter uses this private

17

textual space to explore her feelings and concerns in ways which suggest that she found issues of identity, particularly in the shift from childhood to adult womanhood, difficult and troubling.

An important example of this occurs in an entry from June 1884, when Potter was just coming up to her eighteenth birthday. Following the death of William Gaskell (husband of the novelist Elizabeth Gaskell) for whom Potter had always had a great fondness, she recalls a moment from her childhood in which he was sitting on the doorstep at Dalguise, the house she and her family regularly rented for their summer holidays in Scotland. In memory Potter sees not only Gaskell, but also a childhood version of herself coming into the frame of the picture: a 'little girl in a print frock and striped stockings' who 'bounds to his side' and offers him a bunch of meadowsweet (J: 93). The use of the third person here suggests a sense of separation from her own childhood self and is reminiscent of similar moments in nineteenth-century literature in which Victorian heroines experience a fragmentation or different versions of the self. Indeed, Sandra Gilbert and Susan Gubar, in their groundbreaking critical study, *The Madwoman in the Attic* (1979), identify this as a recurrent trope within nineteenth-century women's writing. They suggest that it relates to anxieties about self-identity in a context in which an adult woman's identity was strictly controlled by the gender mores established by a patriarchal society and would come to be subsumed by marriage (Gilbert and Gubar 1979: 357–9).

That such a reading is relevant here is indicated by the remainder of the passage, which goes on to reflect on the disturbing changes wrought on her 'self' in the intervening years, in particular the loss of physical and imaginative freedom: 'the little girl does not bound about now, and live in fairyland' and occasionally wonder in a 'curious, carefree manner, as of something not concerning her nature, what life means, and whether she shall ever feel sorrow' (J: 94). Shifting from this third-person account of an earlier self she moves to the present tense with the sad affirmation that 'I have begun the dark journey of life' (J: 94). Though early passages such as these record a feeling of being unsettled and an absence of a clear sense of identity, the 'journey' which her **journal** documents, whilst 'dark' at times, is also a journey of the self. In later entries we encounter a young woman who had begun to reach beyond the constrictions imposed on her by her family, class and gender, to achieve a kind of 'psychological emancipation' (Robison 1984: 238) and to perceive the possibility of a very different kind of future to that which she had initially envisaged as her lot in life.

A set of illustrated letters written to children, predominantly the children of her one-time governess, Annie Moore (née Carter), represents another important body of early writing which gives us glimpses of Potter's shifting sense of identity. Within these letters, Potter begins to experiment with a different kind of self-writing. Both in words and in accompanying simple line-drawn self-portraits, the letters reveal a young woman with a wry sense of humour, capable of laughing at herself and others, who leads an active and busy life. The letters depict her engaged in a surprising range of pursuits which include, feeding and interacting with **animals** at the **zoo**, taking photographs, helping to push a loaded gig up a steep road, walking her pet rabbit on a lead, visiting the **circus**, rowing a boat and going out in a storm 'all wrapped up' and wearing 'goloshes' in order to rescue her rabbit and bring him indoors (*LC*: 31–46). Other than those letters in which overtly fictional stories featuring **animal** characters are told, Potter herself appears as the main character in the picture letters of the period and, in a sense, as the heroine of her own stories.

One of the most interesting aspects of Potter's self-construction in these picture letters is the fact that she briefly documents two of the major transformations of her life and identity. Firstly, we witness the early stages of her transition into 'Miss Potter' the author. In a letter to Marjory Moore, she details some of the difficulties faced in early attempts to become a published author (*LC*: 66) and depicts herself in an accompanying sketch as an assertive woman, openly challenging the views and opinions of a male publisher (see Figure 2). It is notable though that she again reverts to the third person here,

Figure 2 Self-portrait sketch from letter (1900).

this time in what we might think of as the construction of a new and not yet fully developed future identity. She refers in the letter to the 'Miss Potter', who has 'arguments' with her prospective publisher, as a separate person to the letter-writer herself, adding: 'I think Miss Potter will go off to another publisher soon!' (*LC*: 66).

A second major identity transformation is also touched on within this body of writing, as we glimpse Potter begin to slowly morph into her new identity as a countrywoman in the **Lake District**. In a letter of 1907 to Louie Warne, her focus shifts to tales of the farm **animals** and her experiences at Hill Top (the Lakeland home she purchased in 1905, which is now managed by the **National Trust**) with a line drawing depicting herself and Mrs Cannon (the farmer's wife) giving medicine to a calf (*LC*: 123). Read alongside her **journal**, these letters offer important insights into Potter's changing sense of self as the years go by.

Whilst the latter instances of textual self-construction appear in private writings, Potter also makes a small number of appearances within her published work. Moments of authorial intervention occur in *Benjamin Bunny*, in which Potter comments that she once bought a pair of Mrs. Rabbit's 'rabbit-wool mittens' at a 'bazaar' (*BB*: 11), and in an addendum to *Mrs. Tiggy-Winkle*, in which she asserts that '*I* am very well acquainted with dear Mrs. Tiggy-winkle' (*TW*: 57). On both occasions Potter writes herself into the imaginative world depicted in the stories and aligns herself with her young readers by affirming the 'truth' of the fantasy elements. These comments are though placed in parenthesis, functioning as 'asides' to the reader, and she does not insert herself into the action of the story itself. In *Samuel Whiskers*, however, Potter appears as a named character within her own fictional world as well as within one of the book's illustrations. We learn that John Joiner has just finished making a wheelbarrow for 'Miss Potter', who has also 'ordered two hen-coops' (*SW*: 65), and Potter then appears in the story in the first person, reporting that 'when I was going to the post late in the afternoon' I looked up and saw 'Mr. Samuel Whiskers and his wife on the run, with big bundles on a little wheelbarrow, which looked very like mine' (*SW*: 66). An accompanying illustration depicts Samuel Whiskers and Anna Maria in the foreground, pushing the loaded wheelbarrow around a corner, and a distant, almost ghostly, figure of Potter in the background (*SW*: 67) haunting the pages of her own story. Though Kutzer suggests that Potter only depicts herself as 'integrated within the animal world' in *Pigling Bland* (2003: 144), in fact she is woven into that world here, albeit in a minor way.

Not only does she witness the two rats running away with her wheelbarrow but also adds that she had not given them 'leave to borrow' it (*SW*: 66). Notably, this first named appearance in her published works occurs during the years in which Potter was starting to spend more time at Hill Top and becoming increasingly comfortable with her newly emerging identity as an independent writer and countrywoman.

We see Potter developing this identity more extensively in *Pigling Bland*, a story about the imaginary adventures of two actual pigs from Hill Top farm in which Potter is certainly a more 'fully participating figure' (Kutzer 2003: 144). She inserts herself as a character in the story, speaking in the first person as she and the elderly pig, 'Aunt Pettitoes', try to deal with a number of young misbehaving pigs. Potter constructs her identity here as that of a practical unsentimental farmer, an identity reinforced by the way in which she is contrasted to Aunt Pettitoes. Whilst the latter sniffs and cries and gives the pigs peppermints for their journey, Potter's character focuses on practical matters, pinning the pigs' licences inside their waistcoat pockets 'for safety' (*PB*: 22) and giving instructions to help them on their journey. It is a self-construction which echoes Potter's account of her lineage in a 1929 essay on the '"Roots" of the Peter Rabbit Tales', in which she writes that she is descended from generations of 'obstinate, hard headed, *matter of fact*' Lancashire folk (*A*: 207). The 'I' we encounter in this story is also clearly an independent woman, occupied with the practical and legal aspects of husbandry. No male figure is shown to be involved with the running of the farm and instead it is Potter's character who both helps drag the pigs out of the hoops of the pig trough and personally secures the necessary legal paperwork. Though Potter does not mention herself by name within the story itself, she inserts herself visually via two line drawings. In the first she is bending down giving a licence to Alexander, which will allow him to travel to the market in Lancashire, in a self-portrait which is remarkably similar to those which appear throughout her illustrated letters to child acquaintances. In the second she can be seen watching the two pigs leave the farm along with Aunt Pettitoes, with Potter standing just inside the doorway of Hill Top. The consistency of these textual acts of self-construction during the early Sawrey years suggests that by this stage Potter's newly emerging identity was one with which she was comfortable and, to some extent, willing to share within the public domain.

By the time *Pigling Bland* appeared in print, however, its author was no longer 'Miss Potter' but 'Mrs. Heelis', a change in nomenclaturic identity which she would insist on for the rest of her life. Not only did she affirm this new identity in private, but also in her next act of textual self-insertion more than two decades later. *The Fairy Caravan* was published in America and Potter felt it to be 'too autobiographical' (*H*: 292) to be published in Britain. In this book though we see Potter making a different kind of textual appearance; here she is 'off-stage' but the **animal** characters themselves talk about her. A group of Herdwick sheep wonder why 'Mistress Heelis' has never given them bells (*FC*: 92) and, at the smithy, the dog blacksmith aligns Mistress Heelis with the problematic 'Big Folk' who have done so much harm to the old ways of life, adding that it serves her right to 'lose her clog!' (*FC*: 178). This clog reference leads to a magical thread which is then pursued throughout the chapter. We hear that initially both of Mistress Heelis's clogs have been seen walking on their own past the smithy and grinning to themselves. However, whilst one clog returns home, the other goes missing and has an adventure, the highlight of which is taking part in an **uncanny** woodland **dance** of shoes, with Mistress Heelis's clog **dancing** around with the rest. In this final textual appearance within her published fiction, not only has 'Miss Potter' been transformed into 'Mistress Heelis', the breeder of Herdwick sheep and the wearer of country clogs, but in the end we are left only with her disembodied **dancing** clog.

The disappearance of the woman, who leaves only an object (her clog) behind, foreshadows Potter's impulse in the last years of her life to fade away without fuss or pomp leaving behind only her stories and the **Lake District** landscapes she had done so much to protect. Indeed, towards the end of her life Potter began to construct a posthumous future which was defined by absence. When reflecting on the possibility of further publications in 1942, just one year before her death, she wrote 'I am very willing to retire into obscurity' (*A*: 176) and in the last days of her life she gave instructions that there should be no marked burial site and no tombstone, with even the place where her ashes were scattered to be kept secret (Taylor 1986: 204). Potter's final impulse was one of anti-memorialization and a complete rejection of the various identities she had experimented with in her life. Her body returned to the land she loved so much without any form of inscription marking the spot where she lay. Legally and officially of course the woman who died on the 22 December 1943 was Helen Beatrix Heelis, a name which meant very little to most people, whilst via reputation and legacy, 'Beatrix Potter' lived on.

C IS FOR CLOTHES

Beatrix Potter was fascinated by clothes and costume all her life and in her **journal** often documents details of clothing worn by family members, people she encountered on holiday and as depicted in artwork. Indeed, one of Potter's earliest pieces of coded writing, dating from 1881, is an account of her 'Grandmamma Leech' and around a quarter of the passage is given over to the latter's clothes, from her wedding dress – which had very large loose sleeves with removable 'swansdown ones under them' – to her bonnet and pelisse and the difficulties presented by crinolines (J: 3). Since clothing is often the first thing Potter focused on when meeting someone new for the first time, her diaries offer glimpses into the sartorial choices of well-known figures from late nineteenth-century intellectual and artistic circles. Oscar Wilde, we discover, wears a 'black choker' instead of a shirt collar and his wife has her front covered with 'great water-lilies' (J: 100), whilst John Ruskin, the great Victorian art critic, comes across as a rather shabby figure, wearing a 'very old hat, much necktie and aged coat buttoned up on his neck' (J: 73). After one extended description of changing fashions in women's clothing Potter excuses herself for having given such a long account of a 'frivolous subject' (J: 211) but the treatment of clothes and costume in her writing is rarely frivolous. In her fictional work, Potter uses costume to establish context, to convey important ideas to the reader and, in some cases, as a crucial plot device. She also displays in her writing an awareness of the function of clothes in relation to issues of identity, role-play and performance.

Potter's abiding interest in historic costume is in evidence in many of her *Tales*, which often depict characters wearing the clothes of an earlier generation, such as Jemima Puddle-duck's poke-bonnet and shawl, and in some texts she uses sartorial references very deliberately to situate a story in a specific historic moment. For example, in *Sister Anne*, Potter's retelling of the fairy tale 'Bluebeard', she uses clothes – along with archaic language and a castle setting – to evoke a medieval context. She pays close attention to the costume worn by Bluebeard's wife and sister-in-law: the 'trailing skirts of green worsted', the 'quaint long-horned head-dress' which points 'forward like a unicorn's horn', the 'bell-shaped sleeves', 'long-toed shoes' (SA: 115) and the 'large embroidered pouches' which hang from the sisters' girdles (SA: 75). As well as locating the story in the distant past, the women's costumes also play a brief but important role in the plot. Having failed to pass the bunch of household **keys** to his wife without her sister intercepting them, Bluebeard asks his sister-in-law to retrieve his glove from under the table; it is while she undertakes an 'awkward crawl to recover the Baron's greasy leather glove', encumbered as she is by her 'voluminous long-skirted gown and high headdress', that Bluebeard manages to slip the bunch of **keys** in his wife's girdle (SA: 92).

Historic costume is also used to establish the temporal setting of *The Tailor of Gloucester* but here clothes are also vital to the story's plot. In the opening lines, Potter introduces the story's eighteenth-century setting through references to costume rather than kings and queens or other more typical signifiers of historic moment:

> In the time of swords and periwigs and full-skirted coats with flowered lappets – when gentlemen wore ruffles, and gold-laced waistcoats of paduasoy and taffeta – there lived a tailor in Gloucester.
>
> (*TG*: 7)

Potter seems to relish the language of unfamiliar fabrics and garments, offering in the original version of the story, written for Freda Moore, a little glossary of such terms which explains, for example, that 'paduasoy' is the 'silk of Padua' (*H*: 113). Potter's interest in the clothes which sit at the heart of the story is indicated by the fact that when working on this book she went to study some 'most beautiful' eighteenth-century garments at South Kensington Museum (*L*: 73), carefully sketching and painting the clothes before reproducing them for the story. Her fascination with the clothes themselves as objects is apparent in the *Tale*, which includes illustrations of close-up sections of the embroidered cloth (*TG*: 33) and also precise written details about the fabric: the coat is of 'cherry-coloured corded silk' which is 'embroidered with pansies and roses' and the satin waistcoat trimmed with 'gauze and worsted chenille' (*TG*: 8). Whilst references to the clothes are woven throughout, by the end of the *Tale*, they seem to have shifted to centre stage, with the jacket, the waistcoat and the embroidered cuff respectively dominating the page in the last three images of the book (*TG*: 53, 55, 56).

C is for Clothes

Whilst Potter lingers over the fabric and embroidery of the costume, the meaning attributed to clothes here is complex. On the one hand, the sheer extravagance of the garments which are being made for the Mayor's wedding points to a problematic social and economic dichotomy. The poverty of the Tailor, who needs to spend his last fourpence on food and a twist of silk to finish the commission, contrasts starkly with the wealth of a man who can afford to pay for such an expensive and luxurious outfit. A reading of the clothes as a symbol of iniquitous social hierarchies is undercut though, both by the extent to which the story fetishizes the beauty of the garments and by the role of the mice, whose kindness saves the Tailor and leads to him becoming rich. Moreover, the mice themselves parade around in equally decadent eighteenth-century clothes made from scraps of the beautiful fabric. Carpenter suggests that the story 'reverses the usual order of power', with both the Tailor and the Mayor being reliant on the 'very lowest creatures' in their society's 'pecking order' (1989: 285), and this reversal is reinforced by Potter's handling of clothes. Whilst the figure of the Mayor remains absent from the main text, appearing in his new outfit only as a paratextual frontispiece, it is the mice themselves who model the expensive costumes which would be worn by the fine ladies and gentlemen of the age within the story itself (see Figure 3).

Figure 3 Illustration from *The Tailor of Gloucester*.

Along with images of the mice dressed in extravagant outfits are ones which show them working at their stitching unclothed, and this juxtaposition also adds a complexity to our understanding of the role of clothes in society, reinforcing the performative and artificial nature of social codes and status. Though clothes often play an important role in Potter's writing, the meaning of this trope is rarely stable and consistent. As other critics have suggested, in **Peter Rabbit** and *Tom Kitten*, clothing functions to suggest maternal and social control (Cosslett 2006: 157; Kutzer 2003: 44). In the former this has particularly disastrous consequences, as the buttons on **Peter's** blue jacket ultimately cause him to get trapped; only by freeing himself from the coat and returning to his natural unclothed state can **Peter** escape. However, it is the wearing of clothes which saves Jeremy Fisher, since the trout who intends to eat him does not like the taste of Jeremy's macintosh and spits him out. A crucial distinction here though is that both **Peter Rabbit** and Tom Kitten are child **animal** characters. The images which show them being dressed in clothes are strongly suggestive of inappropriate levels of physical restriction, with **Peter** looking as if he is being 'strangled' (Kutzer 2003: 44) as his mother fastens his coat, and Tom staring out of the page at the reader, his eyes wide with horror, as his mother fits him into an overly tight blue suit (*TK*: 18).

In *Tom Kitten*, the main plot of the story deals with the unsuitability of the clothes which the child characters have been forced to wear and which impede their engagement with the natural environment. Moppet and Mittens' pinafores trip them up and, in order to climb up the rockery to sit on the garden wall, they have to be turned 'back to front' (*TK*: 24). Tom is wholly unable to jump when walking 'on his hind legs in trousers' and his clumsy progress causes frustration to himself and damage to the natural environment, as he is forced to pull himself up by holding onto ferns which break in the process (*TK*: 27). The negative portrayal of clothes in *Tom Kitten* suggests that the story endorses what might be called a 'natural education' for children, in which they learn and grow through direct interactions with an external natural environment. Such a model of education had been promoted by the eighteenth-century French philosopher and novelist, Jean-Jacques Rousseau, and is famously celebrated by William Wordsworth in his great autobiographical poem, *The Prelude*. Wordsworth describes his early life growing up in the **Lake District** in Rousseauvian terms, in which he, a 'five years' child', made 'one long bathing of a summer's day', running over the 'sandy fields' and 'leaping through flowery groves / Of yellow ragwort' like a 'naked savage'

(Wordsworth [1850] 1953: 498). In *Tom Kitten*, clothes function on one level as a symbol of those forces which deny and prevent the development of a young child through these sorts of experiences.

Whilst Wordsworth's poem celebrates the idea of the growing child being immersed in nature, many popular nineteenth-century cultural representations of children played a role in promoting the wearing of unsuitable and uncomfortable clothing which would restrict such activities. In 1886, two influential cultural texts appeared in which a male child is depicted wearing a velvet suit with ruffled lace collar. One was the portrait by Potter family friend, John Everett Millais, which came to be known as 'Bubbles'. It became one of the most widely reproduced and famous late Victorian works of art after being taken up by 'Pears', the soap manufacturing company, and used on their posters and advertisements. The second was the novel *Little Lord Fauntleroy*, by Frances Hodgson Burnett and the illustrations by Reginald B. Birch, which started an immediate fashion for the 'Fauntleroy suit' in America and Europe that continued until after the turn of the twentieth century. The 'elegant uncomfortable' (*TK*: 16) suit in which Tom is dressed in *Tom Kitten* bears a remarkable similarity to both the outfit worn by the child in the 'Bubbles' portrait and that of Little Lord Fauntleroy in Birch's illustrations, and it is difficult not to read Potter's handling of clothing in her *Tale* as a critique of such overly elegant and restrictive costumes for children which precluded them getting dirty and playing freely outside.

Such a critique may well be informed by personal experiences, since visual and written records of Potter's own childhood clothing suggest that she too had been subject to sartorial cultural influences. In a photograph of a young Potter with William Gaskell, we see her wearing clothes which bear a striking resemblance to those worn by Lewis Carroll's character Alice in illustrations by John Tenniel. Potter herself makes the comparison, noting that she wore 'white piqué starched frocks' and 'cotton stockings striped round and round like a zebra's legs' just like Tenniel's Alice (*A*: 208). It is in fact Tenniel's drawings of Alice from Lewis Carroll's 1871 sequel, *Through the Looking-Glass*, which most closely resemble Potter's outfit. Here Alice is depicted wearing stripy stockings, flat patent black shoes fastened with a strap, and hair held back by a band behind the ears, which would later come to be known as an 'Alice band' in the period after 1871. Though Potter had been fascinated by Tenniel's illustrations (*L*: 369) she focuses on the practical impediments of the outfit when worn by a real child, commenting that the headband hurt (*A*: 59) and the whole costume was 'absurdly uncomfortable' (*A*: 208).

Just as Potter shows awareness of the ways in which clothes can function in an inhibiting way, she also explores how they can be used more performatively, to question existing social positioning and hierarchies. This is most starkly apparent in *The Fairy Caravan*, since here costume is essential for the troupe of **circus animals** in enabling role-play. Paddy Pig uses various props and costumes to take on several different roles, including the Learned Pig, a clown and the Pigmy Elephant (*FC*: 68). **Xarifa**, the dormouse, becomes 'Princess **Xarifa**' with an outfit consisting of a 'doll's parasol, a blue dress, a crimson shawl and a lace handkerchief across her nose' (*FC*: 69–70). The most dramatic transformation of all is that of Tuppenny, the 'ill-used' little guinea-pig, who becomes the 'Sultan of Zanzibar' with a glamorous repurposing of his 'excessive' hair into a turban held by a 'crystal-headed pin' (*FC*: 70).

The significance of costume in relation to matters of identity also emerges within Potter's autobiographical writing. In the 1880s and 1890s Britain began to see challenges to traditional gender roles for women, with articles on the 'Woman Question' regularly appearing in the periodical press (Ledger 2007: 154), and this included discussion of new types of clothing for women which would permit greater physical freedom. One of the most radical developments in this respect was the introduction of the knickerbocker. Originally worn by men, these loose-fitting trousers which gathered below the knee became increasingly popular with women, since they helped to facilitate forms of physical activity which had previously been prohibited, such as cycling. In 1894 Potter gives an account of 'pretty little imp of eight or nine' who rides a bicycle and wears 'the neatest of little blue and pink combination knickerbockers' (*J*: 331). Potter adds jokingly that it is indeed the 'thin edge of the wedge' if children grow up to them but she also records her conviction that we are at the 'edge of the reign of knickerbockers' (*J*: 331). In an extended reflection on the new trend, she compares them to earlier fashions for bloomers and divided skirts, asserting that the problem with these previous fads was the necessity of wearing them underneath existing clothes and making sure they did not show. Whilst Potter disparages the 'pioneers of the movement' who parade around in them in a purely performative way while smoking cigars, she adds that to wear knickerbockers as 'a gymnastic costume, for cycling or other more or less masculine amusement is a different matter', commenting that it seems likely that within a very few years, a lady would be able to appear in them without 'exciting hostile comment' (*J*: 331). Her intriguing observation that they 'make all the difference in the world in the comfort of scrambling', but are 'hot' (*J*: 331), suggests that Potter herself had tried wearing knickerbockers at some point, perhaps while visiting her radically minded young cousin, Caroline Hutton, in Gloucestershire a few months earlier.

Though there is no definite evidence that Potter had worn knickerbockers, an interesting and intriguing change in her costume occurs at around the time this new fashion began to make an appearance for women. Photographs taken during her early adulthood usually show Potter wearing very traditional late-Victorian outfits; however, in the summer of 1889 she appears in a new fitted tweed jacket with matching deerstalker.

The deerstalker would come to be associated in the popular imagination with Arthur Conan Doyle's detective, Sherlock Holmes, as a result of Sidney Paget's influential illustrations of the stories for *The Strand* magazine, but it was not until 1891 that Holmes is first depicted wearing this headgear. Traditionally the hat was worn by country sportsmen or by city-dwellers who were spending time in the country and, as Potter is photographed wearing this headgear on holiday in the **Lake District**, it would appear that she is wearing it for the same reasons. However, like knickerbockers, the deerstalker had traditionally been worn by men, so that Potter's adoption of this headgear in 1889 suggests a slightly different interpretation. In the 1880s and 1890s, images of women wearing deerstalkers along with knickerbockers began to appear in advertising images, including cycling outfits, thus connecting the headgear to wider cultural shifts in women's identity and behaviour.

Potter pairs the hat with a matching fitted jacket and a full-length skirt, so is certainly not wholly embracing this radical new look but, like knickerbockers themselves, the deerstalker has slightly transgressive overtones at this point and gestures towards a different kind of future for women. One of the photographs of Potter taken in the **Lake District** in her new outfit is particularly arresting, not just because of her unusual headgear but also because of the look she gives the camera (see Figure 4). Her stance and gaze are in some ways reminiscent of the female mouse character in *The Tailor of Gloucester* (see Figure 3). Both seem to look out at us in a rather playful and challenging way, and in a manner which suggests an awareness on the part of the female subjects that their costume represents a form of rebellion against social expectations.

Potter's handling of clothes within her published work also points to a very modern understanding of the power of the image. Her strategic use of clothes plays an important role in the commercial success of her characters beyond the pages of the books in which they appeared, most famously and effectively in the case of **Peter Rabbit's** little blue jacket, which makes him

Figure 4 Close-up of Beatrix Potter from a group photograph (c. 1889).

instantly recognizable. One of the reasons why this character has had such a successful cultural and commercial life beyond the pages of his original story is because the cut and precise colour of his blue jacket are so distinctive. We can see the effectiveness of this technique in spin-off publications such as *Peter Rabbit's Almanac for 1929*. Here the reader does not need to be told that the rabbit who appears in the pictures for February, March, May, June and December is **Peter**; we know this is the case because of his blue jacket.

The effectiveness of Potter's 'branding' of **Peter** in this way can be discerned by the extent to which the blue coat has subsequently come to define her most famous **animal** character. In advance of the 120th anniversary of *Peter Rabbit*, Penguin undertook a rebranding exercise, bringing in an artist and a design agency to 'refine' the 'brand for a new generation', by producing a 'refreshed Peter Rabbit logo' (Newson 2021). In an article about this process, which is itself subtitled 'the design evolution of a blue-jacketed icon', the artist is quoted as saying that after the rebranding, the 'blue jacket remains the icon of love, trust and friendship' (Newson 2021). Not only is this a rather unexpected set of associations for a character defined primarily for his rebellious and naughty behaviour, but the phrasing suggests that it is not **Peter** who represents these things, rather they have somehow come to be metonymically embodied in the jacket itself. The fact that the rebranding team focused their efforts and attention so closely on the colour and shape of the jacket indicates just how effectively Potter used this garment in her construction of **Peter's** identity, but the wording also suggests that, in the 120 years since the book's publication, a range of other cultural meanings have accrued around and been absorbed by both the character and his 'iconic' clothes.

D IS FOR DANCING

Perhaps the most famous image of dancing within Potter's work appears on the cover of *Squirrel Nutkin*, where the eponymous squirrel is depicted with front paws in the air and one foot raised off the ground in dance. It is in fact a slight variation of the in-text illustration of Nutkin (*SN*: 46) which accompanies a description of him singing songs to 'Old Mr. B!' and growing 'more and more impertinent', while dancing 'up and down like a *sunbeam*' (*SN*: 47). Earlier in the story, Nutkin not only dances in front of Old Brown, but tickles him with a nettle as he does so (*SN*: 23). Dancing is used here to suggest the taunting and rebellious behaviour of the young squirrel which will, of course, shortly bring about a brutal and **violent** comeuppance, as Nutkin loses his tail to the infuriated owl. Nonetheless, much of the considerable charm of Potter's most famous squirrel character is conveyed by the images of him dancing, along with the unexpected and beautiful idea that he dances like a '*sunbeam*'. Our attention is drawn to the italicized word and the simile is suggestive of the way in which his russet-gold tail catches the light as he moves; it also though subtly conveys the more subversive idea that Nutkin himself is something of a ray of light in the world of the story, in his refusal to conform to the strict feudal order which it depicts. As Kutzer suggests, whilst the other squirrels accept this order, Nutkin is the 'voice of rebellion', but it is Potter's representation of his physical acts of dance, as much as his words, which reinforces the idea that the text offers a 'celebration' of this 'disobedience' (2003: 26, 28), and which helps to position the reader on Nutkin's side.

A similar use of dancing, to taunt a larger and threatening enemy, also occurs in *Miss Moppet*, after Mouse escapes from the eponymous cat. The last line of the story tells us that after his escape, Mouse can be seen 'dancing a jig on the top of the cupboard!' (*M*: 33), now out of harm's reach. The accompanying image depicts a joyful and newly escaped Mouse, with arms flung out and one leg raised in dance (*M*: 32). In *Mrs. Tittlemouse*, the title character throws a party for her mouse friends once she has finally managed to rid the house of unwelcome and messy visitors. The illustration,

D is for Dancing

which shows the mice happily dancing in their best dresses, also depicts a portion of the face of Mr. Jackson the toad who, having failed to gatecrash the party, stares at the joyful mice through the window (*TM*: 54–5). Here and elsewhere in Potter's writing, dancing is celebratory but also points to a refusal to be cowed by life's difficulties, especially on the part of the small and vulnerable.

In *Pigling Bland*, dancing is also suggestive of exuberance and a kind of spontaneous happiness. Brother Alexander doesn't just walk down the road, rather he skips, dances and sings, much in the manner of young children (*PB*: 25). Later, the story's main themes of escape and liberation are reinforced through spontaneous and joyful acts of dancing. As Pig-wig finally sees the Westmorland fells, she stops to sing and dance, as if to celebrate all that this region represents for herself and Pigling (see Figure 5).

As they walk together into their new life 'hand in hand', a final line drawing of the two pigs shows them dancing together '**over the hills and far away**' (*PB*: 80–1). As well as using dance here to emphasize the happiness and relief of the pigs as they escape into their new lives together, the style of dance depicted within the accompanying illustrations also helps to situate

Figure 5 Illustration from *The Tale of Pigling Bland*.

their story in a particular socio-cultural context. This is not the sort of dancing performed within polite Edwardian London society circles, but rather a type of dance suited to the characters in question and with distinctly rural and north-country roots. As we can see in Figure 5, Pig-wig is shown performing a small jumping step with one arm/front leg extended in the air and the second holding up her skirt. In the final image of the book, Pig-wig has both arms on her hips while Pigling Bland has one arm on his hip and the other raised (*PB*: 81). In other words, the images show that the pigs are dancing in the style of a reel or a jig. Potter makes more explicit references to the north-country dances she had in mind in *The Fairy Caravan*. When Tuppenny joins the **circus** troupe, **Xarifa** tells him that both Paddy Pig (who plays a fiddle) and the Scottish terrier, Sandy (who plays the bagpipes), do 'step dancing' whilst Paddy Pig dances jigs, Sandy dances reels, and all of us do 'country dances' (*FC*: 29).

References to dancing of other kinds also occur throughout *The Fairy Caravan*. Little Mouse is gifted a 'pair of lady's slippers' by the **fairies** so that she can dance at a wedding (*FC*: 58), there are songs of shepherds who 'dance and skip! / O'er the hills and valley trip' (*FC*: 90) and, in an allusion to Wordsworth, even the 'wild daffodillies' dance in the wind (*FC*: 127). The **fairies** descend from the **trees** they love on moonlit nights and dance together on the ground (*FC*: 157), and Pony Billy prances 'to the tune of the smithy song' as he heads back from the village and amuses himself with 'step-dancing' over the shadows of the hedgerow **trees** (*FC*: 189–90). Within *The Fairy Caravan* the motif of dancing is almost always suggestive of joy and happiness and, in the most extended passage on dancing in the book, we see various **animal** species of different ages come together at a rural festive community event:

> They trod a circle on the snow around the Christmas tree, dancing gaily hand in hand. Rabbits, moles, squirrels, and wood mice – even the half-blind mole, old Samson Velvet, danced hand in paw with a wood mouse and a shrew, while a hedgehog played the bagpipes beneath the **fairy** spruce.
>
> (*FC*: 143)

A similar treatment of dance-gatherings as forums in which social divides of different kinds can be crossed occurs within a more mysterious dancing scene in *The Fairy Caravan*. In Chapter 17 we encounter a secret magical dance floor in 'the middle of the great wood' which shines 'like a moonlit mere' (*FC*: 182). Adding to the **fairy**-like quality of this space is the fact that the light was always 'streaming upwards' from the ground, not 'downwards from the sky above' and, on this spectral dance floor, there are hundreds of dancing shoes (*FC*: 182). In his essay on 'The Uncanny', Sigmund Freud suggests that 'feet which dance by themselves' have something 'peculiarly **uncanny** about them' (Freud [1912] 2017: 752) and shoes which dance by themselves certainly have this potential too but, as so often in Potter, the otherly or strange is reconfigured as something beautiful. Potter compares this woodland dance to the 'Hall of Lost Footsteps' in a deserted **fairy** palace in France 'where ghosts dance at night'; there is a sadness about the latter, whilst this **uncanny** 'dance among the oak woods' is one 'of joyous memories' (*FC*: 182).

As in the Christmas **animal** gathering which occurs earlier in the book, this dance also allows for normal boundaries and social distinctions to be forgotten. Here are 'Shoes of fact and fable', glass slippers, cavalier boots, red slippers and every manner of other footwear:

> Round about them danced other shoes, other shoes dancing in hundreds. Broad shoes of slashed cloth; and long-toed shoes with bells [...]; buckled shoes, and high-heeled shoes; jack-boots, and buskins, and shoes of Spanish leather, and pumps and satin sandals that jigged in and out together.
>
> (*FC*: 184)

All the shoes, regardless of the status they represent or the context to which they belong, come together in this magical woodland dance and 'round about them – clump, clump, clump! – danced Mistress Heelis's clog, clog-dancing like a good one' (*FC*: 185).

This autobiographical intervention is a reminder of Potter's own personal love of community folk dances, which she discusses in detail in her final published essay, 'The Lonely Hills' (1942). In it she recalls the folk-dance revival of the 1920s and details precise memories of dances which were rooted in her life in the **Lake District**:

> For me the pretty jingling tunes bring memories of Merry Nights and of our English Folk-Dance Revival twenty years ago. The stone-floored farm kitchen where first we danced 'The Boatman' and heard the swinging lilt of 'Black Nag.' The loft with two fiddles where country dancers paced 'The Triumph,' three in arm under arched hands. [...]

Coniston, and the mad barbaric music of the Kirkby-Mazzard Sword Dance, when a beheaded corpse springs up and holds a wheel of wooden swords aloft. [...] The Morris bells and baldricks! The plum cake and laughter. Fat and thin, and high and low, the nimble and the laggard, the toddler and the grey-haired gran – all dancing with a will.

(*A*: 210–11)

As other critics have suggested, Potter's memory of these dances and her 'admiration of the folk traditions are parallel to many of her commentaries about the land, historic buildings, and ancient furniture – all of which she was concerned to protect and preserve for future generations' (Page and Smith 2021: 52). The passage also indicates though that one of the things Potter valued so much in these traditions, and a crucial part of what she wanted to protect, was the spirit of democracy which was manifest within such rural community gatherings. It is clear from the passage that part of the charm and significance of the village dance for Potter was its capacity to cross all divides and hierarchies, in a carnivalesque spirit of joy and laughter. There is something **circus**-like in her description of summer festivals at which the dancers appear 'in converging strands of colour to weave a tapestry that glistened like shot silk', and of a pageant in Grasmere where dancers 'in their hundreds from all over the north' appear like a 'rainbow-hued kaleidoscope' (*A*: 211). Within this same passage Potter's writing becomes increasingly personal as she seems to relive the experience of the dance in memory, capturing its rhythms and excitement in patterns of alliteration and assonance:

[G]ive me the swinging, roaring, reels – the sparkling pretty long sets – the maze of intricate dances surprisingly remembered – follow the fiddle, forget your feet! [...] Give me reels and spontaneous, unsophisticated country dancing all the time for dancing in a north country village.

(*A*: 211)

Given Potter's emphasis on 'unsophisticated rural dancing' within her writing, one rather unexpected development in terms of Potter's cultural legacy was a 1971 filmed ballet production of the *Tales of Beatrix Potter*. In many ways the ballet, which has traditionally been considered a highbrow and sophisticated mode of dance, is positioned at the opposite end of the cultural spectrum to the sorts of dance which Potter celebrates in her

D is for Dancing

writing. Indeed, ballet is more closely associated with the sorts of acceptable social entertainments endorsed by the circles in which her parents moved.

Not surprisingly perhaps, Warne originally turned the ballet project down, but was later won over to the idea. In the end, the ballet production of Potter's work proved to have considerable popular appeal and did, in many ways, succeed in translating the mood of the books onto stage and screen. The ballet film was choreographed by the ballet dancer and director, Frederick Ashton, and featured the British dancer, Wayne Sleep, as both Tom Thumb and Squirrel Nutkin. Ashton himself had some reservations about the production, later observing: 'I was not certain that with films dominated by violence and sex the time was right for such an explosion of sheer charm' (Bernheimer 1971), but in fact *Tales of Beatrix Potter* subsequently proved to be one of the top ten most popular movies of 1971 at the British box office (Harper 2011: 269).

The film's success seems partly to have been the result of Ashton's sensitive attention to the 'quirks' apparent in Potter's own handling of the anthropomorphized **animal** characters. As one contemporary reviewer notes:

> The stories are told simply and directly and with a certain almost clumsy charm. Instead of going for perfection in the dancing, the Royal Ballet dancers have gone for characterizations instead. The various animals have their quirks and eccentricities, and they are fairly authentic: The frog dances like a frog, for example, and not like Nureyev.
>
> (Ebert 1971)

In the production, characters from different *Tales* interact together on stage in a way that is reminiscent of the way characters from across the little books come together in dance in a drawing Potter made for a Christmas card in 1932. Produced for the Invalid Children's Aid Association, 'They Trod a Circle on the snow around the Christmas **tree**' depicts several of her best-known **animal** characters, including **Peter Rabbit**, Mrs. Tiggy-winkle, Jemima Puddle-duck, Squirrel Nutkin, Mr. Jeremy Fisher, all dancing together around the **tree** (see Figure 6).

Though the **animal** characters are not performing ballet steps here, the depiction of their pointed feet is strongly suggestive of ballet's 'point technique', in which a fully extended foot touches the floor, usually bearing the body weight. Moreover, the style of dancing shown on the card is very

Figure 6 Christmas card design by Beatrix Potter (1932).

similar to the dance steps performed in the 1971 film production, including Jeremy Fisher dancing 'like a frog'. In some ways then Potter's own drawing foreshadows not only the idea of characters from across her *Tales* coming together in dance but also elements of the way in which dance style would be used so effectively to convey those characters within Ashton's choreography.

Twenty years after the film was screened, the ballet was brought to the stage by ballet dancer and former artistic director of the Royal Ballet, Anthony Dowell. It premiered at the Royal Opera House in December 1992. However, the stage-production never received the same level of favourable response from critics as the film, and indeed is often compared unfavourably to the original film in reviews. Later Christmas revivals of the stage-show in 2007 and 2010 also resulted in some negative commentary, including a particularly vitriolic piece published in the *Financial Times* by the British dance critic, Clement Crisp. He writes scathingly of the December 2010 production at the Royal Opera House in which he claims that the Royal Ballet's dancers 'trip and tittup into view' in 'bloated' costuming and, 'I venture, sweat like the pigs they represent under a burden of quaintest frockery' (Crisp 2010).

Whilst the increasingly caustic tone of the review can, in part, be attributed to Crisp's personal cultural preferences and prejudices, there is nonetheless a sense that the charm of Ashton's original choreographic production was not so effectively transferred to later stage productions. Moreover, by the late twentieth and early twenty-first centuries, major new cultural reworkings of *Peter Rabbit* and the *Tales* were taking a very different turn, often relying on the alternative representational possibilities offered by computer-generated imagery (CGI) to bring Potter's imaginative constructions to new audiences.

E IS FOR EATING

The fact that virtually all Potter's *Tales* contain references to eating and food is not in itself surprising since these are central and recurring tropes in children's literature, from the school midnight feasts and holiday picnics of Enid Blyton to magical feasting in J. K. Rowling's fictional world of Hogwarts. However, in Potter's work representations of food and experiences of eating are rarely straightforward, nor are they predominantly pleasurable. The matter of what constitutes food is frequently problematized, not least because her main characters are themselves often perceived as food by both humans and other **animal** characters. Moreover, though some eating experiences in Potter's stories offer comfort, more often eating is connected to feelings of anxiety, fear or frustration.

It is notable that Potter resists what is perhaps the most dominant food trope in children's literature, that of feasting. Carolyn Daniel argues that food 'in seemingly never-ending quantities is a regular feature in classic British stories for children' and suggests that in 'early' canonical texts this can be seen as a reaction against the 'austerity of the traditional nursery upbringing', which advocated an 'extremely bland and restricted diet for children' (2006: 11). One of the most famous examples of this within Potter's own Golden Age period is the picnic scene in Kenneth Grahame's *The Wind in the Willows*, in which Ratty serves up a memorable riverside feast for Mole. It is a schoolboy fantasy of excess, in which the foods merge together in a litany of Edwardian picnic-hamper treats. Along with 'cold chicken' there is 'coldtonguecoldhamcoldbeefpickledgherkinssaladfrenchrollscresssandwidge spottedmeatgingerbeerlemonadesodawater' and Mole, 'in ecstasies', cries out that it is 'too much!' (Grahame [1908] 1994: 12).

Such a celebration of food abundance never occurs in Potter's writing and excessive consumption does not function in her work as a source of ecstatic happiness. This in itself suggests that her treatment of food is unusual within the contexts of literature written for children and is all the more intriguing since Potter was herself aware of the vicarious pleasure of reading about gastronomic treats. In remembering a book called *Little Sunshine's Holiday*

E is for Eating

(1871) by Dinah Craik, which tells the story of a not quite three-year-old child who is taken on holiday, Potter recalled that her enjoyment of the story stemmed partly from the connection she felt with the child character who travels by train at night, 'just like the journeys on which I was taken' (*A*: 196), but her dominant memory of the book is a food passage which was in stark contrast to her own experiences. On arrival at the holiday house, 'instead of having bread and milk to supper', Little Sunshine is given 'a basin of cream with a large spoonful of strawberry jam floating in it' (*A*: 196). Both cream and jam constitute indulgent epicurean treats for a very young child, and Potter's own relish for this imaginary supper is suggested by the fact that the food came to be exaggerated in her mind, with the 'tiny bit of jam' in the text (Craik 1871: 29) becoming a 'large spoonful' in memory.

The cream and jam supper offered to Little Sunshine is clearly very far from Potter's own childhood dietary experiences and, in this respect, she offers a counter-reading to Daniel, suggesting that her stories *reflect* her own food experiences rather than offering a fantasy of forbidden excess. Potter's memory of the Craik passage causes her to observe that she herself has never been a 'greedy person' perhaps 'because my own upbringing was so spartan' (*A*: 196) and, within Potter's own work, it is usually very frugal meals, often consisting of wild hedgerow ingredients, which produce happy and positive meal experiences. These tend also to be shared acts of eating, representing community and a coming together over food, but stripped of any middle-class formality (such as china teacups, tea-tables and tablecloths). **Peter's** sisters, Flopsy, Mopsy and Cotton-tail, enjoy the blackberries they have gathered from the hedgerows for supper along with bread and milk (*PR*: 68). Timmy Willie and Johnny Town-mouse share an ear or two of corn during the latter's visit to Timmy's home (*JTM*: 56) and Mrs. Tittlemouse hands round 'acorn-cupfuls of honeydew' to her party guests (*TM*: 57). When Tuppenny runs away from the Land of Green Ginger and meets **animals** from the travelling **circus**, their first act of welcome is through food. Jenny Ferret fills up the teapot from a 'kettle on the fire' and gives Tuppenny a 'mug of hot balm tea and a baked apple' (*FC*: 18). Not only is a simple frugal diet celebrated in Potter's work but, in a rare passage which appears to describe a luxurious abundance of food, the usual enjoyment of feasting to be found in children's books is thwarted. In *Two Bad Mice* the elegantly laid-out dinner of 'two red lobsters and a ham, a fish, a pudding and some pears and oranges', which makes the two mice squeak 'with joy' (*TBM*: 11 and 19), is in fact merely a simulacrum of food and provides then with no sustenance or pleasure at all.

As well as steering away from celebratory images of feasting, Potter's work also often focuses on the negative consequences of overeating. In **Peter Rabbit's** case, his overconsumption of radishes results in him feeling sick and needing to be put to bed with camomile tea. Though Kutzer suggests that the story is about the 'pleasures of appetite and the rewards of risking danger' (2003: 41), it is difficult to read the story as a positive affirmation of giving into our food appetites since the image of **Peter** blissfully gorging on radishes is followed by one in which he is clearly unwell; he holds a paw over his stomach and his eyes are downcast (*PR*: 23, 25). Overeating in Potter's fictional world also frequently causes sleepiness, often with dangerous results. After 'stuffing' themselves with the 'soporific' (*FB*: 27) lettuce leaves, the Flopsy Bunnies 'are overcome with slumber' (*FB*: 19), and it is this which renders them vulnerable to capture by Mr. McGregor. Timmy Willie falls fast asleep in the vegetable hamper after eating a quantity of peas and ends up being transported into a hostile urban environment (*JTM*: 8), and Pig Robinson finds himself cast out to sea after consuming too many muffins, which he went on eating 'until he fell asleep' (*LPR*: 88).

The story of Pig Robinson continues to emphasize the dangers of overeating since, once at sea, the ship's cook begins to feed the pig on huge amounts of porridge and potatoes in order to fatten him up for the captain's table. References to apple sauce and Captain Butcher's birthday meal make Pig Robinson's fate apparent to the reader but he is too busy enjoying his abundant meals to notice. The ship's **yellow** tom-cat tries to warn the pig of his fate by lecturing him on the 'impropriety of greediness' and about 'the disastrous effects of over-indulgence' (*LPR*: 94) but this lesson on greed is complicated by the fact that a young reader potentially identifies with the **animal** both as character and as food. Moreover, the references to pork accompaniments, such as the ingredients for stuffing and apple sauce, also mean that here the reader is in some sense implicated in the pig's fate.

Along with problematic scenes of excessive eating, Potter's stories also deal with experiences of hunger and quests for food which are stressful, with both motifs often pointing to forms of social inequality. In order to be allowed to gather nuts on Old Brown's island, the squirrels in *Squirrel Nutkin* have to run the gauntlet of approaching the owl to present him with gifts. Benjamin and Flopsy have a large family and there is not always 'quite enough to eat' (*BB*: 11), so Benjamin borrows cabbages from **Peter**, but when there are none to spare his children have to scavenge food from Mr. McGregor's 'rubbish heap' (*BB*: 15). The lettuces are a rare treat and the sort of food usually available here is far less appetizing: 'mountains of chopped

E is for Eating

grass from the mowing machine (which always tasted oily) and some rotten vegetable marrows' are mixed in with other inedible detritus, such as 'an old boot or two' and empty 'jam pots' (*BB*: 16). Other creatures from the bottom of the social hierarchy are also forced to scavenge here, such as the 'little old mouse', who picks 'over the rubbish among the jam pots' (*BB*: 20).

Even creatures from higher up the food chain (if not the social hierarchy) are shown to suffer from hunger and lack of food in Potter's *Tales*. In *Mr. Tod*, Tommy Brock

> complained bitterly to Mr. Bouncer about the 'scarcity of pheasants' eggs and accused Mr. Tod of poaching them! And the otters had cleared off all the frogs while he was asleep in winter – 'I have not had a good square meal for a fortnight, I am living on pig-nuts. I shall have to turn vegetarian and eat my own tail!' said Tommy Brock.
>
> (*T*: 14)

The last line comically and oxymoronically conflates two common exaggerated claims for an absence of food but the idea of taboo meat consumption, if not actual cannibalism, haunts this story, which involves one of Potter's most disturbing treatments of **animals** as food. Though Tommy Brock occasionally eats rabbit-pie, he does so only when 'other food was really scarce' as he was 'friendly with old Mr. Bouncer' (*T*: 10). Since Tommy is hungry, he comes to view his friend's grandchildren as a viable meal and this is all the more horrific because their extreme vulnerability as well as their proximity to human babies are emphasized in the text: the 'little rabbit babies were just old enough to open their blue eyes and kick' as they lie on their 'fluffy bed of rabbit wool and hay' (*T*: 12). This description renders the meal preparations particularly disturbing, as does the laying out of more 'civilized' dining accoutrements, such as the 'pie-dish of blue willow pattern', the tablecloth, a 'salt-cellar' and mustard, alongside a 'large carving knife' (*T*: 30), a juxtaposition which adds to the horror of the projected consumption of the baby bunnies.

Daniel argues that 'when we give fictional animals language, we accord them full subjectivity' and because 'talking animals are subjects, their flesh, like human flesh, is neither morally nor ethically edible'; she goes on to argue that because of this, stories which feature talking **animals** tend to uphold arguments for a 'vegetarian diet' (2006: 29). This is very far from being the case in Potter's writing, however, with many of her **animal** characters living in almost constant threat of being eaten by each other or by humans.

The latter fate is the one facing Pig Robinson who is being fattened up for Captain Butcher's birthday dinner. Moreover, in the language of the book, he is converted from living subject to food object by the captain, who demands the pig is covered up while sleeping on the deck since he doesn't fancy 'loin of pork with sunstroke' and because this scorches the skin and 'spoils the look of the crackling' (*LPR*: 101). As in *Jemima Puddle-Duck*, in which the foxy gentleman requests ingredients for a sage and onion stuffing, the clear boundary between **animal** as character and as food is threatened. In this respect, Potter's stories can be seen to conflate the dominant 'rules' of the talking-animals genre with the more disturbing eating tropes that occur in fairy tales. In 'Hansel and Gretel' by the Brothers Grimm, for example, there is both a process of fattening up (as we see in *Pig Robinson*) and the entrapment of child character who is destined to be eaten (as depicted in *Mr. Tod*).

As well as offering frequent reminders that **animals** often become food, Potter's stories also make regular references to what we would call the 'food chain', by exploring how the eater of one species becomes the eaten of another. This is an important thread in *Jeremy Fisher*, since the frog, who consumes minnows, butterflies, ladybirds and grasshoppers, is himself nearly eaten by a trout. The idea is more disturbingly handled in *Samuel Whiskers*, in which the cats eat the baby rats, and the grown-up rats then nearly eat Tom Kitten. Despite anthropomorphically framing some of the eating practices of the **animals** via typical Edwardian cooking and food presentation practices (such as serving roasted dishes with a sauce or encasing food in a roly-poly pudding), Potter's stories display a careful attention to actual **animal** traits and diet via the trope of eating. The picnic in Grahame's *Wind in the Willows* is problematic in this respect since it represents what Tess Cosslett has called 'excessive humanisation' (2006: 172), with a rat and mole enjoying a fully human diet. Cosslett compares Grahame's picnic with Potter's handling of food, which explicitly points to a distinction between **animal** tastes and those of humans. For the most part, acts of eating in Potter involve the typical diet of particular species, so that frogs eat insects, squirrels eat nuts, rabbits eat garden produce and cats eat mice. The latter is a regular feature of the stories, occurring perhaps most humorously in *Ginger and Pickles*, whose mouse customers are 'rather afraid of Ginger' and Pickles has to serve them, because they make Ginger's 'mouth water' and it would 'never do to eat our own customers' (*GP*: 11). In Potter's refusal to set aside **animal** instincts and their place in the food chain, here even the shop's customers are threatened with being consumed. Potter also makes explicit references to the distinction between **animal** food and human tastes in *Jeremy Fisher*. When Jeremy serves up his dish of roasted grasshopper with ladybird sauce, an authorial intrusion adds that though frogs consider this a 'beautiful treat […] I think it must have been nasty' (*JF*: 57). The plight of pigs is, however, particularly difficult to negotiate in the world of talking-animal stories since they are a farm **animal** kept for human consumption and Potter engages with this dilemma in *Pigling Bland* and *Pig Robinson*. Both stories make clear that these creatures form part of the human diet through references to the process of them being or becoming food (such as 'bacon', 'apple sauce' and 'fattening up').

Given the rarely celebratory and often deeply complex handing of food and eating in Potter's work, one rather surprising aspect of her cultural legacy has been the publication of Potter-themed cookbooks. Whilst a number of recipe books inspired by a nostalgia for the evocative depictions of food within children's literature have been published (Slothower and Susina 2009: 21–38), a body of writing which includes rat- or kitten-filled puddings and 'mouse pie' might not seem an obvious source of culinary inspiration but, even here, the market for Potter-related spin-off texts has found an outlet. *Peter Rabbit's Natural Foods Cookbook* by Arnold Dobrin was published in 1977 but 'Rabbit pie is noticeably absent' (Slothower and Susina 2009: 27), with the focus on getting children to eat healthier foods via recipes such as the 'Fierce Bad Rabbit's Carrot-Raisin Salad'. *Peter Rabbit's Cookbook* by Anne Emerson (1985) and *The Peter Rabbit and Friends Cookbook* by Naia Bray-Moffat (1994) are both aimed at young cooks with recipes such as 'Pigwig's Conversation Peppermints' (Emerson 1985: 8), whilst *Beatrix Potter's Country Cooking* (1991) by Sara Paston-Williams is targeted at an adult audience but largely sidesteps the problem represented by acts of eating within the books themselves by focusing on the kind of dishes which Potter might have encountered during her life in the **Lake District**. The blurb suggests the recipes are inspired by 'the works of Beatrix Potter and her love of traditional British cooking', but in fact the introduction steers away from the complex treatment of food in the works themselves, and focuses on biographical clues which suggest that the 'Heelises enjoyed simple traditional country dishes using fresh produce' and that 'Beatrix loved collecting wild plants, fruits and nuts from the surrounding countryside' (Paston-Williams 1991: 9). However, a recipe for 'Old English Rabbit Pie' does make an appearance and there is a nod to some of the more acceptable dishes (in terms of human consumption) which appear in the books, including 'Duchess's veal and ham pie'. Within this latter publication, the difficult and challenging ideas about eating and food found within the *Tales* are mainly ignored, and the Potter brand is used instead to represent a particular kind of English culinary tradition which is what we might think of as the implied background to many of the acts of cooking and eating represented in the *Tales*.

A more significant and controversial aspect of Potter's legacy in relation to food is the fact that this has recently been implicated in helping to shape those Western attitudes to food production which have been seen to contribute to a global environmental crisis. In his 2023 book, *Regenesis*, journalist and environmental activist George Monbiot offers a critique of contemporary farming and food production methods. He argues that a 'pastoral myth' of farming as a wholly positive and harmonious world is upheld in the twentieth and twenty-first centuries by both television and children's books. In relation to the latter, he claims that a 'remarkable' number of books for children tell stories of a farmyard

> with or without a rosy-cheeked farmer, in which the animals talk to themselves or to the reader. In most cases, there is one cow, one pig, one horse, one chicken, one dog, and one cat, living together as if they were a family. There is of course no hint of why the animals might be kept on a farm, what happens to them in life, or how and why they die. At the very dawning of consciousness, we learn that the livestock farm is a place of comfort and safety, a harmonious world removed from stress and conflict.
>
> (2023: 238)

Though Monbiot does not refer to Potter by name in the book, he has elsewhere identified her with the promotion and perpetuation of an agro-pastoral way of life in the **Lake District** (Monbiot 2017). Moreover, Potter's talking-animals picture books might well be seen to represent an early and deeply influential instance of the 'pastoral' farmyard scenes, as depicted in children's books, which he critiques here. However, there are important distinctions between her work and what Monbiot describes, especially in relation to the treatment of **animals** as food. Whilst Potter's books usually present us with small-holdings rather than examples of farming on an industrial scale, she does depict working farms not wholly artificial 'family' units; in the background to illustrations within *Jemima Puddle-Duck*, for example, we see two calves in a pen and three cows as well as multiple chickens and ducks in the yard (*JPD*: 9, 56). Potter's **animals** may talk but their potential role as food is rarely far from the surface of her stories, with references to pigs going to market as well as via her recurring focus on the 'stress and conflict' caused by **animals** trying to evade the prospect of becoming food. As Nicki Humble suggests, this is the 'central aim' of Potter's **animal** protagonists and Potter's own immersion in the 'pragmatic logic of a farming community' results in her not drawing a veil over the 'life-and-death realities of animal husbandry' (2014: 64). Whilst Potter's work certainly does not ask us to question meat consumption or related farming practices, it does lay bare the meaning and implications of these choices to her young readers.

F IS FOR FAIRY

In her essay on the '"Roots" of the Peter Rabbit Tales', Potter identifies the young Scottish nurse who looked after her as a child as a crucial influence on her writing. The nurse had a 'firm belief in witches, fairies, and creed of the terrible John Calvin'; Potter notes that, though the creed 'rubbed off', the 'fairies remained' (*A*: 207). The extent of this nurse's influence on Potter's early imaginative development is clear from her later acknowledgement that 'I used to half believe and wholly play with fairies when I was a child' (*J*: 435). Towards the end of her life Potter reflected on the extent to which this belief in 'fairy' had, in particular, shaped her engagement with the natural world: 'I do not remember a time when I did not try to invent pictures and make for myself a fairyland amongst the wild flowers, the **animals**, **fungi**, mosses, woods and streams, all the thousand objects of the countryside' (*L*: 423).

There is evidence of Potter perceiving elements of the natural world in this way within her **journal** and, although there is an attempt on the part of the young woman to distance herself from these perspectives, as belonging to childhood, some passages suggest that she was in fact still experiencing the natural world in a similar way as a young adult. In an entry written at the age of eighteen, Potter begins by using the past tense: 'I have thought the whole countryside belonged to the fairies' and that they come out of the woods by moonlight into the fields (*J*: 357). As the passage continues, however, Potter playfully reaffirms these beliefs by adding that hedgehogs are 'fairy beasts', and asking how, 'without the aid of the fairy-folk', could there be so 'little mildew in the corn'? (*J*: 357).

It seems clear from her writing that no small part of the strong attraction Potter felt towards the natural environment was the access it gave her to a private magical world, and that this in turn informs her perception of the value and importance of nature. Her readers are themselves invited to enter this magical world via the imaginative portal which is accessed by opening and turning the pages of her books. Indeed, this process is made explicit in ***Peter Rabbit***, in which the reader first encounters a drawing of the rabbit family without **clothes** and presented on all fours (*PR*: 6) but, on turning the page, finds a transformed group of anthropomorphized rabbits wearing **clothes**, standing upright, with the children being handed baskets by their mother (*PR*: 9). In *Mrs. Tiggy-Winkle*, the process occurs in reverse, so that at the beginning of the tale, Lucie – a human child-character – encounters the anthropomorphized figure of a washerwoman in cloth cap and apron who is busy with her laundry. At the end of the story, however, Lucie looks back and sees 'nothing but a HEDGEHOG' – a line which is accompanied by a drawing of an unclothed hedgehog running away on all fours (*TW*: 58–9). Even here though, we are confronted with Potter's reluctance to dismiss and explain away the magical elements completely. She ends the story with an authorial intrusion, observing that 'some people' believe that Lucie dreamt of her encounter, but adding: '*I* have seen that door into the back of the hill called Cat Bells – and besides *I* am very well acquainted with dear Mrs. Tiggy-winkle' (*TW*: 59). These words appear next to the final drawing of the non-anthropomorphized hedgehog, but the effect of this direct authorial message allows a young reader's belief in the possibility that hedgehogs are indeed 'fairy beasts' to be reinforced.

So effectively is the idea of imaginative access to some sort of magical experience of nature presented within Potter's public and private writing that when Chris Noonan came to make *Miss Potter* (2006), his biographical drama of Potter's early life for the big screen, he took steps to reaffirm and represent this idea for a twenty-first-century cinema audience. Using CGI, Noonan filmed scenes with Renée Zellweger as Potter talking to an animated version of her drawing of **Peter**. However, this aspect of the film drew down criticism from reviewers (Bradshaw 2007; French 2007) and does not successfully convey the more subtle idea presented in the writing. A crucial problem with the scenes is that 'Potter's' verbal response to her characters on screen ('Peter, do behave!' and 'Jemima, stop that!') comes across as that of a prim school mistress dealing with naughty children rather than the more intimate and usually non-hierarchical imaginary encounters with talking-animals suggested by Potter's own writing. The scenes which depict 'Potter' speaking to a CGI **Peter Rabbit** also have the effect of trivializing Potter's reading of the natural world itself as a special, magical space and the potentially powerful function of this on young readers.

One of the reasons why Potter's development of her anthropomorphized **animals** is so effective is because the characters are informed by her own underlying sense of magic in the natural world and the creatures around her. The ancient talking-animals trope has been seen by contemporary critics as having the capacity to encourage an early environmental awareness in children (Buell 2014: 2). The trope is all the more effective when developed by a writer like Potter, whose personal sense of joy in, and imaginative connection with, these creatures results in the production of many appealing and likeable characters. Potter develops the technique in some of her stories by also anthropomorphizing plants and **trees**, depicting them too as magical beings or as closely affiliated with such beings, in ways which have the effect of encouraging young readers to make further connections between themselves and the nonhuman world. Perhaps Potter's most interesting use of this latter approach appears in a story called 'The Fairy in the Oak', the final chapter in *The Fairy Caravan*. As with many of Potter's *Tales*, 'The Fairy in the Oak' had its origins in a story invented for real children – in this case one written some eighteen years earlier for the daughters of an acquaintance from New Zealand (*H*: 351).

That this story had an ecological impetus from the outset is suggested by the fact that within the notebook in which the first version was written, Potter has added in pencil: 'For 'tis my faith that every flower enjoys the air it breathes' (*H*: 351). The line is taken from Wordsworth's poem, 'Lines Written in Early Spring', in which he connects the human with the nonhuman world and offers a critique of human actions:

> To her fair works did Nature link
> The human soul that through me ran;
> And much it grieved my heart to think
> What man has made of man.
>
> (Wordsworth [1798] 1953: 377)

In her story Potter takes the idea of the flower's sentience as expressed in the poem to offer an extended ecological account of what 'man has made' of nature.

The story tells of the felling of an ancient north country oak, which was already a 'fine upstanding tree in Queen Elizabeth's reign' (*FC*: 254). The **tree** stands on a corner near an old highway where it has witnessed many social changes. In the early twentieth century though, when cars have arrived to replace the old carts and gigs, the district council decides to cut the oak down in order to widen the road. In its critique of the destruction of the **tree** for these purposes, the story can be situated in the long line of environmental conservationist writing, spearheaded in the **Lake District** by Wordsworth himself, who in 1844 campaigned against the development of the Kendal to

Windermere railway line. Indeed, the first half of Potter's story voices similar concerns about those who would undertake such developments as having 'no sentiment' and 'no respect' for the natural world (*FC*: 257).

Though in many ways Potter's handling of this act of destruction to make way for cars echoes anxieties expressed by Wordsworth a generation earlier, a crucial difference occurs via Potter's introduction of the female fairy figure. This figure is shown to embody the experience of the oak as it is felled, so that the brutal **violence** enacted on the tree by the male council employees (who 'hacked and sawed', who 'swung their heavy axes and drove iron wedges with sledgehammer blows into the great tree's heart') is registered as physical suffering on the part of a female figure, the 'harmless' and 'timid' fairy of the oak who 'sobbed and cried with pain' (*FC*: 259–60). **Xarifa**, who narrates the story, emphasizes the suffering of this figure in her account of the destruction of the tree, commenting that each 'dull, dead thud of the axe hurts the little green fairy that lives in its heart' (*FC*: 256). Left homeless, this pitiful figure wanders around till her 'leaf-gown was tattered and torn' (*FC*: 262), in a powerfully gendered image of the physical consequences of **violent** acts of destruction on the natural world. Ian Thompson observes that some 'critics have seen [...] the stirrings of feminist environmentalism' in Potter's *Tales* (2010: 202) and Marion Copeland argues that 'Ecofeminism's concern with the domination of nature and of all animals, wild and domestic, human and nonhuman, lies at the heart' of Potter's work; Copeland also suggests that Potter formulates connections between 'the oppression of women and the domination of nature' (2004: 71) and nowhere is this more fully explored than in this story, with its portrayal of a magical gendered figure as the embodiment of the oak tree.

In this respect though, it is worth noting that one of the most significant changes which Potter made to the story in her revised 1929 version was in the handling of the fairy. In the original story, dating from *c*.1911, the fairy in the oak is more clearly derived from representations of such figures in ancient folklore, being both dangerous and powerful. We learn that though she had been a 'peaceful little spirit' for many hundred years, she was now so angry, she 'nearly killed three men and lamed a horse' (*H*: 353). Though there are some lingering traces of the fairy's magical powers in the later version, they are far less explicit. In the earlier story, the mood of the fairy quickly shifts from distress to vengeful fury; growing 'fierce and angry' she uses her magical powers to snap the chains holding the oak and knock a 'woodman on the head' (*H*: 354). The fairy's anger is palpable and, even when she can no longer resist the forces pitted against her, she **dances** and screams with rage (*H*: 354–5). The experience of something 'strange' occurring when the men try to remove the oak leaves them feeling unsettled and 'glad to get away alive' (*H*: 355).

Although the original version of the story gives agency to a feminized image of nature and is, in some ways, a more satisfying representation of this magical figure, even here the fairy is ultimately ineffectual against the dominant forces of patriarchy operating within culture. Moreover, this portrayal serves to emphasize what has been described in recent ecofeminist scholarship as the 'longstanding dichotomy crafted between nature and culture', which 'has invariably privileged the latter term', with nature deemed to be 'wild' and 'disorderly', in contrast to the 'cultural arena's status as measured' and 'rational' (Murphy 2019: 13). Potter's revised treatment of the fairy in the later published version continues to use the fairy figure to reinforce the link between the oppression of women and the natural world, but it shifts away from this more problematic alignment of the female and nature with the irrational and disorderly.

Potter's questioning of the nature/culture dualism, on which ecofeminists argue models of oppression are founded, is also suggested by the unexpected end to 'The Fairy in the Oak'. Had Potter concluded the story with the destruction of the **tree** and the fairy's enforced flight, the moral and message would have been clear: we would read the story as a thoroughgoing reinforcement of Wordsworthian principles of landscape protection in the face of incoming modernity and industry, a position we know that Potter, influenced by her friendship with Canon Hardwicke Rawnsley (co-founder of the **National Trust**), supported. Such an ending would also though have left the fairy permanently cast outside social spheres and located within a liminal space of increasingly threatened 'wilderness'. However, the story does not conclude here. Instead, the fairy wanders out of the wood and comes to the banks of a flooded stream where a new bridge to the farm is being built, 'a wooden bridge with a broad span across the rushing river', and the 'straight brave timbers' that spanned it were 'made of the fairy's oak' (*FC*: 263).

This rather surprising conclusion to the story deploys the happy-everafter language of the fairy tale but combines it with a more pragmatic image of the future, informed no doubt by Potter's complex understanding of the human relationship with the natural environment derived from her two decades of farming experience. The fairy is now happy again and has made her home in the bridge:

She lives there, contented and useful; and may live there for hundreds of years [...] The bridge stands sure and trusty, where never before a bridge stood. Little toddling children take that short cut to school; and Something guards their footsteps by the bank of the flowery pool. The good farmhorses bless that bridge that spares them a weary road; and Something leads them over, and helps to lighten their load.

(*FC*: 263)

Crucially, by the end of the story, nature is firmly intertwined with culture. Notably the positive shift in the story occurs when the wood from the oak is reclaimed for farming and community purposes, and the new bridge is shown to be of benefit to both humans and nonhuman creatures, so that there is a reconciliation of these two communities. Judith Page and Elise Smith argue that, in 'both her imaginative writing and her practical work, Potter views nature as complex and interconnected with human life' (2021: 37) and within this story Potter presents these connections in ways that also reinforce the **Lake District** functioning as what UNESCO defines as a 'Cultural Landscape' – in other words a landscape which is shaped and defined through the 'combined works of nature and of man'. Though the story encourages a conservationist outlook and environmental awareness via its deeply negative handling of the felling of an oak to facilitate faster modes of human travel, it goes on to use the oak fairy to provide an image of reconciliation, embedding both women and nature within culture, and rejecting the nature/culture dualism in favour of a message about mutual reliance and connectivity.

G IS FOR GINNETT'S CIRCUS

In April 1885, an eighteen-year-old **Beatrix** Potter was staying in the **Lake District** with her family and she made the following short entry in her **journal**: 'Went to Ginnet's [sic] Travelling Circus. Very good, wonderful performing bull' (J: 146). This particular circus (in fact spelt Ginnett's) was one of the largest and best-known touring circuses of the Victorian period. The troupe performed for Queen Victoria and continued touring until the outbreak of the First World **War**, when the circus horses were requisitioned for the **war** effort. Though famous, Ginnett's was only one of a number of circus companies which flourished in the Victorian era, a period which saw a rapid rise in the popularity of circus entertainment. In August 1895, Potter – now aged twenty-nine – once again visited Ginnett's circus and on this occasion observed: 'I would go any distance to see a [circus] Caravan', adding 'it is the only species of entertainment I care for' (J: 397). It is worth pausing over this claim and reflecting on Potter's handling of the circus in both her private and public writings, to consider just what the experience and idea of the circus meant to her and quite why she found it so very appealing.

One answer of course relates to the circus **animals**. According to historians, a last major phase in the evolution of the Victorian circus occurred between 1880 and 1900, and during this period 'wild animals became a star feature' of the major circuses, who purchased 'lions, tigers, and elephants from the far corners of the globe', thus offering many people their 'first glimpse of the strange and the wonderful' (Assael 2005: 5–6). It is to this period of circus history that Potter's experiences belong and, although Ginnett's had its origins in horsemanship and equestrian display, it is clear from Potter's extended account of 1895 that a close-up encounter with exotic **animals** was a crucial feature of her own circus experience, since she mentions seeing lions, elephants and a brown bear (J: 397). Though Potter herself had already encountered many such creatures during visits to the **zoo**, it is nonetheless apparent from the **journal** descriptions that her interest in the circus was partly to do with the **animals** themselves. This is unsurprising given her fascination with nonhuman creatures and in her written accounts of these circus encounters she often notes species behaviour patterns and characteristics, such as two small lion cubs who played 'like kittens' (*J*: 252).

Though never sentimental about **animals**, there is a clear concern for aspects of their welfare within Potter's private writings about the circus. In a visit to a different circus ('Bostock & Wombwell's Menagerie') in Dunkeld during August of 1892, she observes that the '**animals** were splendid, so much healthier and fresher looking than most at the [**Zoological**] Gardens', going on to add that they had a 'variety of beasts' and the only **animal** which looked out of condition or unhappy was one of the pair of performing elephants, who was 'deplorably ill with a cold' (*J*: 252). Potter was clearly interested in the sick elephant's fate, since she records that the 'poor thing' died three days later (*J*: 252). In this same entry Potter also observes that she had 'no desire' to see the performance because of the lion-taming, which 'I object to' – a revulsion which no doubt stemmed from being told as a teenager that people who tame and exhibit lions and tigers have a red-hot rod inside their whip (*J*: 11).

Alongside the opportunity to study **animal** behaviour close at hand, a second source of appeal in the circus for Potter lay in the astonishing physical skills and appearances of the troupe. In her account of the visit to Ginnett's circus in 1895 she describes the 'skilful' performances of two men on parallel bars and 'Herr Wartenburg the Barrel King', who climbed onto a high seat then 'laid himself on his velveteen back with his heels in the air, and **danced** the wrong side up to the tune of *The Keelrow* against a cylinder' (*J*: 398). Alongside such feats of physical prowess, Potter was interested in the idea of performance itself, especially the function of **clothes** and costume in role-play and identity construction. Potter's perceptive gaze takes in and observes what the glamorous clothing fails to hide – the hard and rather drab life of the circus performers. She records that the 'scornful' Madame Ansonia, 'arrayed in blue and silver', stops to put her goloshes on in the ring, and a 'fair-haired enchantress' displays her dogs in an 'anxious cockney accent' and twinkles about in 'high-heeled French boots and chilly apparel', adding that tights 'do not shock me in a tent associated with damp grass' since here they 'suggest nothing less prosaic than rheumatics and a painfully drudging life' (*J*: 397).

In one sense, the circus show functions as what Judith Butler describes as the 'kind of gender performance' which enacts and reveals 'the performativity of gender' itself (1990: 139), but only perhaps to someone as perceptive as Potter. Indeed, her description of the female circus players here is reminiscent of Angela Carter's much more overt portrayal of this process of performativity in *Nights at the Circus* (1984). At the beginning of that novel, Carter's Victorian cockney circus character, 'Fevvers', the winged '*aerialiste*', is depicted peeling off the costume and make up which help to create her glamorous and exaggeratedly feminine stage persona, until she is left wearing a 'grubby dressing-gown, horribly caked with greasepaint around the neck' (Carter 1984: 19). In Potter's account, the distinction between the performed self and the 'prosaic' self beneath is less stable and the costumes are barely able to conceal a real life of 'rheumatics' and drudgery from Potter's sharp eyes.

Despite Potter's awareness of the more tragic aspects of the lives of the **animals** and people involved in the troupe, the humorous aspects of these performances also gave her a rare experience of shared laughter and fun. The circus was at the opposite end of the cultural spectrum from the more highbrow and emotionally repressive world in which she usually moved and Potter's private accounts of these circus visits, which are themselves very funny, demonstrate how much she enjoyed the ridiculous and absurd. She writes of Madame Ansonia ignoring 'her company (and half the scarves which she ought to jump)' and of an old iron-grey mare who was 'so very, very old that I was apprehensive about its rising when it curtseyed' (*J*: 397–8). There is in Potter's account a seamlessness between the activities on and off stage, and the joy she experiences in being a part of this mixed, slightly anarchic and strangely democratic gathering of humans and **animals** under a canvas roof is palpable:

> There was a great sale of sweets and the occasional variety of streams of rain through the tent, and the opening of umbrellas. The circus-dogs who mingled freely with the audience were demoralised by a fox terrier on the stalls [...] One bench of school-children was overturned by Joey [the horse].
>
> (*J*: 398)

Potter's enthusiasm for the circus – or this 'scene of joy' as she calls it (*J*: 398) – is connected to her love of old traditions, since the circus grew out of a range of pre-existing and pre-industrial forms of cultural recreation, including the medieval village fair. The circus also though represented something which appealed to Potter's democratizing spirit, since it took place in 'spaces such as the street or park' and crossed 'important class and spatial boundaries' (Assael 2005, 2, 9).

G is for Ginnett's circus

Potter's **journal** descriptions suggest that her reading of the circus had much in common with that of Dickens, whose novel, *Hard Times* (1854), contains the most famous Victorian literary depiction of the circus. In the novel, 'Sleary's Circus' becomes a powerful emblem of all that has been excluded from the new modern urban and industrial world, as represented by the fictional 'Coketown' with its school board superintendent, Thomas Gradgrind, and his strict observance of facts. Gradgrind stands in opposition to 'Fancy', a term used by Dickens to encompass a wide range of meanings, including human imagination and love. Although Potter's father was no Gradgrind and encouraged his daughter's love of the arts, a sense of oppression regularly emerges within the pages of her **journal** and there are subtle links between Gradgrind's daughter, Louisa, and Potter herself. Louisa's powerful speech to her father about her need to 'exercise her fancy' and her claim that such freedom would have made her 'a million times wiser, happier, more loving, more contented' (Dickens [1854] 1969: 240) echoes, in some ways, Potter's own need to break free of the restrictions of her home life into an imaginative world of 'fancy'. As Brenda Assael suggests, Victorian circuses were 'physical embodiments of that quintessentially Dickensian love of "fancy," an inalienable human desire generated by spontaneity, freedom, release, enjoyment, curiosity, and the wonder of life' (2005: 1) and such associations surely explain a significant part of the attraction for Potter.

Potter herself also recognized the potential appeal of the circus to young readers, since a couple of weeks after her 1895 visit to Ginnett's circus she humorously recounted the experience in a picture letter to Eric Moore (*LC*: 36–7). The idea of an **animal** character running away to join a circus was also developed quite early on in *The Tale of Tuppenny* (1903), which concludes with a guinea-pig protagonist selling himself to a 'travelling show-man', who 'goes about the country with a tent; and a brass band; and a menagerie of five Polecats and Weasels; and a troupe of performing fleas; and the Fat Dormouse of Salisbury; and TUPPENNY the HAIRY GUINEA-pig who lives in a caravan' (*H*: 308). However, this story remained unpublished and it would be nearly another three decades before Potter published a book which drew explicitly on the trope of the circus.

When putting together a collection of stories in the late 1920s for her American publisher, Potter finally returned to Tuppenny's tale and it is his story which opens *The Fairy Caravan* (1929). Though this text has received comparatively little interest from critics it is, in many ways, a fascinating collection which brings together Potter's experiences of actual circuses with her interest in **fairy** and magic. Kutzer describes the book as a 'a loose set of stories centred on a traveling animal circus', adding that 'the story of such a caravan might have been the basis for a good short illustrated tale but here it becomes simply a vehicle for Potter to string together a number of stories she found amusing or illustrative of life in the Lakes' (2002: 162-3). Though the circus caravan does provide a 'vehicle' or a framework for an eclectic group of tales, it is also rather more than this and, at intervals within the collection, Potter returns to the idea of the circus and what it represents.

Potter's treatment of the motif of the circus in *The Fairy Caravan* has a magical dimension from the outset, since the **animals** 'carry fern seed' to ensure that the circus is invisible to humans (*FC*: 30). Potter later emphasized the story's grounding in magic and fantasy in her essay, 'The Lonely Hills', in which she writes that it was the discovery of '**fairy** footmarks on the old drove road' which 'first made me aware of the Fairy Caravan' (*A*: 212). This fantasy element is important since it allows Potter to move beyond the poverty and drabness of real circus lives, and effectively realize the imaginative potential of the circus in terms of personal transformations and freedom.

The Fairy Caravan begins as a story of oppression and escape, with the story of Tuppenny the guinea-pig who lives in the town of Marmalade. Tuppenny is a sad figure of 'dilapidated appearance' who 'suffered from toothache and chilblains' and whose hair is 'thin and patchy', probably as the result of 'ill treatment' (*FC*: 5-6). After his fellow guinea-pigs have poured a whole bottleful of a hair-growth treatment onto him, Tuppenny's hair begins to grow at an alarming rate and the guinea-pig's already unhappy life becomes much worse with taunting and further mistreatment. Tuppenny decides to run away and, after a long journey, which takes him far away from the town and into the countryside, he comes across a 'curious little encampment' with a **yellow** caravan on which is painted 'ALEXANDER AND WILLIAM'S CIRCUS', featuring 'The Pigmy Elephant! The Learned Pig! The Fat Dormouse of Salisbury! Live Polecats and Weasels!' (*FC*: 15-16). Here Tuppenny finds a group of **animals** seated around a fire who, in stark contrast to the inhabitants of Marmalade, display the traits which Dickens attributed to members of the circus: a 'remarkable gentleness' and an 'untiring readiness to help and pity one another' (Dickens [1854] 1969: 77). Sandy the dog is instructed to carry the 'cold and wet' guinea-pig to the fire so that he can 'warm his toes'; he is given food and finds himself 'much comforted by the warmth of the fire, and by their kindness' (*FC*: 18).

Crucially, the circus company also show interest rather than revulsion or mockery in response to Tuppenny's unusual appearance and his abundance of hair. They 'admired it prodigiously' and the dormouse describes it as 'truly mar-veel-ious' (*FC*: 20). In this world, all are accepted and embraced for what they can contribute to each other's lives and to the troupe, from **Xarifa** the tiny dormouse – who regularly falls asleep but also entertains them all with stories – to Paddy Pig, an 'important member of the circus company' who plays several parts: the Learned Pig that could read, in spectacles; the Irish Pig that could **dance** a jig; and the clown in spotty calico (*FC*: 68). The pig's most significant role is his performance of the 'Pigmy Elephant' – a delightful Potteresque play on words, and also a humorous take on her interest in the possibilities of **clothes** in enacting transformations and role play. As this is a very small and low-budget circus troupe, the only way to incorporate exotic **animals** in the performance is through disguise, so Paddy Pig wears tusks which are 'shaped from white peeled sticks out of the hedge' and a 'black stocking' which is 'stuffed with moss for a trunk' (*FC*: 68).

The idea of identity transformation enacted through costume and performance is made most explicit in the story through the radical transformation of Tuppenny himself who, in the next show put on by the troupe, rides on the 'Pigmy Elephant' dressed up as the Sultan of Zanzibar. He wears a 'scarlet bandana handkerchief robe, a brass curtain ring round his neck' and at gala performances his whiskers are dyed pink; as the narrator observes, no-one 'would have recognized him for the miserable, ill-used little guinea pig who ran away from his home in the city of Marmalade' (*FC*: 70). Here costume is used much more effectively than in Potter's experiences of real circuses. Within the context of her fictional circus, even the lowliest figures in society can be transformed into the most exalted and glamorous. This subversion of hierarchies relates to the idea of the 'carnivalesque' as explored by the Russian philosopher and literary critic, Mikhail Bakhtin, in *Rabelais and His World* (1965). Through his study of the work of the French Renaissance writer, François Rabelais, Bakhtin developed a theory of the subversive potential of carnivals and folk festivals, with their emphasis on laughter, a playful overturning of hierarchies and an undermining of the authority of official culture. Potter's handling of the 'transformation' of Tuppenny in *The Fairy Caravan* suggests that part of the appeal for her in the circus was indeed the humorous way in which it 'disrupted the order of things' (Assael 2005: 13).

Though Potter began to prepare some additional stories for a sequel to *The Fairy Caravan*, she did not explicitly revisit the trope of the circus elsewhere in her writing. However, the impulse to playfully overturn hierarches and explore imaginative transformations, alongside a mood of joyous carnivalesque celebration, recurs many times within her *Tales,* and is often explored through the related trope of **dancing**, via her handling of **clothes** and costumes, and through repeated motifs of freedom and liberation. In many of Potter's stories there is a challenge to forms of social oppression and a celebration of the less inhibited and more imaginative modes of life, both of which are linked thematically with her interest in the circus.

Whilst Bakhtin's study of Rabelais informed an understanding of the carnival as something which ultimately functions to reinforce 'the "official" order by inverting it only temporarily', as Assael suggests, the Victorian circus 'defied the limits of "a mere holiday mood"' and, 'rather than inverting power relationships for a day or a week, had a more permanent role to play in this society' (2005: 8). Since the circus functioned as part of the Victorian commercial leisure market, it was regularly on hand, 'functioning to overturn the sacred in favour of the profane any day of the week and throughout the year' (Assael 2005: 8). Given the carnivalesque possibilities offered by the circus, it is perhaps no wonder that Potter 'would go any distance to see' one and identified it as 'the only species of entertainment' for which she cared (*J*: 397).

H IS FOR *HORN BOOK*

The *Horn Book* or *Horn Book Magazine* is a bi-monthly review which was founded in Boston, Massachusetts by Bertha E. Mahony (later Bertha Mahony Miller) in 1924 to discuss and identify the best in children's literature. Its title derives from the single-sided tablet which was used as a primer for learning the letters of the alphabet during the medieval and renaissance periods, and which was known as a 'hornbook', but in her first editorial Mahony plays on the meaning of the term by indicating that the mission of the *Horn Book Magazine* was to 'blow the horn for fine books for boys and girls' (Hahn 2015: 289). Just one year after its first appearance Potter wrote to Mahony to describe the *Horn Book*, rather underwhelmingly, as 'pleasantly written' (*A*: 9), but she came to see is as a 'splendid publication' (*L*: 370) and her subsequent engagement with this magazine, as well as with American librarians, booksellers and publishing houses, would result in several important late works being published in America at a point at which Potter's 'little book' project with Warne had all but come to an end. These include *The Fairy Caravan* and *Sister Anne* (both published by the Philadelphia-based publisher, David McKay Co.) and *Wag-by-Wall* (published posthumously by Horn Book Inc.). Potter's new ties and a growing American readership also resulted in two editions of *Little Pig Robinson*, since she offered this story to both Warne and McKay, with the American edition featuring more of her illustrations. Indeed, Potter preferred the McKay book, which reminded her 'pleasantly of old favourites of nursery days' (*A*: 40).

Potter's first encounters with American readers and visitors in fact pre-date the appearance of the *Horn Book* but relate to the same impetus: a growing interest in children's literature on the part of American librarians, booksellers and readers. In 1921 and at a time in which Potter had begun to shun her identity as '**Beatrix** Potter' in favour of 'Mrs Heelis', farmer and breeder of Herdwick sheep, she received a visit from Anne Carroll Moore, superintendent of Children's Work at the New York Public Library. Moore had just returned from a charitable trip to France to help rebuild libraries in villages devastated by **war**, and she had ordered fifty copies of the French translations of *Peter Rabbit* and *Benjamin Bunny* from Warne to be sent over. What this initial meeting revealed to Potter was the extent of transatlantic interest in her own work as well as the many important developments in children's literature which were taking place in America.

Indeed, one of the reasons why Potter quickly came to enjoy discussing her work with American correspondents was that she felt, for the first time, her books were being taken seriously, whereas in Britain her *Tales* were viewed as 'toy books – not literature' (*A*: 31). As early as 1904 Potter had an intimation that her books were read differently in the States, as a 'lady in Pittsburgh' wrote to Warne to say that *Peter Rabbit* is 'exquisite literature' (*L*: 90) and, through extensive dialogue with American booksellers, librarians and reviewers in the 1920s, Potter began to perceive that her books were indeed viewed differently across the Atlantic. Potter later wrote that 'New Englanders understood and liked an aspect of my writings' which is not appreciated by those who sell the books in Britain, recognizing that there is more in the books than 'mere funniness' (*A*: 96). In 1934, one of her American contacts published *The Children's Almanac of Books and Holidays*, which presented the history of children's literature via a series of landmarks. **Peter Rabbit** appears on the cover and the foreword includes Potter's work in an overview of 'some of the truest writing' that has been done for children; unsurprisingly, Potter found the publication 'delightful' (*A*: 60).

The very existence of a publication such as the *Horn Book* was evidence of a different attitude towards literature for children in the United States. As Potter observed, there is nothing like this 'to direct the choice of children's reading in this country' and, as a consequence, British children were being encouraged to 'like things grotesquely ugly' (*A*: 31). Over the next few years Potter began to reflect on developments in children's literature in Britain from her own childhood to the present. At the core of her findings was the belief that, though this country had produced some classics, such as Lewis Carroll's *Alice in Wonderland* and Charles Kingsley's *The Water-Babies*, in 'the main children's literature has not been taken seriously over here' (*A*: 49). Indeed, she found herself in full agreement with a 1934 article in the *Horn Book* on 'English Children's Literature', commenting that British authors used to 'write down' to children and now write 'twaddling dull' stories or 'odious slangy stuff' (*A*: 57).

Potter's American correspondents shipped new books over to her so that she could read, by way of contrast, the sorts of books which were being published in America for children, and she clearly found developments in American children's literature much more promising. Such texts included

And to Think That I Saw It on Mulberry Street (1937) by Dr. Seuss, which she thought 'delightful' (*A*: 83), and *Doctor Dolittle* (1920) by Hugh Lofting, which she found a 'most amusing clever book' (*A*: 39). Potter rapidly came to believe that in America 'writers take more pains with juvenile literature', whereas in England they seem to think 'anything is good enough for children' (*A*: 66).

For the first time in her career, Potter found herself in a position to engage in discussion, analysis and critical reflection on the field of writing to which she had committed so much of her creative energy. She embraced the opportunity, reading everything she was sent and offering her own perceptive analysis on what she felt worked well in the context of children's fiction. She writes that too many 'story books for children are condescending self-conscious invention', whilst in Seuss there is a 'natural truthful simplicity of the untruthfulness', which she compares to her own successful strategy of 'spontaneous natural bare faced' lying (*A*: 84). Potter was particularly interested in books which explored **animal**/human relations. She found Marjorie Kinnan Rawlings' Pulitzer prizewinning book, *The Yearling* (1939) – which tells of a young boy's powerful but ultimately tragic relationship with a deer – 'alive' and 'splendid' but 'too painful for satisfaction' (*A*: 86, 92). However, she thought that Elizabeth Coatsworth's *Here I Stay* (1938), a historical novel which depicts a girl's long winter with virtually no human contact but constant interaction with **animals** and the natural world, was very powerful. Potter comments on how effectively the author has conveyed the 'strength and beauty of the girl's character' and on the 'poetry of the great lonely places and wood' (*A*: 93). During this period, Potter was also reading many American classics, thinking about literary style and how writers achieved certain effects. She read Sarah Orne Jewett's *The Country of the Pointed Firs* (1896) 'repeatedly', trying to understand 'how it was done', finding the style 'artless and simple' and the book 'perfect as a work of art' (*A*: 53).

Well aware that books for children needed to be targeted at certain age ranges, Potter also discussed the paucity of more serious British books for 'middle aged children', along the lines of *Adventures of Huckleberry Finn* (1884). She recalled reading novels which focused on the 'realistic portrayal of children's lives' (Hahn 2015: 392) by Juliana Ewing and Mary Molesworth herself as an older child, but observed that this realist genre of writing has had 'no successors' for a very long time (*A*: 104). She does though identify Arthur Ransome's *Swallows and Amazons* series as a positive development for this age range within British children's publishing, describing it as 'more like' the kind of thing she had in mind and adding 'I am sorry I never met the author' who 'used to live near Windermere' (A: 104).

As well as participating in stimulating discussion about developments in children's literature with her American contacts, Potter also enthusiastically embraced acts of cultural exchange. She was delighted to discover that a reading of *The Tailor of Gloucester* had become a Christmas Eve tradition in many children's libraries and homes in New England (Morse 1982: xi), and would go on to provide other stories which might be absorbed into that tradition, suggesting that the 'Demerara Sugar' chapter from *The Fairy Caravan* might work as a Christmas story for American children (A: 27), and later including Christmas references in *Wag-by-Wall* for the same reason (H: 328). In return, Potter immersed herself imaginatively in a 'real old fashioned' American Christmas via a newly published book by Anne Carroll Moore (A: 7). After reading *Nicholas, A Manhattan Christmas Story* (1924), Potter observed that she had no idea New York was 'so "Christmassy"' (A: 7) and the following year wrote to say: 'We will read his book again on Christmas Eve and think of his merry doings across the Atlantic' (A: 8). The use of 'we' here suggests that the story was to be read out loud at Castle Cottage, so that while American readers were encountering a *Tale* set in an English city on a snowy Christmas Eve, a New York Christmas was being experienced by the Heelises in a remote corner of northern England.

Despite Potter's interest in the new writing being published in America for children, an important point of connection between Potter and her American correspondents was their shared love of older stories emanating from British and European traditions, with Potter observing that you 'love the same old tales that I do' (A: 35). John Goldthwaite claims that this is 'most certainly' a reference to the *Uncle Remus* books by Joel Harris Chandler (1996: 305) but in fact Potter's letters to her American correspondents make no reference to these books at all, and the term 'old tales' here seems to refer to much older nursery classics and fairy tales. As Potter herself observed, '*I* like *fairy* tales, and so do American readers' (A: 42), and it is notable that the books which she published in America are those which are steeped in more ancient literary traditions. These are books which feature stories about magical woodland spaces where shoes **dance** without their owners, tales of fairies who live in **trees**, and of Bluebeard in his castle.

The books which Potter wrote for an American audience are also those which draw inspiration most explicitly from the landscapes and culture of the north of England. Aware that her American readers were drawn to her books and to the **Lake District** partly because of their love of an old rural order with its 'simple country pleasures' (Morse 1982: xi), she presented them with stories which celebrated such a world. Indeed, the writing Potter published in America is some of her most local and geographically grounded work. In *The Fairy Caravan* she doesn't transport the reader to the famous lakes or **Lake District** tourist centres, but to those (then) little-known spots around her own home: Wilfin Beck, Codlin Croft, Pringle Wood and Troutbeck Tongue – places which had remained relatively unchanged and untouched by tourism or modernity. In a sense, this book was a kind of love letter to the places she had come to know best and to care about the most, written for readers whom she believed would appreciate such landscapes.

Though this interest in overseas readers via the *Horn Book* and other American contacts is vital in terms of the development of Potter's writing at the end of her career, this was far from Potter's first engagement with child readers from other countries. Around 1909, Potter met a family from New Zealand who were staying briefly in London and she corresponded with the mother and her two daughters (Kitty and Hilda) after they returned home, eventually writing 'The Fairy in the Oak' for the two girls. Though a revised version of the story would later appear as the final chapter in *The Fairy Caravan* for an American market, its original readership was 'two New Zealand fairies' (*LC*: 150) and Potter later dedicated *Cecily Parsley's Nursery Rhymes* to their young cousin, 'little **Peter** in New Zealand'.

Potter's awareness of growing international markets for her work and her interest in reaching out to those readers is also suggested by the publication of *Timmy Tiptoes* in 1911, a story which is dedicated to 'many little unknown friends', and features non-English **animal** characters, including the grey squirrel (already present, but not widespread in Britain), a chipmunk and a brown bear. That Potter was particularly targeting American readers with this publication is indicated by the fact that she went to the **zoo** to draw an American black bear, and consulted a book called *American Animals* to find out about chipmunk behaviour. Always interested in species accuracy, Potter was clearly influenced in her handling of Chippy Hackee by the account of chipmunks in the book, which portrays them as very companionable and having a tendency to care for and protect each other (Stone and Cram 1902: 162–8).

From an early stage, Potter and Warne had also begun to explore the possibility of her *Tales* being sold in non-English speaking countries via translations. By 1907 Warne had considered approaching French and German publishers to produce translated editions of **Peter Rabbit**, but the project stalled (*L*: 154). Warne later decided to publish translated editions themselves and, during 1913, Potter was quite occupied with this project, taking as much care in checking over the translated words as she had in producing her original English ones. She observed that 'Mrs Tiggy is perfectly charming in French' (*L*: 201) but her favourite was *La Famille Flopsaut* (*The Flopsy Bunnies*). Potter's work had already reached readers outside Britain by this date and in fact by the time Warne began to work on these editions, Dutch translations of **Peter Rabbit** and *Jemima Puddle-Duck* had been published (*H*: 264).

By the beginning of the twenty-first century, **Peter Rabbit** had been translated into an astonishing thirty-six languages, including Icelandic, Afrikaans and Welsh. Uniquely, it has also been translated into hieroglyphics (using the script of Middle Kingdom Egypt), Ancient Greek and Latin. The cover of the latter gives the title, rather delightfully, as *Fabula de Petro Cuniculo*, and the author as Beatricis Potteri. Linder describes this text as having been produced for 'teaching purposes' (*H*: 266) which suggests that familiarity with the original is so extensive, it provides a means of learning some basic Latin words and phrases. Almost like a latter-day Rosetta Stone, the base text of **Peter Rabbit** functions here as a **key** to these ancient languages.

A year before Warne first began to explore the possibility of editions of **Peter Rabbit** in other languages, an unauthorized translation had, however, already been published in another non-English-speaking country, marking the first steps in what would become perhaps Potter's most far-reaching global influence. In 1906 a Japanese language version of **Peter Rabbit** appeared in a section of an agricultural magazine in Japan which was dedicated to pastoral literature, and multiple other versions of the story were published in Japan between 1906 and 1971 (Wallace 2013: 395). Authorized translated editions of Potter's *Tales* began to appear from 1971, with six titles published that year (Yoshida 2002: 191). Whilst this relates to the wider cultural project of translating European children's classics into Japanese in the post-**war** period as part of an ongoing process of 'westernization', the particular popularity of Potter's work is indicated by the fact that by the beginning of the twenty-first century, 'no non-English speaking country except Japan has such a complete set of translations of Potter's works' (Yoshida 2002: 191).

In accounting for this development, Shin-ichi Yoshida makes quite significant claims about the particular qualities of Potter's writing, qualities which are rarely attributed to the work of individual literary figures other than Shakespeare. Yoshida suggests that Potter's books 'speak to human beings everywhere' and are both 'quite English and also very universal'

(2002: 190 and 191). Though this may be true, there is also a more particular socio-historical factor involved here, which helps to explain the appeal of Potter's work in both Japan and America (especially New England). Both countries had experienced rapid industrialization and urban development, and a crucial part of the appeal of Potter's work seems to lie in its evocative depiction of rural landscapes and a pre-industrialized way of life.

Potter recognized this in relation to her American readers from an early stage and tried to harness their desire to protect this fast-disappearing world by raising funds for **National Trust** land purchases. It is evident that this aspect of her books was also vital in developing widespread Japanese cultural interest in Potter's work. Yoshida writes that these books 'appeal to us to return to nature quietly but strongly' and are 'all the more valuable in the present society where industries are developing and cities are expanding quickly' (2002: 195). Reinforcing such a reading is Catherine Butler's claim that Japanese tourists are particularly attracted to those places in Britain which represent a stark contrast to urban Japanese life; they are seen as a 'retreat from the pressures of modernity' where people seem to 'live together with nature in a peaceful atmosphere' (2023: 156) and, in many ways, the **Lake District** of Potter's books is a powerful evocation of such a place.

Potter's *Tales* were written in the early years of a new century which followed the period in which Britain had itself gone through unprecedented levels of change as a result of the industrial revolution. As the first country in human history to undergo the process of industrialization and urbanization, Potter's generation was still dealing with the anxieties and social transformations associated with this change. In part, her texts are a response to a half century of disquiet about the loss of older rural rhythms and ways of life and, as such, it is perhaps inevitable that her books would go on to speak so powerfully to readers from other nations who were themselves beginning to emerge from that same process.

I IS FOR ILLNESS

After several weeks of dealing with ill-health on the part of her mother and father, **Beatrix** Potter confided to her **journal** in 1895 that she was 'feeling very much down' and had turned to books and literature for comfort. She writes of deriving 'quiet pleasure' from reading Matthew Arnold's letters and 'much consolation' from Wordsworth (*J*: 411). Potter's understanding of the ways in which reading could help provide emotional and psychological support during difficult times is also apparent in the fact that some of her earliest attempts at imaginative writing for children are prompted by illness on the part of young readers. Noel, the eldest child of Potter's one-time governess, Annie Moore, and the recipient of many of her early picture letters, was frequently unwell as a child and later contracted Polio (*LC*: 15). A few months before Potter made this entry in her **journal** about her own recourse to reading and literature, she had written to Noel during one of his periods of illness, and used the letter to tell a comforting micro-story of sickness and recovery. A small mouse appears first in bed, being visited and cared for by Doctor Mole and Nurse Mouse, before being shown wrapped in a blanket and well enough to 'sit up in a chair by the fire' (*LC*: 30–1).

Several of Potter's published *Tales* also incorporate illnesses of some kind or other and present a young reader with similar narratives. Daphne Kutzer reads Mrs. Rabbit's sickbed nursing of her son as an extension of maternal control in **Peter Rabbit** (2003: 46) but Potter presents more overtly positive acts of caring in other stories and images, especially alongside motifs of friendship. In *Timmy Tiptoes*, for example, the eponymous squirrel is looked after by Chippy Hackee and an illustration depicts the squirrel tucked up comfortably in a mossy bed and being brought food by his friend (*TT*: 33). An early instance of this motif of being cared for and nursed back to health by friends occurs in an illustration which Potter produced for *Alice in Wonderland* in the early 1890s, which depicts Bill the lizard after he has been kicked out of a chimney. Whilst the original Tenniel drawing focuses on Bill flying out of the top of the chimney, Potter's illustration turns to what happens next. She portrays a group of **animals** looking on in concern and

I is for Illness

caring for the apparently unconscious lizard, with two guinea-pigs gently holding onto his two front legs, as if holding the hands of a sick patient, and preparing to give him some brandy (*Art*: 254). Though privately Potter rejected a romanticized view of nursing, observing acerbically in her **journal** that there is supposed to be some 'angelic sentiment' in tending the sick, but 'personally I should not associate angels with castor oil and carrying slops' (*J*: 407), she clearly recognized the positive psychological effect of stories and images which depict those who are sick or injured being cared for.

Potter's awareness of the value of such representations, along with her sympathy for poorly children, is no doubt influenced by her own prolonged periods of illness in childhood and early adulthood. Potter is often depicted as having been a sickly or 'delicate child' (Taylor 1986: 21) and her **journal**, begun when she was in her mid-teens, makes reference to regular bouts of colds and other minor illnesses throughout the early 1880s. Indeed, Linda Lear describes her as suffering from 'a systematic infection' during this period (2007: 66). As well as using reading as a means of providing emotional and psychological support, Potter also turns to writing to give expression to private frustrations about the impact of ongoing health issues on her life. On the run up to Potter's nineteenth birthday most of her hair had fallen out and she had to have the remaining locks clipped short. Though recorded in a matter-of-fact tone in her **journal**, the distress this caused emerges in a sorrowful reflection on the lost hair: 'I have seldom seen a more beautiful head of hair than mine' which last summer was very thick and 'more than a yard long' (*J*: 143-4). She also writes of her frustration at the restrictions which illness placed on her daily life, asking herself rhetorically how it is that these 'high-heeled ladies', who 'dine out, paint and pinch their waists to deformity', can 'racket about all day long' whilst 'I who sleep o'nights' and can 'turn in my stays' am so tired towards the end of the afternoon that 'I can scarcely keep my feet?' (*J*: 146).

Though Potter often uses her private **journal** to record her thoughts and feelings, we encounter very few passages in which she writes in any detail about the illnesses themselves or her physical symptoms. A rare exception is an entry from 1887, which records that she had been 'very ill' with something 'uncommonly like rheumatic fever' while the family were away on holiday in Grange-over-Sands (*J*: 203). The passage provides an unusual level of detail about the onset and nature of the illness, which began with pain in one foot that spread from her toes to ankle and then knee. She describes being 'feverish' and the pain as 'fearful', with the result that a doctor is called out to her in the early hours (*J*: 203). Taken back to London, she is bedridden for three weeks with pain 'continually moving backwards and forwards, up and down each leg' so that she could not be turned in bed without 'screaming out' (*J*: 203).

The fact that this record of painful and no doubt traumatic physical suffering is so unusual within the **journal** indicates that writing rarely functioned as a recourse or outlet for Potter while she was in the midst of serious illness, since such periods usually prevented her from writing. Indeed, on this occasion, we find out that the entry is written retrospectively; the bout of rheumatic fever occurred in April, but Potter records this account of her illness in June (*J*: 203). This unusual entry therefore helps us to be more attuned to the silences and significant gaps in Potter's journalling, which often point to periods of illness. In December 1886, for example, Potter makes her first diary entry since the April of that year and acknowledges again that illness had prevented her from writing: 'I made a last feeble attempt at notes in July last' but since then have not put 'half a dozen words on paper' (*J*: 201). This passage is a powerful reminder of the impact of physical illness on her psychological state. She makes clear that the inability to write is a combination of both physical and mental factors, since she adds that while part of the time I was 'too ill' to write, since then 'lazinesss and unsettledness consequent on weakness' have 'demoralised me' (*J*: 201). The following year, in which she suffered from the serious bout of rheumatic fever, Potter produced little **journal**-writing at all – a scant two and a half pages all year – and subsequent bouts of illness can be identified by significant gaps in the **journal**. Linder notes that there is very little code-writing 'from 1888 until the beginning of 1892', adding, it is believed that this is due to 'ill-health' (1966: xxii), and this reading is supported by evidence in the text itself. In 1889 the family spent their holiday at Holehird in the **Lake District** and Potter leaves no diary account of this visit. However, when the family returned to this house in 1895, Potter opens her holiday **journal** with the observation that they last stayed here in the summer of 1889 when 'I could hardly walk at all' (*J*: 391). In another entry (from 1890), she mentions having to make a visit to a prospective publishing house with her uncle by hackney carriage as she was 'not well enough to stand the Underground' (*J*: 213).

Whilst it is clear that Potter suffered from very serious and debilitating bouts of illness during her teenage years and early adulthood, it also seems evident that the narrative of her being weak and sickly was subsequently reinforced by her mother as a means of controlling the behaviour of a daughter who was inclined to be rebellious and who wanted to engage in physical outdoor pursuits of which her mother disapproved. In June 1894, Potter – now coming up to her twenty-eighth birthday – received an invitation to go and stay with her younger cousin, Caroline Hutton, and her family at their home in Gloucester. At this point Potter had not been away on her own for five years, but this opportunity for independent travel very nearly didn't happen since her 'relations' made it appear 'such an undertaking' that she began to have anxieties about the trip and developed a 'sick headache' (*J*: 319). In the end, the visit only went ahead because of her cousin's more forceful personality; as Potter puts it, Caroline 'carried me off' (*J*: 319). In Caroline's own later account of the incident, we get a clear sense of the way in which Potter's 'frailty' was used by her mother as a controlling narrative. Caroline writes: 'I am always glad that in spite of her mother's objections I managed to get her to my old home. She said *B*. was so apt to be sick and to faint; and I, regardless of the truth said, I was quite accustomed to all that' (*J*: 319, n. 2). It is notable that Potter's sick headache seems to have disappeared as soon as she was away from her mother, since the two cousins talk animatedly on the train journey to Gloucester. Moreover, Caroline's account makes clear the extent to which such claims about Potter's tendency to illness and delicacy in her late twenties were exaggerated by her mother, adding that 'of course' during the visit 'she could do most things, quite long walks included' (*J*: 319, n. 2). Caroline's first-hand account suggests that Potter's mother encouraged a narrative of invalidism and induced some psychosomatic symptoms on her daughter's part. It is perhaps no coincidence that Potter's level of independence seemed to increase after this visit and, though she still experienced bouts of fatigue from time to time, in an entry from 1896, she records feeling 'much younger at thirty than I did at twenty; firmer and stronger both in mind and body' (*J*: 427).

Nonetheless, given her own experiences, it is unsurprising that motifs of illness appear regularly in Potter's writing for children. However, her **animal** characters tend to become ill not as a result of dangerous infections or fevers, but due to injury or because of **eating** the wrong foods. The latter is touched on in several stories, including *Johnny Town-Mouse*, in which Timmy Willie begins to feel ill because his 'teeth and digestion are unaccustomed' to the food he is given by the urban mice (*JTM*: 36). In *The Fairy Caravan*, Paddy Pig is found 'sitting huddled up inside the tree with his fore-trotters pressed against his tummy', having eaten what he thinks are 'Tartlets' but which are in fact toadstools from Pringle Wood (*FC*: 162). Potter's work also though offers a sensitive and subtle engagement with factors which affect our emotional and psychological well-being. In *Benjamin Bunny*, for example, we encounter a **Peter** who is still recovering from the trauma of barely escaping from Mr. McGregor's garden with his life. When Benjamin meets **Peter** at the beginning of the *Tale*, the latter looks 'poorly' and is huddled up in a red handkerchief (*BB*: 14–15). As the story progresses, it becomes clear that **Peter** is not so much suffering from the aftermath of his overeating but from psychological trauma and shock. Benjamin encourages his cousin to re-enter the garden and rescue his **clothes** but as soon as he returns to the scene of his recent ordeal, **Peter** looks terrified, his neck strains upwards and he stares away into the distance (*BB*: 25). Whilst Benjamin is 'perfectly at home' (*BB*: 31) in the garden, **Peter** cannot enjoy himself at all; he keeps 'hearing noises' (*BB*: 28), is unable to eat and wants to go home (*BB*: 32).

Potter also touches on social inequality through the theme of illness. In *Wag-by-Wall*, we learn that the central character, Sally Benson, had lived comfortably while her husband was alive but now has a 'hard struggle', since her husband's 'long illness had left debts' (*WBW*: 10), and the impact of illness for those less well off in society is addressed more extensively in *The Tailor of Gloucester*. The 'poor old tailor', having spent his last fourpence, becomes 'very ill with a fever, tossing and turning' in his bed for three days and nights (*TG*: 32) and were it not for the intervention of the mice, he would have been left with an unfinished commission and no money on which to survive following his illness. Potter's sensitivity to the link between poverty and illness, or rather the greater impact which sickness had on the lives of the poor, resulted in one of her most sustained charitable activities. From the mid-1920s until her death, she used the '**Peter Rabbit**' brand to raise money for the Invalid Children's Aid Association (ICAA), an organization which helped provide medical treatment for the 'seriously-invalided and crippled children of the poor' (*LC*: 206). When first approached by the charity, she wrote to Warne and observed there could not be a 'kinder' cause (*L*: 284). As well as granting permission for the '**Peter Rabbit**' brand to be used for money-raising activities, she produced regular Christmas cards between 1925 and 1941 to support the work of the ICAA (see, for example, Figure 6).

Along with poverty, Potter also recognized that urban contexts, and especially London – a 'horrid place' (*J*: 158) – had a negative impact on health. She always caught 'bad colds' there (*L*: 220) and when in the city her impulse was to get out of the house and go on carriage drives which might give her access to some (relatively) fresh air. Such outings were clearly perceived by Potter as essential to both her mental and physical well-being, and she connected being confined to the house with increased risk of infection, noting in one entry that, having been 'indoors almost continually', I caught a '**violent** cold in my head' (*J*: 407).

From an early stage, Potter came to believe that quiet and 'fresh air is everything' (*J*: 49), and associated not only being outside but also away from London with better health. It comes as little surprise that, as an adult, she chose a life for herself far away from the metropolis, in a place which offered less polluted air as well as daily opportunities to spend a great deal of time outside, tending her **animals** or going on long walks with her dog. This sort of lifestyle did not of course prevent Potter being ill; indeed, her later years were plagued with recurrent bouts of bronchitis and heart issues, as well as appendicitis and gynaecological problems. However, what is clear from her late letters is the extent to which engagement with the natural environment helped her to deal psychologically with periods of illness. The letters written in the last decade of her life linger over **seasonal** changes and convey a sense of peace brought about through observation of the natural world. Even when long-term illness and old age restricted her ability to take long walks outdoors, she continued to find comfort in the memory of her earlier regular encounters with the natural environment in favourite spots. In 1937 she wrote to her beloved cousin Caroline to say: 'Thank God I have the seeing eye' and, even when lying in bed, can still 'walk step by step on the fells and rough lands seeing every stone and flower and patch of bog and cotton grass where my old legs will never take me again' (*L*: 384). Potter reiterates this source of consolation in another letter to Caroline, written during the last weeks of her life, observing that it is 'some years ago since I have walked on the beloved hills, but I remember every stone & rock' (Lear 2007: 439). The lines recall those from an 1832 poem by Dorothy Wordsworth called 'Thoughts on my sick-bed', which had been published in a 1933 biography of the writer:

> No need of motion or of strength
> Or even the breathing air;
> I thought of Nature's loveliest scenes
> And with memory I was there.
>
> (De Selincourt 1933: 388)

In a **journal** entry made during a visit to **Lake District** decades earlier, Potter had recorded that William Wordsworth is always referred to as '*the poet* in these parts' but adds that local tradition says that 'Dorothy Wordsworth was the greater poet' (*J*: 145). At eighteen Potter could have had no idea of the ways in which she, like Dorothy Wordsworth, would come to be intimately connected to this region, nor that she too would come to walk its landscapes on a daily basis. There are many fascinating parallels between **Beatrix** Potter and Dorothy Wordsworth, not least their habits of journalling, but also their walking practices, their love of being outside, and their close and detailed attention to the natural world. The lines in Potter's letter and in Wordsworth's poem suggest that these two women also shared a vital capacity to recall in vivid detail the memory of their earlier physical encounters with the natural world and that, in both cases, this recourse brought them a significant amount of consolation during times of illness.

J IS FOR JOURNAL

Beatrix Potter's most sustained body of writing is the coded journal she kept between 1881 and 1897. Little attention had been paid to the 'mysterious bundle' of coded notebooks and papers, until Leslie Linder, an engineer and Potter enthusiast, began to attempt to crack Potter's code in the 1950s (Linder 1966: xviii). As a result of his efforts, the decoded journal – amounting to around two hundred and fifty thousand words of prose – was finally published in 1966, exactly one hundred years after Potter's birth. It was accompanied by a prefatory essay in which Linder provided an account of Potter's code-writing, details of how a **key** was found to crack the code, and insights into the journal manuscripts (Linder 1966: xxvii–xxiii). Despite having now been in the public domain for several decades, Potter's journal has, however, yet to receive detailed critical attention or full recognition as an important body of autobiographical writing by one of the most popular children's authors of the twentieth century. Indeed, whilst Linder suggests that when reading the journal we forget 'about Beatrix Potter the author of the *Peter Rabbit* books, and became conscious of a charming person called Miss Potter, who lived at Number Two Bolton Gardens, London' (1966: xx), this text has tended to be read in terms of the insights it provides into Potter's published writings. John Goldthwaite, for example, describes it as a 'curious piece of work' but suggests that, via the journal, we can 'see in that short span of years in the 1890s some little of what was going on when the essential imagining was done and only the making of the books remained' (1996: 292–3), and Daphne Kutzer reads Potter's *Tales* in the 'context of her coded journal' (2003: 2).

Yet Potter's journal, with its experimental shifts of style, subject matter and register, deserves to be considered as an important piece of journal-writing in its own right, to be ranked alongside other vital autobiographical texts such as Dorothy Wordsworth's *Grasmere Journals* and Virginia Woolf's *Diaries*. As Roselee Robison suggests, in a rare scholarly essay on the journal, it is 'one of the most intriguing documents amongst the vast array of nineteenth-century diaries' (1984: 232). Moreover, Potter's journal was written at a crucial moment of socio-cultural history, as the nineteenth century came to a close and during the period which has come to be referred to as the *fin de siècle*. The journal offers a fascinating, witty, lively and – at times – subversive account of this moment, at which Britain was on the cusp of change, from the perspective of a deeply intelligent and unusual young woman.

The fact that the early years of the journal were written on any sort of paper available, including loose sheets later sewn together and single scraps of paper (Linder 1966: xx), is suggestive of Potter's overwhelming need to write. This is apparent also in the way in which later journal entries shift away from larger writing with quite carefully formed letters into a more relaxed (and, at times, tiny) handwriting, once Potter was able to 'write fluently and at high speed' in her coded hand (Linder 1966: xx). Moreover, Potter later observed, in her only known reference to the coded journal, that it began because she had 'the itch to write, without having any material to write about', adding humorously that the 'modern young author is not damped by such considerations' (Linder 1966: xvii). It is in the pages of this journal that Potter takes her first steps as a writer and begins to experiment with prose-style, voice and subject matter. Here we find confessional passages which document her moods and feelings, bitingly witty observations about people and society, art criticism, travel writing, socio-political commentary, scientific notes, nature writing and much more.

Lear notes that Potter 'poured out her thoughts and observations, both trivial and momentous' into her journal for fifteen years and what we know about her between the ages of fourteen and thirty 'comes almost exclusively from her private revelations' (Lear 2007: 48). In fact, so vivid and engaging is the Potter we encounter here that the reader feels almost bereft when the journal ends suddenly and without explanation on Sunday 31 January 1897, at a moment when Potter was deeply embroiled in her study of **fungi**. Though the majority of Potter's journal after 1892 is contained in ten exercise books, the final extant material (22 December 1896 to 31 January 1897) is written on the four sides of a single sheet of folded paper which has been taken from an exercise book, and it opens eleven days after the last entry in the previous book. These last sections are dominated by notes relating to Potter's mycological work and it is notable that her long diary-keeping impulse came to an end at a time when she was beginning to explore other forms of writing, including a scholarly scientific paper. From this point onwards and for the remainder of her adult life, we no longer have access to Potter's wholly 'private revelations'.

J is for Journal

Whilst personal diary keeping was a common activity within intellectual and educated circles of society in the Victorian period, what makes Potter's journal so unusual is the fact that it is written throughout in a secret code of her own invention, made up of interchanged letters of the English alphabet, imaginary symbols and numbers, as well as characters resembling the Greek alphabet and German script (Linder 1966: xx). When Dorothy Wordsworth began her *Grasmere Journal* in May 1800, she famously wrote that she had decided to keep the journal because 'I will not quarrel with myself, & because I shall give Wm Pleasure by it when he comes home again' (Wordsworth 2008: 1). Like Potter, Dorothy Wordsworth used the journal to process her thoughts and emotions in words, but in Wordsworth's case the journal was never wholly private since it was written with at least two readers in mind. In being written in code, Potter's journal constitutes a more completely private form of writing in which the only intended reader is herself. The importance of this, in providing her with a space in which she could express her private feelings and views, comes through in several entries. In one she 'fearlessly' expresses her negative opinions of a Michaelangelo painting, adding 'No one will read this' (J: 117), and on another occasion she notes that though she keeps quiet about her views in public, 'to myself I say what I like' (J: 94). Humphrey Carpenter suggests that her journal presents us with someone 'very determined and independent-minded' who displays a 'vigorous contempt for most of the accepted Victorian values' (1989: 279) and it is the code-writing which gave Potter the freedom to express those views which she felt unable to voice out loud.

Perhaps the best-known female author of a coded diary, other than Potter herself, is Anne Lister (1791–1840), who was famously portrayed on screen in the 2018 BBC television series, *Gentleman Jack*. Like Potter, Lister devised her own coded language as a teenager, which was made up of Greek, Latin and mathematical symbols, as well as punctuation and zodiacal signs. Unlike Potter though, Lister only wrote certain sections or sentences of her diary in code, including those dealing with her homosexuality and lesbian experiences. In other words, Lister encodes those aspects of her private writing which she felt needed to be kept secret. What makes Potter's journal so interesting in comparison is the fact that it is written in code throughout. Whilst this certainly gives Potter the freedom to scatter humorous and often scathing comments throughout her writing, the vast body of material in the extant journal is innocuous and would not need to be kept secret. The decision to write in code throughout suggests that secrecy was not so much a necessity but rather something Potter enjoyed, granting her, as it did, a fully private space in which to explore her thoughts and ideas. There is nonetheless evidence that as a young woman Potter edited and destroyed some material from her earlier teenage journal entries. Clues to this include fragments of a torn-off page and pencil annotations on some of the remaining material. On one page, for example, she has written 'looked over – all right' and alongside some earlier passages of art criticism she has pencilled 'silly sentiments', but adds that she found them 'amusing' and so has preserved 'the greater part of them' (Linder 1966: xxi–xxii). Such evidence of editorial excision is intriguing, and perhaps indicates that Potter did at least consider the possibility of someone else reading the journal at some point in the future.

The rare occasions in her life when Potter was encouraged to express herself more freely were (as the journal itself reveals) when she was in dialogue with her 'pickle' (*J*: 360) of a cousin, Caroline Hutton, and though Potter did not confide the existence of a secret journal to her cousin during the years in which it was being kept, it was in a letter to Caroline that Potter made her only known reference to the coded diaries. Written just five weeks before her death, the letter describes them as 'exasperating and absurd compositions' written in a 'kind of cypher shorthand' (Linder 1966: xvii). Reflecting back, rather vaguely, from this distance of more than sixty years, Potter also comments that the decision to keep a journal was 'apparently inspired by a united admiration' of those two well-known earlier diarists, Boswell and Pepys (Linder 1966: xvii); however, the journal itself points to a rather different line of influence. Beginning in 1890, Potter wrote a small number of epistolary journal entries which are addressed to 'My dear Esther' (*J*: 209). In a footnote, Linder comments that this is believed to be an imaginary person, perhaps 'inspired by Fanny Burney's sister, Esther, whom Fanny Burney addressed in her own diaries' (*J*: 211, n. 7). Such a reading is supported by other evidence within the journal but in ways which suggest that Burney's influence on Potter's development as a diarist was rather more extensive than this.

Burney's reputation as a diarist began to emerge in the mid-Victorian period, following the publication between 1842 and 1846 of a popular seven-volume edition of her later journal (covering the period from 1778 onwards). Her youthful journal, from 1768 to 1778 (when Burney was aged between fifteen and twenty-five), was then subsequently published in two volumes in 1889 as *The Early Diary of Frances Burney*. Potter had clearly read this 1889 edition before visiting Teignmouth in 1892, since she notes that this was where Fanny Burney kept her 'sprightly journal in 1773' (*J*: 242), and this particular section of Burney's journal was not published in the earlier edition. There is, however, some evidence that Potter had also read the 1842–6 edition, not least the fact that Burney's switch to writing journal letters to her sister (usually in fact to her sister Susanna rather than Esther) occurs more frequently after 1778. Moreover, though Burney's youthful diaries were not published in full until 1889, the first volume of the 1842–6 edition opens with an 'Author's Introduction', which (as the accompanying textual note tells the reader) is made up of 'the opening passages of Miss Burney's Diary, which she commenced at the age of fifteen years' (Burney 1842: 2). In this first diary entry, Burney famously states that her journal will be an 'account of my thoughts, manners, acquaintance and actions', in which she will 'confess my *every* thought' and 'open my whole Heart!' (Burney 1842: 1). She states that she will perceive herself to be 'talking to the most intimate of friends – to one whom I should take delight in confiding', and concludes that she must address the journal to 'Nobody', since this is the only person to whom she would 'dare to reveal my private opinion of my nearest Relations' and 'my own hopes, fears, reflections and dislikes' (Burney 1842: 1). The similarity between the approach outlined by a teenage Burney and that taken by Potter within her own journal just over a century later is striking, and suggests that an encounter with Burney's first diary entry may well have inspired Potter to commence her own journal project at almost exactly the same age. Like Potter, Burney was 'extremely shy', whereas the tone of her diary is 'humorous, playful' and 'irreverent' (Sabor and Troide 2001: xiv, xvii), and in both cases the journals become textual spaces in which these intelligent but shy women could confide their more subversive thoughts.

That Burney's own diaries encouraged Potter to write about the world around her in a playful and witty way is suggested in particular by those experimental passages addressed to Esther, in which Potter adopts a Burneyesque narrating voice. The first entry for 1890 describes a visit to the Winter Exhibition at the Royal Academy and opens with a description of Potter's Uncle Thomas who, she writes, appeared as if he had been 'put in a **clothes** bag and sat upon', adding 'I never saw a person so creased' (*J*: 209). The next entry addressed to Esther describes the momentous visit to Hildesheimer & Faulkner. This resulted in Potter's first drawings being accepted for payment and so gave her a glimpse of a future involving some kind of financial independence. The 'letter' opens with an overt nod to Burney as a published woman writer and thus a direct source of inspiration: 'My dear Esther', it is an 'odd consideration' that 'one of the first events I have to write to you about should be a stroke in humble imitation of my heroine Fanny Burney' (J: 211).

In 1892 Potter wrote in her journal, 'I who have lived so much asleep and out of life that the old world of books is almost as tangible as the new world of the *times*' (J: 244). However, in some ways the journal itself works against this idea and presents us instead with a woman who, for social and familial reasons, kept her private reflections to herself but who nonetheless engaged intelligently with the world around her. The Potter who emerges from the pages of the journal is abreast of contemporary social and political issues, interested in developments in art and culture, and sharply responsive to everything from the latest fashion trends (which she often laughed at), to debates over Irish independence. Potter biographers have also tended to portray her living a deeply lonely life in the upper floor nursery of Bolton Gardens, but the young woman we encounter in the journal, like Burney herself, spends a great deal of time out and about. In the years covered by the journal, we see her experiencing much of what London life had to offer: visiting art exhibitions, galleries and museums, as well as leisure venues such as the Kensington swimming baths, the theatre and the **zoo**.

Like Burney, Potter also travelled around the country a great deal and her account of these experiences within the journal constitutes a lively body of travel-writing. The Potter family usually took a winter holiday, an Easter holiday and an extended holiday over the summer, and it was these experiences which inspired some of Potter's most detailed journal entries. Between 1881 and 1897 Potter visited the **Lake District** several times for lengthy summer holidays but also spent time at other places, including Scotland and a variety of popular Victorian seaside resorts, such as Ilfracombe, Torquay, Falmouth and Weymouth. Through Potter's accounts we glimpse fascinating details of the late Victorian upper-middle-class visitor experience at these seaside resorts in their heyday. Burney's accounts of her own travel experiences never seem far from Potter's mind, and on the occasions when she visits somewhere Burney had previously visited, she alludes to this in her journal (J: 242, 374). It is clear though that Potter was also conscious of working within a wider tradition of travel-writing, at one point establishing her more modern perspectives on landscape by noting that one is 'apt to smile' at descriptions of 'terrific cliffs and horrid gorges' in the late-eighteenth-century picturesque guides, where real nature 'on enquiry presents very ordinary rocks' (J: 220).

Though some of Potter's travel diaries were written during the time away, on other occasions she writes an extended account of the holiday from

J is for Journal

memory following her return. A good example of this is Potter's account of an Easter trip to Falmouth in 1892, which runs to some twenty-three pages and reveals her lively interest in almost everything she encountered. This Falmouth journal entry ranges between details about travel, weather, flora and fauna, landscape, historic buildings and sites, industry, language and dialect. It offers reflections on the appearance and character of the town and its inhabitants, often recounted with a Burneyesque liveliness and wry humour. She observes that the policemen all seem to have 'bunions, or very mis-fitting boots' and comments that everything in the town has a 'nautical flavour', with sailors who loll about in the main street 'spitting on the pavement' and an air so pure it transmits every smell within twenty yards, 'from wall-flowers to fish' (*J*: 220–4).

Like Burney, Potter was sharply attuned to her own cultural moment and to the particularities of day-to-day life. Potter's holidays are facilitated by the era of advanced railway tourism, in which speedy travel up and down the country had begun to alter the experience of both travel and place. Not only are she and her family able to be far away from London in a matter of hours, but their first encounters with new locations were often via rapidly changing framed scenes viewed in glimpses from the carriage window. As she heads to Cornwall, Potter writes that on the left the railway 'skirted the coast', alternately looking down on 'little creeks and harbours down below', then offering a 'first sight of the green Cornish sea' (*J*: 220). This sense of the excitement of movement and new sights glimpsed as a series of snapshots, carries over into much of Potter's travel-writing, even when she is journeying by carriage rather than train. An experience of movement is often at the fore, so that at times Potter's experience of the landscape unrolls before us like a film reel:

> Down the wooded lanes, round the twisting of the Helford creeks, between banks smothered in primroses, up again along a steep hill with the sun slanting through blackthorn hedges, past a great old-walled farm and high closed gateway, and a white cat basking in the sunset at a barn door high up in the wall.
>
> (*J*: 317)

Humphrey Carpenter has observed that Potter's *Tales* belong to 'the modern age rather than the Victorian', suggesting that there are 'moments when her work even bears resemblances to the modernists' (1989: 296). Potter's experimentation with a prose which tries to capture the experiences of a new modern world began, however, in her journal and came to the fore in her travel-writing. It is perhaps ironic that, in turning back to a diary written in the previous century for inspiration, Potter would come to produce passages of writing which would herald the new century to come.

K IS FOR KEY

Keys and related tropes, such as locks and doors, appear regularly in Potter's writing and function in a variety of ways but within her children's books they most often function to represent opposing ideas of entrapment and safety. The latter motif is used to particularly good effect in *The Tailor of Gloucester*. Having prepared the expensive cloth for the Mayor of Gloucester's waistcoat and coat, the Tailor carefully locks the windows and takes away the key to keep the fabric safe overnight. In this story, however, there are a group of creatures for whom these methods of boundary control have no relevance. The 'little brown mice' (*TG*: 12) do not need keys to enter the building. Using instead their own subterraneous means of access, they 'run in and out without any keys through the old houses of Gloucester!' (*TG*: 32). Crucially though, the locked door creates a space of safety for the mice themselves in which to work, since the Tailor's predatory cat, Simpkin, cannot enter via these routes and is subject to domestic spatial constraints, needing the key to gain access. While the mice sew, laugh and sing merrily inside the shop, Simpkin can only scratch at the door and, as 'the key was under the tailor's pillow' (*TG*: 44), cannot get in. In this story then the locked door makes the shop a secure space for the mice, in which they are free to concentrate on their intricate stitching and do good work for the Tailor.

Elsewhere in Potter's stories though, a key and locked door represent a means of entrapment for those inside. In **Peter Rabbit**, as **Peter** tries to escape from Mr. McGregor, he comes across a 'door in the wall' but finds the door 'locked' (*PR*: 48). An emotive accompanying image depicts a tearful **Peter** stood upright against the door, with one paw reaching upwards to a key he cannot reach (*PR*: 50). In another **animal**/human encounter, in *The Fairy Caravan*, Pony Billy is also trapped by a lock and key. Having failed to carry the fern seed which renders him invisible to the 'Big Folk' (*FC*: 30), the pony is captured by two policemen and locked in the 'pound, or pinfold', a round enclosure with a 'high circular wall, built of cobblestones', to which the key hangs upon a 'nail at the police station' (*FC*: 39). The matter of how to release the pony occupies the attention of his **animal** friends for some time as they discuss whether they can get hold of the key or pick the lock. Meanwhile Billy walks in circles round the pound, in a way that suggests his entrapment within human society and its rules, and contrasts with the freedom he experiences when he is invisible to humans.

Much more terrifying than these depictions of locked spaces is the central act of entrapment in *Mr. Tod*. Benjamin Bunny's babies have been stolen by the badger, Tommy Brock, and are subject to a double imprisonment. Not only are they locked up by him within Mr. Tod's stick house – which is something 'between a cave, a prison, and a tumble-down pig-stye' (*T*: 29) – but they are also 'shut up' in the oven (*T*: 37). Outside this oven and making clear the fate intended for them is a table set for supper and implements which cause Benjamin to 'shudder' (*T*: 30). Inside their prison the young rabbits await their dreadful fate as Tommy Brock sleeps and Benjamin, along with his cousin **Peter,** wrestles with various locks and bolts to try to gain access to the house and effect a rescue. When this does finally take place, it occurs amidst one of the most **violent** scenes in Potter's work, as Mr. Tod returns home and a fight breaks out between the fox and Tommy Brock. Very briefly at this point, the oven-prison functions as a means of safety for the 'trembling' baby bunnies, who are perhaps 'fortunate they were shut up inside' (*T*: 70). Nonetheless the horrors of their place of imprisonment, the extended anxiety caused by first Benjamin and **Peter** not being able to break in, and then the fight, make the final rescue of the bunnies, still mercifully 'warm and wriggling' (*T*: 77), one of the most moving moments in Potter's work.

A further crucial function of keys, particularly within the fairy-tale tradition, is as the keeper of secrets, as well as the means by which secrets can be discovered. Nowhere is this seen more clearly than in *Sister Anne*, Potter's retelling of Charles Perrault's 'Bluebeard' story. It was published in 1932 when Potter was in her sixties, and it would be the last book-length work to appear in her lifetime. *Sister Anne* was originally published in America and has never been republished, partly because the text has tended to be criticized or neglected by Potter scholars. Margaret Lane's commentary on the story in her early Potter biography set the tone for much later discussion; she describes it as a 'long and wearisome re-telling of the Bluebeard story', of 'little interest', and amounting to a 'pretentious failure' (1946: 145). Daphne Kutzer later mentions it in passing as a 'gothic retelling of the Bluebeard story' which reflects Potter's 'lifelong love of fairy tales' (2003: 166). Potter herself described *Sister Anne* as certainly not 'food for babes' (*A*: 47) but ten years after its publication records having reread it 'with enjoyment and

K is for Key

detached interest' adding, by way of contrast, that she was 'sick of *Peter Rabbit*!!' (*A*: 163).

Other than the unusual length of the tale (it is around seven times the length of the original) and its **uncanny** handling of geographical setting, Potter makes two important revisions to the original story, both of which position *Sister Anne* as an early feminist retelling of a fairy tale, a tradition which would come to include Angela Carter's influential 1979 collection, *The Bloody Chamber*. The first and most important revision which occurs in Potter's version is a shift in focus to the wife's sister, Anne: 'a big dark browed capable woman, with strong arms, and a quick wit' (*SA*: 50). Only mentioned briefly in the Perrault original, here Anne is moved to centre stage, becoming an important figure in her own right. She is depicted throughout as a strong and empowered woman, who contrasts strongly with her sister, Fatima, Bluebeard's nervous and timid wife. Indeed Potter's depiction of Anne has led to some more positive recent critical interest in her story, with Rose Lovell-Smith seeing Potter's 'revisionary reading of Perrault' as a 'distinctive and distinctly feminist' version of the tale, which 'stands between Victorian women's and later twentieth-century feminist revisions of fairy tales'; Lovell-Smith focuses on the story's emphasis on 'sisterhood and womanly solidarity' and on the depiction of 'a heroine who is a strong-minded, courageous, competent and energetic single woman' (2013: 15, 17).

A second important revisionary element in Potter's version though relates to the handling of the keys themselves, the central symbol and plot device within Perrault's original story. In Perrault the keys are given to the wife as a test and come to represent her curiosity and guilt. Having been given a bunch of keys by her husband, the wife is told that she can use them to 'open everything and go everywhere, except for this private room' (Perrault 2009: 164). However, she opens the door to this forbidden room because her curiosity is so 'keen', and here finds a grisly scene of horror: the dead bodies of several of Bluebeard's other wives and a floor 'clotted with blood' (Perrault 2009: 165). Having dropped the key in her terror, the wife makes desperate attempts to remove the blood stains from it but, however 'much she washed it, and even scoured it with sand and pumice, the blood stayed on it' (Perrault 2009: 166). The blood on the key which cannot be removed speaks of her guilt, with Perrault adding a few lines of verse to the story which outline 'The Moral of the Tale' as being a warning to the curious: 'Curiosity's all very well in its way, / But satisfy it and you risk much remorse' (2009: 170). This is further developed to become a warning to women, in a long-standing cultural reinforcement of the peril of female curiosity unlocking terrible knowledge, with Perrault adding: 'The feminine sex will deny it, of course' but 'the knowledge you looked for is not worth the cost' (2009: 170).

In Potter's version, though the key trope remains central to the story, its meaning is rewritten. As in Perrault, Bluebeard tries to give his wife the bunch of keys in order to trick her, but he is initially thwarted in this impulse by Anne herself who, seeming to recognize the inherent danger they represent, repeatedly intercepts the keys. The husband finally passes them to the wife by an act of trickery, distracting Anne and slipping the keys into his wife's girdle. Lovell-Smith suggests that the keys in Potter's story do not have magical properties and are just 'an ordinary bunch of household keys' (2013: 10), but in fact there is something strange and **uncanny** about them from the outset. As soon as Fatima begins to carry the keys, they start to affect her rather like an evil spell; she becomes 'uneasy', more 'than usually languid and querulous', her eyes 'haggard' and the 'pouch with the heavy bunch of keys' drags 'at her waist' (*SA*: 94). Potter's depiction of the negative physical and psychological effect of the keys on Fatima functions to transform the story's overall meaning, since her actions, far from being motivated by mere curiosity, are shown to be governed by the malign force of the keys themselves.

As soon as Fatima disappears in quest of the secret room, Anne – already worried about the keys and their 'foreboding evil' – goes in search of her sister on a Gothic journey through the labyrinthine passages of the castle, finally treading on the bunch of keys which Fatima has dropped and finding her sister 'lying like one dead' at her feet (*SA*: 109). The focus of the story at this point shifts to Anne's rescue of her sister, with the significance of the keys further altered by the fact that Potter removes all references to the wife desperately trying to clean the key. Fatima here is barely capable of action following her gruesome discovery and, though herself 'white to the lips', Anne simply hands the keys over to Bluebeard when he demands them (*SA*: 117). Whilst the keys still tell their tale in *Sister Anne* – covered as they are in tallow grease and a 'stain that smells like blood' (*SA*: 118) – the crucial shift in emphasis, away from the wife's attempt to hide her 'guilt', alters the story's meaning in significant ways. In Perrault's version the keys function as a reminder of the woman's guilt, but in Potter the focus is on the wife's traumatized response to what she has seen and Anne's desperate attempts to save her sister from this **violent**, abusive and murderous husband, thus shifting the reader's attention (rightly we might think, given the enormity of his crimes) on the husband's own guilt and brutality. Far from functioning as a warning against curiosity, *Sister Anne* seems to suggest that it is better for the women to find out the terrible secret which the keys hide before it is too late.

In 'Bluebeard' keys function as a gatekeeper of secrets, they keep secrets locked away and give access to hidden and possibly taboo places. But, as this story shows, just as keys can keep secrets, they can also reveal them. Potter's own life is marked in many ways by various acts of secrecy, most notably the coded **journal** which she kept from her mid-teens until the age of thirty. It was the painstaking work of Potter scholar, Leslie Linder, in finding the key to this code-writing in 1958 which gave us access to this previously secret body of writing. In a strange parallel to Perrault's Bluebeard who – rather than hiding or throwing away the key of the room in which his secrets are hidden, instead gives it to his wife as a test – Potter, rather than destroying the words she had kept secret for so long, left the 'large bundle of loose sheets and exercise books written in cipher-writing' along with her other papers at Castle Cottage, where they were found following her death (Linder 1966: xviii). Given the extent of her fame and the desire for privacy which we witness in many aspects of her life, Potter's decision to leave this material behind is rather intriguing. Perhaps she believed that no-one would ever manage to find a key to crack the code but, in leaving the documents to be found, she was in a sense setting her own test. Though Linder writes that Potter 'did not leave a key to the code' and observes that 'she probably thought these writings would never be read by anyone else', he also notes that after cracking the code, he subsequently discovered the 'perfect clue' (1966: xix) in the form of a page headed XC, on which is written the opening lines of the ninetieth psalm written in code; Linder describes this page of coded text as a 'simple and straightforward key to the code!' (1966: xx). It would seem then that, though Potter used a code to keep this body of writing secret, she also provided those with sufficient intelligence, patience and insight, the key to access it.

L IS FOR LAKE DISTRICT

Potter first came to the Lake District at the age of fifteen in 1882 when her family took Wray Castle on the western shore of Windermere for the summer and she celebrated her sixteenth birthday there one week later. The Potter family would spend a number of holidays in the Lakes over the next thirty years, staying in a variety of grand houses in different Lakeland landscapes, including Lingholm and Fawe Park on the shores of Derwentwater. It is a somewhat surprising fact that Potter's early period of holidaying in the Lakes overlapped with that of the other most influential writer of literature for children with a Lake District setting, Arthur Ransome. Though more than twenty years younger than Potter, Ransome first came on his own family's annual summer holidays (to Nibthwaite, near Coniston) as a very young child, and so his holidays, which spanned the period $c.1884$–97, cover almost exactly the same timeframe as Potter's own. In both cases, those holiday experiences were inflected by late-Victorian middle-class contexts, with an emphasis on gentrified pursuits such as picnicking and boating; they were also shaped by gendered expectations of the period, with Ransome's holidays dominated by fishing expeditions with his father, whilst Potter's main holiday pursuits included gathering botanical specimens and the production of watercolours. Photographs taken of Potter during her Lakeland holidays function as a graphic reminder of the impact of gender on holiday experiences in the period since, even when participating in a physically demanding activity like rowing, she wears a restrictive full-length walking costume, buttoned to the neck, its distinctive shape achieved through the wearing of stays, a boned undergarment. Nonetheless, in their personal engagement with the Lakes during these holidays, both Potter and Ransome experience a late-nineteenth-century version of a 'natural education', in which the child learns through interactions with the natural world. Such an education also relates to Wordsworthian legacies, since having been promoted by the late-eighteenth-century French philosopher and novelist, Jean-Jacques Rousseau, it was first modelled in a Lake District setting by Wordsworth in his autobiographical poem, *The Prelude*.

Later in life, Potter claimed that 'it was not the Lake District at all that inspired me to write children's books' (*A*: 207); nonetheless, the holiday experiences of her late teenage and early adult years clearly inform her imaginative life in important ways. Lake District landscapes, buildings, people, flora and fauna, as well as patterns of daily life and speech, regularly appear in her writing for children. Several of the *Tales* depict recognizable Lake District landscapes, including St Herbert's Island on Derwentwater in *Squirrel Nutkin* (*SN*: 15) and the Newlands valley in *Mrs. Tiggy-Winkle* (*TW*: 15). Some *Tales*, including *Tom Kitten*, depict Potter's own house, Hill Top (*TK*: 9, 21), and the shop in *Ginger and Pickles* is modelled on the village shop in Near Sawrey. Specific place-references also pop up from time to time, anchoring the story in a known geographical space. In *Pigling Bland*, for example, the title character looks out over 'peaceful green valleys' where 'little white cottages' are nestled and his companion, Pig-wig, says that's 'Westmorland' (*PB*: 68) – a reference to one of the two historic counties whose landscapes would later be encompassed by the boundaries of the Lake District National Park.

The presence of the Lake District in many of Potter's best-known *Tales* is well documented (Davies 1988; Thompson 2010) but its appearance in her later, less well-known writings reveals the extent to which these landscapes continued to play a crucial part in her imaginative life to the end of her life, often informing her process of revision and re-engagement with older stories. In *Sister Anne*, for example, instead of the never-never setting of Perrault's original, Potter sets her story in and around the landscape of Morecambe Bay, with some actual locations – such as Kentmere and the Eagle's Head Inn (at Over Kellet) – mentioned by name. In her retelling, the **uncanny** possibilities of this liminal landscape provide an important backdrop for the events which unfold. Later in life Potter also considered inserting her own voice within the long tradition of Lake District place-writing with a guidebook. In 1930 she admitted to having had rather a 'fancy to do a Lakes-guide-history-description' and was asked by Warne to write something along these lines, but in the end found herself 'shying' at a job which she felt was too much of a task for her 'declining years' (*A*: 40). The never-written Potter guidebook would have been a fascinating text to read alongside Wordsworth's *Guide to the Lakes* but, given her self-depreciating attitude to her own work, is unlikely to have made reference to her own role in helping to construct visitor perceptions of this place.

Though later in life Potter denied that the Lake District had inspired her children's books (*A*: 207), there is a great deal of evidence as to the powerful influence her textual construction of this region had on readers, with many identifying Lake District landscapes closely with Potter's *Tales* in a way that clearly demonstrates the formative role of children's literature on the development of cultural values and myths about place. That this process had begun in her own lifetime is suggested by references on the part of two significant twentieth-century poets, W. H. Auden and Kathleen Raine, which point to the influence of Potter's work on their own experiences of place in the first half of the twentieth century. Auden acknowledged that his idea of the 'North' was shaped initially by his 'nursery library', including 'the work of Westmorland's Beatrix Potter' (Mendelson 1996: 329) and the poet Kathleen Raine, who settled briefly in the vicarage at Martindale near Ullswater in 1940, described the region as the 'Westmorland of Beatrix Potter' (1975: 122). The connection would go on to be reiterated in numerous topographical guidebooks. Norman Nicholson for example writes in *Portrait of the Lakes* that 'Esthwaite has its Beatrix Potter woods' (1963: 24), and Molly Lefebure depicts the Lakes landscape as if inhabited with Potter's imaginary creations:

> Beyond the village [of Near Sawrey] lies the grassy cart-track which Jemima Puddle-duck took to the woods where she met the courteous foxy-whiskered gentleman [...] Here are the fox-gloves in the glades, the late spring sunshine; if you search hard enough you will find the tumbledown house with the old bucket turned upside-down for a chimney [...] Everything is here, deliciously and, in a way astonishingly; just as it was when that hand of genius painted it.
>
> (1964: 61)

By the later years of the twentieth century and into the twenty-first, the close association perceived by readers between Potter's work and the Lake District had spawned several well-illustrated books, with titles such as *Beatrix Potter's Lakeland* (Davies and Pemberton-Piggot 1979), *Beatrix Potter: At Home in the Lake District* (Denyer 2000) and *Beatrix Potter's Lake District* (Cooper 2007). Not only do these books point to locations relevant to Potter's biography, such as Hill Top – the first property she owned in the Lake District – but also the various locations in which her characters and scenes from her stories can be 'found'. A similar process occurs in visitor guidebooks such as *Walking with Beatrix Potter*, which overtly links real places with imaginary characters, describing Esthwaite Water, for example, as the 'probable home of Jeremy Fisher' (Buckley and Buckley 2007: 33).

The effect of these books, with their combination of contemporary photographs of real geographical locations, alongside Potter's drawings of anthropomorphized **animals** situated within these recognizable landscapes, reinforces the close connection, already established by Potter's own writing, between the stories and the landscape in which they are set.

The extent to which Potter continues to be connected to the Lake District in the public imagination is indicated by media coverage of the Lake District's inscription as a UNESCO World Heritage Site in 2017. An article published in *The Guardian* newspaper just a few days after the announcement, for example, had the following subheading: 'Wordsworth's daffodils, Beatrix Potter's Peter Rabbit, Ransome's Swallows and Amazons – Cumbria has been fertile ground for countless writers' (Guest 2017). Given this level of close popular identification, it is perhaps not surprising that in the immediate aftermath of the UNESCO announcement, those opposed to the World Heritage inscription also turned to Potter as a kind of shorthand for certain sets of ideas. George Monbiot took issue with both the Lake District nomination document and the region's UNESCO status in a controversial *Guardian* think-piece, in which he argues that the World Heritage designation, with its focus on the landscape as an agro-pastoral landscape, 'protects sheep farming, and nothing else'; this 'blatant assault on nature', he claims, will turn the area into a 'Beatrix Potter-themed sheep museum' (Monbiot 2017). The use of 'Beatrix Potter' here as an adjectival prefix is, in part, a reference to her role as a breeder of Herdwick sheep, but also to what Linda Lear describes as 'the primary aim of her stewardship' of the Lakes within her lifetime and via her bequest to the **National Trust**: 'the preservation of a culture of hill faming and sheep stocks' (Lear 2007: 445). However, Monbiot's description of the process which has led to the region being constructed in this way points also to the role of her books in promoting a 'fairytale with great cultural power' (2017). He describes the way in which the Lake District has been presented as a 'seat of innocence and purity; an Arcadian refuge from the corruption of the city, an idyll in perfect harmony with the natural world' (Monbiot 2017). Though for most Potter scholars, the *Tales* in fact offer a much more complex and less idyllic treatment of rural environments than these claims would suggest, Monbiot's use of Potter in the article is revealing in its acceptance of her influence on popular perceptions and myths about the Lake District.

Given the close connection presented in the media between Potter's *Tales* and the region achieving World Heritage inscription as a 'Cultural Landscape', it is particularly ironic that the nomination document has very little to say about Potter's contribution in terms of her writing for children. Whilst the co-authored nomination makes clear that perceptions of the Lake District have been profoundly shaped by writers, it is a Wordsworthian legacy which is emphasized and, when the document turns to Potter, the focus is very different. Whilst the handling of other literary figures, and in particular the Lake Poets, results in several pages of analysis of their writings and the way in which the ideas contained within them helped to shape cultural responses to the landscape, none of this is to be found within the main Potter section. 'Beatrix Potter-Heelis' is granted slightly less than a page of commentary, which focuses almost exclusively on her farming work and her massive contribution to the conservation of the Lake District via her bequest to the **National Trust**. No sense of Potter's wide-ranging contribution to shaping perceptions of this landscape through her writing emerges and indeed the latter is dismissed in the following sentence: 'Beatrix Potter's successful series of children's books were often written against a backdrop of English Lake District scenes and from observations of local wildlife' (Lake District National Park Partnership 2015: 225). Elsewhere in the document her land purchases are identified as having helped to perpetuate an agro-pastoral way of life in the region (136, 487) but there is no attempt at all to acknowledge or reflect on the significance of her writing in terms of its contribution to the evolution and development of this 'Cultural Landscape' in a post-Wordsworthian context.

In this respect, the treatment of Potter contrasts sharply with the handling of William Wordsworth and the literary figures who gathered round him during the early years of the nineteenth century, where the writing itself is repeatedly emphasized and given global significance. Central to the claims put forward in the nomination document is that Wordsworth wrote poetry which was directly inspired by the English Lake District and its inhabitants, and was 'based on a new and internationally influential view of the relationship between humanity and landscape' (Lake District National Park Partnership 2015: 53). Wordsworth and his circle (consisting here of Wordsworth's sister, Dorothy, and fellow poet Samuel Taylor Coleridge) are further credited with the foundational development of ecological thinking: 'Modern historians of the environmental movement have traced the origins of the idea of human ecology to the writings of these two authors and William's sister, Dorothy' (2015: 186).

Given the document's focus on Wordsworth as a founding figure of these ecological perspectives, part of the sticking point for the authors may well have been a difficulty in clearly mapping and articulating Potter's work and her ecological credentials in relation to this central Wordsworthian line of influence. Judith Page has pointed to connections between Potter's interest in preserving and protecting the landscape and a Wordsworthian vision, suggesting that it is her 'focus on restoration that most clearly links Potter to Wordsworth and to the Lakeland landscape that united them across time and change' (2012: 103). Nonetheless there are crucial differences, not least the fact that, 'Unlike Wordsworth, who famously wrote about Lake District rustics, Potter did not write about shepherds, she became one herself' (Page and Smith 2021: 54). Potter's perspectives, drawn from her own experiences of working closely with the land and with **animals**, produce in many ways a very different ecological vision, as does her approach to exploring ideas about the environment through the lens of magic and **fairy** figures. Though Potter's writing about nature certainly takes what might be called a Wordsworthian legacy in new directions, the omission of any acknowledgement of the significance of Potter's actual writings on the development of this region as a 'Cultural Landscape' is a startling one, given that her work offers a sustained engagement with the natural landscape of the Lakes and **animal**/human relations for young readers.

The scant attention given to Potter in the document is also surprising in relation to the tourist economy, since Lake District visitor attractions data indicates that very high numbers of visitors to the region are interested in Potter-related sites. The nomination document itself presents data from 2013 and 2014 which shows that the 'World of Beatrix Potter' attraction at Bowness-on-Windermere and Hill Top received respectively, roughly three times and two times the number of visitors to Dove Cottage, home of William Wordsworth (1799–1808) and the premier Wordsworth visitor attraction in the Lake District (Lake District National Park Partnership 2015: 564). More recent figures confirm this trend, with 2021 data placing Hill Top in the top five of the most popular visitor attractions in Cumbria and the second highest attraction within the historic house and garden category (*VisitBritain/ VisitEngland*: 2023). Moreover, a recent 'geographical text analysis' of the Lake District claims that Potter now represents a more significant lure for visitors than her literary predecessors. The study suggests that though figures such as Wordsworth, Robert Southey, Thomas De Quincey and John Ruskin were 'celebrated as being a core part of the Lake District's identity when the National Park's boundaries were being established', today 'many more visitors are attracted to the Lakes by the lure of Beatrix Potter's legacy than any of the elder Lake Poets' (Taylor and Gregory 2022: 7–8). Despite the failure of the nomination document to identify Potter's 'significant literary and cultural influence over the Lake District fells', Joanna Taylor and Ian Gregory argue that this has 'contributed to the wider development of important trends in landscape, science, aesthetics, and environmental thought to which the Lakeland landscape was integral' (2022: 7–8). Potter's depiction of a Lake District landscape as the scene of adventures for a group of vividly drawn anthropomorphized **animals**, along with the subsequent reinforcement of this construction in various coffee-table books and visitor guidebooks, has indisputably contributed to the development of what John Urry calls the 'place myth' of the Lakes (1995: 193–210), overlaying a pre-existing Wordsworthian construction of the Lake District as a place of profound tranquillity and beauty, with new elements, including a magical dimension which appeals to a child's capacity for imaginative engagement with the natural environment. The legacy of Potter's writing is also significant in terms of a World Heritage inscription because the global reach of her *Tales* has encouraged a much more diverse visitor demographic in the Lake District than has been typical in Britain's national parks, which the recent DEFRA (Department for Environment, Food and Rural Affairs) *Landscapes Review* describes as an 'exclusive, mainly white, mainly middle-class club' (2019: 15). By contrast, the Lake District has seen a 'boom in Japanese visitors' in the twenty-first century, a trend which is attributed by cultural geographers to the 'popularity in Japan of the Beatrix Potter "Peter Rabbit" books', where they are used to teach English in schools (Walton 2013: 33). It is clear from both visitor demographics and figures, as well as popular identification of the region as 'Beatrix Potter's Lake District' from the mid twentieth-century onwards, that her role in shaping responses to this landscape has been significant and lasting. However, whilst the part she played in the protection of the Lake District through her conservation work is widely acknowledged (Kelly 2022; Lake District National Park Partnership 2015: 55, 136, 225, 294–5), the role played by her books in helping to shape of perceptions of place remains marginalized in accounts of the development of this 'Cultural Landscape'.

M IS FOR MYRIADS OF FAIRY FUNGI

The Potter family spent the summer of 1896 at Sawrey in the **Lake District** and in her final **journal** entry of the holiday Potter writes of the 'myriads of fairy fungi' that start into life in the autumn woods, adding that her pleasantest memory was of sitting on Oatmeal Crag with all the 'little fungus people singing and bobbing and **dancing** in the grass and under the leaves' down below (*J*: 435). When read alongside other **journal** entries from that summer we see just how closely imaginative and scientific perspectives on the natural environment were woven together in Potter's mind, since these reflections on 'myriads of fairy fungi' and the 'fungus people' occur at a point at which she was deeply immersed in serious mycological study. In other entries from that summer she records an important success with spore germination (*J*: 430) and documents her developing understanding of the hidden life of fungi, in particular the realization that they must have some 'other form' to take them over the winter months (*J*: 431). She even writes of her pleasure in contradicting the keeper of Botany at the Natural History Museum with her new findings (*J*: 431).

Just two months before setting off for the **Lake District**, Potter had paid her first visit to the mycological experts at Kew Gardens and had begun to engage in more concentrated research into spore germination. Despite their refusal to engage in any meaningful way with her work and theories, she persevered and produced a research paper, 'On the Germination of the Spores of *Agaricineae*', which was presented at the Linnean Society on the 1 April 1897. Sadly, and rather mysteriously, not only her final paper but all draft versions of this text have subsequently disappeared; however, mycological experts have pieced together information from Potter's **journal** and letters as to the argument contained in her scientific paper (Fortey 2021; Watling 2000) and for the most part, her findings have been verified. The dominant view today is that 'Potter might have spent the rest of her life as a pioneer mycologist' (Fortey 2021: 90) had it not been for difficulties encountered in making inroads into a male-dominated and closely guarded scientific community in the Victorian period. Detailed accounts of her experiences in this respect, including her treatment at the hands of first the Director of Kew Gardens and then the Linnean Society, have been published (Lear 2007 104–29; Noble 1992) and a century after her paper was presented to them, the Linnean Society issued a posthumous apology to Potter, which acknowledged the sexism displayed in the handling of her research and in its policy regarding the contributions of women more generally.

We might ask ourselves though what it was about the field of mycology which so particularly fascinated Potter, and the specific direction taken by her research suggests that her interest was stimulated by the mystery at the heart of the life cycle of fungi – the very mystery in fact which had connected them for so long in ancient folklore with a kind of **fairy** magic. Mushrooms and toadstools seem to lead a secret life and there is something rather **uncanny** about the way in which they appear suddenly overnight, apparently out of nowhere, often disappearing again just as quickly. The sense of secrecy, encoded in their very existence, is even captured in the nomenclature of the field of study. Potter is often now referred to as an amateur mycologist but, though the British Mycological Society had been founded in 1896, Potter did not use this term herself. Potter referred to George Massee, the expert she most wanted to consult at Kew, as a 'fungologist' (L: 40); however, Massee's official title was in fact 'Principal Assistant in Cryptogams'. Potter was familiar with this scientific term not only through Massee but also because the Cryptogamic Society of Scotland had been set up in 1875 and her original mycological mentor, Charles or Charlie McIntosh (a retired Scottish postman and self-taught naturalist), had some involvement with that group (Noble 1992: 62). The wider taxonomic division of 'cryptogams' comprises all plants that have no true flowers and do not produce seeds, reproducing instead by spores, with the term 'cryptogam' referring to their 'hidden' methods of reproduction. This group includes fungi but also ferns, mosses, algae and lichens, and it is notable that Potter's own interests extended to other plants within this taxonomic group. Not only was Potter drawn to a branch of botanical study which is defined by the existence of hidden or unknown elements, she became fascinated by the possibility of helping to find the **key** to unlock these secrets through her own research.

Potter quickly came to realize that fungi with fruiting bodies, like mushrooms and toadstools, must have some sort of underground form. This is known as the mycelium and Potter began to successfully grow this connective substance (Lear 2007: 112–13). In so doing she began to better understand it as a network of filaments which connects the living forms that are encountered on the surface of the earth. Reading Potter's reflections on these processes in her **journal** not only shows how she moves between the imaginative and scientific, but also indicates that the former sometimes helped to stimulate the latter. As Erica Kalnay argues, Potter's reference to 'wonder' when speculating about such processes 'demonstrates the enduring importance of the imagination to her scientific […] mycological work' (2019: 176). After a long drive in Scotland alongside 'lonely' fields and 'deep silent woods' Potter writes of a sense of a **fairy** presence in the landscape, noting, as evidence of this 'the green sour ringlets whereon the ewe not bites' (*J*: 357). This is a quotation from *The Tempest* and the passage describes those whose 'pastime / Is to make midnight mushrooms' and who by 'moonshine do the green sour ringlets make' (5.1.37-40). These words, with their suggestion of secret nighttime processes, stay in Potter's mind and a few days later she comes back to the idea, this time having reached a scientific conclusion: 'I see no mystery in the enlarging ring myself' since the 'funguses grow from the mycelium, not the spore direct, and the mycelium grows from that spore which falls outwards on unexhausted ground' (*J*: 365). Potter's **journal** entries suggest that in the case of cryptogamic species, where reproductive processes occur out of sight and in some cases beyond human understanding, developments in knowledge can be stimulated by imaginative reflections.

Potter began painting fungi in the late 1880s, but 1893–8 was her main period of focused study, and this runs in parallel with a significant stage in her creative development, in which she began to produce illustrations for books and wrote her first stories about **animal** characters in picture letters to children. In other words, Potter's imaginative and scientific worlds are deeply entangled from the outset and the day before writing her famous picture letter about **Peter Rabbit**, Potter had been painting one of her rarest mycological finds to date, the 'Old Man of the Woods'. Moreover, the letters she was sending to Charlie McIntosh at this time function as another kind of picture letter, in which she incorporates quick ink sketches of fungus shapes (Fortey 2021: 90). Symbiosis is a biological process with which Potter was familiar; indeed, she has been identified as the first person in Britain to realize the symbiotic nature of lichens (Hobbs 1989: 19). Her understanding of this process, by which two different organisms live in some way attached to each other, each contributing to the other's support, may well have contributed to her easy acceptance of the complementary nature of scientific knowledge and the human imagination, and perhaps suggested the importance of these working together in a similar way.

Potter's mycological drawings have been noted by contemporary and later experts for their technical brilliance and scientific accuracy, but they also seem to come alive in a way that is unusual within the field of botanical illustration. Kate Chandler observes that an 'energy emanates' from them (2005: 12) and Linda Lear suggests that they are 'lively illustrations of nature's handiwork, rather than cold objects of natural history' (2007: 88). Part of this is to do with the way in which Potter often depicts fungi in their natural setting, growing out of leaves or moss, as well as at different stages of growth within the same image, so that they come across as both alive and part of a wider ecosystem (see Figure 7).

The unusual 'energy' of Potter's mycological drawings is also though to do with the fact that Potter had a vividly imaginative response to the beauty of many of the fungi she encountered. Indeed, this was an important point of connection between Potter and Charlie McIntosh since, at their first meeting in 1892, he spoke with quite 'poetical feeling' about their 'exquisite colours' (*J*: 305). When Potter herself writes about fungi she does so in both a scientific and a figurative way, observing that the specimens Charlie had sent her were 'particularly beautiful', one 'almost like a pansy' and another 'very handsome' (*L*: 18). She is attentive to colour and texture: one is a 'bright chesnut [*sic*] colour & rather velvety' (*L*: 37), another has gills of a 'deep **yellow**' (*L*: 40), and one a 'round, slimy, purple head' (*J*: 338). She finds 'troops of gigantic

Figure 7 *Cantharellus Umbonata* by Beatrix Potter (1893).

Cortinarius' and a 'crisp **yellow** *Peziza*' (*J*: 357). She also turns to figurative language and especially astronomical imagery when describing 'myriads' of fungi, in ways which help to convey the fact that their number and variety exceed human comprehension; on entering a wood she writes that they 'starred the ground apparently in thousands' (*J*: 337) and on another occasion comments that 'I do not often consider the stars', it is more than enough that there should be 'forty thousand named and classified funguses' (*J*: 421).

Just as Potter's imagination plays an important role in her engagement with mycology, so does the latter have an impact on her non-scientific art and literature and, though fungi feature surprisingly rarely in her stories for children, we can trace the influence of her scientific studies on her imaginative development in a variety of ways. An illustration which Potter produced for 'Red Riding Hood' in 1894, for example, suggests that she was thinking about the way in which fungi could be used symbolically to convey meaning in a work of art. In her drawing, the wolf stands behind a slate slab and inside an area which seems devoid of life, whilst on the young girl's side of the wall there is ecological abundance: **trees**, shrubs, grasses, ferns and fungi surround her, and she holds a bunch of flowers in her hand (Hobbs 1992: 147, fig. 176). Moreover, the fungi in the foreground appear to be of the Mycena family (Hobbs 1992:147) - a group more commonly known as 'bonnets', since they have a distinctive cap. In other words, they seem to subtly connect to Red herself who, in the version of the story published by the Brothers Grimm, is known as 'Little Red Cap'.

Shortly after the publication of **Peter Rabbit**, Potter had begun to discuss a nursery rhyme book with Norman Warne and it is clear from her original draft manuscript that she was at this point interested in incorporating fungi in a book for children. One of the illustrated rhymes was to be 'The Toad's Tea Party', for which Potter produced a beautiful watercolour. It is perhaps the most vividly realized instance of her scientific and imaginative perspectives coming together, depicting as it does a group of anthropomorphized toads deep in conversation and seated on accurately rendered 'bracket fungus' chairs (*Art*: 259). The rhyme which was to accompany this image also contains subtle mycological references, chosen to emphasize the magical fairy-tale world of the picture. Instead of sugar, the toads have 'honey dew', a substance produced by the ergot fungus, and they **eat** 'tansey cake' with pats of 'witches' butter' (*H*: 230), the latter being the name of a distinctive black fungus which Potter had previously painted in its natural state (Hobbs 1992: 150, fig. 180).

A second mycological-themed rhyme and image planned for the book is perhaps more significant though in that here Potter actually personifies the mushrooms themselves in ways which recall her **journal** entry about the 'fungus people singing, and bobbing and **dancing**' (*J*: 435). Here, the rhyme and image work to convey to a young reader the idea of these organisms being alive and sentient (see Hobbs *et al.* 1987: 154, fig. 339). Norman Warne went through the dummy nursery rhyme book which Potter produced and marked those rhymes and images which he thought would work well, but he did not mark the 'Nid Nid Noddy' mushroom rhyme, perhaps not seeing the marketable potential of anthropomorphized fungi. Potter, however, tried to draw his attention back to it, explaining: 'I meant it for mushrooms **dancing** in the moonlight with little faces peeping underneath their caps', and adding 'I think it might be pretty' (*L*: 121). Norman Warne would tragically die just a few weeks after this letter was written and the nursery rhyme project was put to one side. However, Potter seems to have continued thinking about the book and especially the fungus-inspired rhymes, since a few months later she wrote to Norman's niece to say, 'I am going to put a picture of mushrooms in a book' (*LC*: 120).

Potter's nursery rhyme book was finally published as *Appley Dapply's Nursery Rhymes* in 1917, but this collection is very different to the one originally planned, with neither of the fungus-themed rhymes included. In fact, the only one of Potter's little books to feature fungi is *Squirrel Nutkin* and here they play a very minor role indeed, being used primarily – along with pine-cones, **yellowing** leaves and nut-gathering – to situate the story in a particular **seasonal** moment. We do see here the influence of Potter's earlier mycological illustrations though, in the way in which she depicts a group of toadstools growing naturally out of the leaves and moss which cover the edges of the **tree** stump on which Nutkin is playing marbles (*SN*: 26).

Despite the almost complete absence of fungi within her published *Tales*, Potter's mycological studies can nonetheless be seen to inform this body of work in other important ways. As Kalnay suggests, many of Potter's illustrations, though 'technically not microscopic in scope […] produce a comparable effect', with the 'circular vignetting' we find in many stories, evoking the 'view through a microscope' and a sense of 'peering inward into a tiny, fairylike realm' (2019: 165). Potter's studies do seem to have encouraged her vivid awareness of the existence of miniature hidden worlds-within-worlds and this is also explored in the books. When we enter Mrs. Tittlemouse's house in 'a bank under a hedge' (*TM*: 7), or Jeremy Fisher's house 'amongst the buttercups at the edge of a pond' (*JF*: 7), or **Peter's** home in the 'sand-bank' under the roots of the fir **tree** (*PR*: 7), our perspective shifts down to those tiny worlds which we would not usually see, so that an awareness of those other nonhuman lifeforms which exist all around us is conveyed to a young reader.

This sense of being able to peer into hidden lives is also achieved in Potter's late work, *The Fairy Caravan,* in which another cryptogamic plant, the fern – or rather its mythological seeds – is used to render the **animal** characters invisible to humans. Potter also though weaves her earlier mycological interests into this book more explicitly with a humorous story about the adventures of her **circus** pig, Paddy, who **eats** toadstools with hallucinogenic properties (*FC*: 163). Here this merely provides an amusing interlude, but the wider 'Fairy Caravan' project produced Potter's most detailed piece of imaginative mycological writing, 'A Walk amongst the Funguses', which was intended to form part of a sequel to *The Fairy Caravan*. Here Potter teaches respect for, and understanding of, the natural world through encounters which are both imaginative and scientific.

In a model which seems to hark back to older educational books for children produced in the late eighteenth century by writers such as Anna Barbauld, **Xarifa** takes Tuppenny for a walk, during which the latter learns about the natural environment from someone who is older and more informed. As was the case with this format from the outset, there is a tendency towards didacticism but, whilst this story does adopt a slightly more teacherly approach than we usually find in Potter's writing, there is a quiet enchantment about the natural encounters described which helps to maintain an overall sense of mystery and magic.

In the story, the **animals** who travel in the **Fairy** Caravan are on holiday, and **Xarifa** and Tuppenny the guinea-pig go for a walk hand-in-hand. Just beyond a fringe of ferns at the edge of the wood they encounter a 'colony of **yellow** funguses spotted about on the turf'; Tuppenny wonders if they are made of butter but **Xarifa** tells him that they are 'funguses called Boletus' (*H*: 314). Tuppenny seems afraid of these strange and mysterious lifeforms from the outset and acts with **violence** towards them, throwing a nut at the nearest Boletus. **Xarifa** tries to counter Tuppenny's negative reaction by both naming and personifying the other fungi they encounter; she tells him that Cantharella 'plays about among the beech leaves in September' and this approach helps Tuppenny shift from a **violent** response to one of care: he reflects on how sweet the mushroom smells and covers up her toes 'with more leaves' in case the sunbeams are too hot for her (*H*: 315). Within the story, the dormouse also conveys a powerful message of respect for a natural world which is often beyond our comprehension. She tells Tuppenny that 'it is injudicious to throw nuts at things we do not understand' and she herself curtseys to the Boletuses (*H*: 314). Crucially, **Xarifa** displays wisdom but also insists on the limitations of her knowledge of other species. When Tuppenny asks if Cantharella **dances**, she replies 'I really cannot tell you' and when he enquires if they are 'fairies', she merely replies 'hush' (*H*: 315). The story does convey knowledge about the habits and names of the fungi encountered but, more importantly, it suggests that we must show respect to the natural environment whilst accepting that we cannot expect to fully understand all of its mysteries.

At the end of her final summer holiday **journal** entry from 1896, Potter writes that the most vital thing is to retain 'the spirit-world of childhood' but 'tempered and balanced by common-sense' and to 'feel truly and understand a little, a very little, of the story of life' (*J*: 435). It is a growing understanding of the 'story of life' and specifically what the environmental writer, Timothy Morton, refers to as the 'total interconnectedness of things' (2010: 53), which emerges during Potter's research into the hidden lives of fungi. Kalnay suggests that Potter's work provides a space for 'imagining agencies and interconnections that often pass unnoticed under the dominance of conventional anthropocentric modes of perception' (2019: 161), and this is certainly encouraged by her mycological research. Her study of mycelium provided insights into the way in which surface life forms are connected at a subterranean level, and Potter's speculations about the way 'mixed fungi' could be growing 'upon a mixed network of mycelium' (*L*: 39) suggest an enhanced awareness of complex modes of ecological entanglement.

Moreover, Potter's response to these living organisms seems to foreshadow recent scholarly thinking about the importance of fungi in our environment, with current research pointing to the fact that they 'form a major and diverse component of most ecosystems on earth' and interconnect 'different levels of biological and ecological organisation', to the extent that their 'complex and dynamic ecological interactions' indicate an 'importance and ubiquity across Earth's ecosystems' (Bahram and Netherway 2022: 1). When Potter was in her seventies, news about penicillin's antibiotic potential was being widely discussed in the media and she evinced no surprise at this, writing in a notebook: 'So penicillium has arrived at last?' (Lear 2007: 432, 536, n. 11). If Potter were to read of the work being done by scientists today on the ways in which her 'myriads of fairy fungi' are fundamentally entangled with most aspects of life on earth, she would no doubt have felt herself to be on equally familiar territory.

N IS FOR NATIONAL TRUST

A short obituary, published in *The Guardian* the day following **Beatrix Potter**'s death in December 1943, describes her as a 'writer of children's books and the originator of the well-known Peter Rabbit books' but also makes passing reference to the fact that she had 'made a number of gifts to the National Trust' ('Obituary' 1943: 2). Behind the scenes, Potter's last Will and Testament was being processed and in due course the enormity of these 'gifts' would become clear. Potter bequeathed around 4,000 acres of land in the **Lake District**, located mainly in the prime locations of Windermere, Coniston and Esthwaite, to 'be held by the National Trust as an inalienable property' (Potter 1944: 2). In 1944 the Trust informed its members of the 'Heelis Bequest' and the extent of this acquisition began to receive national media coverage, including a piece on 'Beatrix Potter's Gifts to the Nation' with accompanying photographs in *The Times* (1944: 6).

Although Potter's earlier actions in purchasing the substantial Monk Coniston estate and handing over a portion of this to the National Trust had been reported in newspapers in 1930, her massive testamentary bequest made much more impact. This has been seen as a 'pivotal moment' in the conservation of areas which define 'the character of the **Lake District** landscape' (MacFarlane 2021: 161), but it was also a 'pivotal moment' in terms of Potter's public identity and legacy. The sheer scale of this bequest as well as its practical impact on the future of the Lakeland landscape has, in some ways, come to overshadow the role played by her books in shaping perceptions and reinforcing the cultural value of that region. Matthew Kelly suggests that Potter's bequest 'ensured that she left her mark on the physical characteristics of the **Lake District** to a degree unmatched by any modern figure', comparing her to Wordsworth and Ruskin, who, 'for all that they influenced how people thought about and experienced the region', did not 'acquire extensive tracts of **Lake District** land and property, and by those means seek to control its future' (2022: 78). Though this is undoubtedly true, the role played by Potter's textual representations of a rural **Lake District**, in influencing how people think about and experience the region, should not be underestimated.

The seeds of Potter's involvement with the National Trust were sown during the holiday she spent at Wray Castle, on the shores of Lake Windermere, as a teenager. The place clearly made an impression and, when revisiting Wray three years later, she wrote that the place looks as 'beautiful as ever' (*J*: 145). More importantly though, during that first extended summer holiday in the Lakes, the Potter family befriended Hardwicke Rawnsley, at this date a young man of thirty and vicar of the parish church at Low Wray. Rawnsley was also a writer and Wordsworth enthusiast, passionately committed to preserving Wordsworth's legacy as well as the **Lake District** which had inspired his work. Rawnsley's own thinking in this respect had been shaped by his encounters, as an undergraduate at Oxford, with John Ruskin, and both Ruskin and Rawnsley play an important role in carrying aspects of Wordsworth's legacy forwards into the late nineteenth century and beyond. Rawnsley became a lifelong friend of **Beatrix** Potter and his influence can be clearly seen in the trajectory of her own work and thinking.

Just one year after Potter and Rawnsley first met, Rawnsley proposed the formation of a Lake District Defence Society (later to become The Friends of the Lake District) at a meeting of the Wordsworth Society. He maintained that, for the sake of Wordsworth's literary heritage, it was necessary to take care of the landscape which had inspired him. The stated aim of the society was 'to protect the Lake District from those injurious encroachments upon its scenery which are from time to time attempted from purely commercial or speculative motives, without regard to its claim as a national recreation ground' (Ranlett 1983: 202). Rawnsley soon became convinced that the surest means of protecting the land was not legislation or localized lobbying but actual ownership and, when several important properties in the **Lake District** came up for sale in 1893, this idea gathered momentum. Rawnsley, along with Robert Hunter and Octavia Hill, proposed a 'national trust', with Rawnsley appointed as secretary. 'The National Trust for Places of Historic Interest or Natural Beauty' formally came into being in January 1895.

Traces of Rawnsley's preservationist influence on Potter's thinking can be identified even within her early **journal** writings. In the year in which the Trust was founded, for example, she writes of the 'horrible' little launches on Windermere which 'ruin the lake for boating' (*J*: 404), but her own growing love of this region and its traditional ways of life began to emerge more fully in her published work, especially in the stories she wrote after her purchase of Hill Top in 1905. The 'Sawrey' books, as they are sometimes known, begin

N is for National Trust

with *Mrs. Tiggy-Winkle* and end with *Pigling Bland* in 1913, and are very much 'about the country and the village around her', which proved 'rich in inspiration' (MacDonald 1986: 87–8). These books subtly reinforce the special qualities of **Lake District** landscapes and its rural communities, with their depictions of small Westmorland farms and cottages, the fields and lanes edged by dry-stone walls, and local flora and fauna. In a single image from *Tom Kitten*, we see several of these ingredients coming together. Moppet and Mittens are clambering up a traditional dry-stone wall, against which ferns are growing; in the background there is a Westmorland cottage and a small copse of **trees**, and behind this a larger tree plantation with a narrow country lane winding into the distance (*TK*: 25). All of these elements constitute important components of the Lakeland ecosystem and 'Cultural Landscape' which Potter would in due course set out to actively protect via her developing relationship with the National Trust. Her textual handling of place though plays a crucial role in cultivating an appreciation of this landscape and a particular rural agro-pastoral way of life to the outside world in the early years of the twentieth century, just as Wordsworth's poetry had done one hundred years earlier.

At the tail end of her 'Sawrey' books period, in which she had begun to encourage an appreciation for these landscapes in a new generation of readers, Potter went on to intervene publicly in a 'classic preservationist campaign' being led by Rawnsley (Kelly 2022: 110). In 1912 there were proposals to construct an aeroplane factory at Cockshott Point, an area of lakeshore on the eastern side of Windermere, and one hydroplane was already being used on the lake. Privately Potter gave vent to her anger and 'bad language' at the 'beastly fly-swimming spluttering aeroplane' (*L*: 192). She also though went public on her views, writing a letter on 'Windermere and the Hydroplane' to the editor of *Country Life*, very much in the spirit of Wordsworth and Ruskin's public letters to newspapers on the matter of railway development in the Lakes a generation earlier. Having cited the ancient mode of lake travel, the ferry boat, which 'time out of mind' has taken parties across and still offers the most 'cheerful and pleasant' way of crossing the Lake (*L*: 193), Potter puts forward similar arguments to Wordsworth and Ruskin, as to the way the hydroplane – like the railways – negatively affects the quiet character of the place:

> Our peaceful lake is disturbed by the presence of a hydroplane [...] The existing machine flies up and down in the trough of the hills; it turns at either end of the lake and comes back. It flies at a comparatively low

level; the noise of its propeller resembles millions of blue-bottles, plus a steam threshing engine.

(*L*: 193)

Moreover, in describing the possibility of further planes and the development of an 'aeroplane factory' here as 'deplorable', she specifically evokes Wordsworth in formulating her opposition. Potter reminds her readers that Cockshott Point is infused with literary and cultural history: this is 'where Wordsworth, Scott, Canning and Christopher North embarked upon the lake with their host' in 1825 to celebrate Scott's birthday (*L*: 194). Going on to argue that aeroplane testing should take place over the sea, she turns to Wordsworth's poetry to help explain why such activities are so unsuitable over an inland lake:

> A more inappropriate place for experimenting with flying machines could scarcely be chosen. The noise is confined by the hills:
> 'echoes
> Redoubled and redoubled; concourse wild' (*L*: 194).

The quotation is taken from the famous 'Boy of Winander' passage in Book Five of *The Prelude*, in which Wordsworth describes a young boy who blows 'mimic hootings to the silent owls' and they:

> Responsive to his call, with quivering peals,
> And long halloos, and screams, and echoes loud
> Redoubled and redoubled, concourse wild
> Of jocund din[.]
>
> (Wordsworth [1850] 1953: 525)

Just as the owls' hootings are echoed around the lake by the confinement of the hills, so now the terrible sounds of the hydroplane are carried around in a nightmarish twentieth-century technological re-enactment of the natural sonic effect captured in the poem. It is a clever sleight of hand on Potter's part, since the quotation evokes Wordsworth's cultural authority on this latest threat to the **Lake District** and her dystopian repurposing of the line shows how the joyous sounds of nature are now being drowned out by technological intervention. The quotation is cut off, so that the 'jocund' sounds described by Wordsworth are absent and we are left with a very different kind of 'concourse wild' echoing around the valley.

N is for National Trust

A few years later Potter intervened again in a matter relating to the protection of Cockshott Point and, in this later campaign, we see how the textual construction of this landscape in her books was already starting to cultivate an appreciation of the region in international contexts. When Potter began to hear from and speak to American librarians, booksellers and reviewers of children's books in the 1920s, she realized that a significant part of the appeal of her writing for those readers was their love of her Lakeland settings. Potter wrote to one American correspondent to say that the 'New Englanders' she had met on their visits to the **Lake District** 'appreciate the memory of old times, the simple country pleasures, – the homely beauty of the old farm house, the sublime beauty of the silent lonely hills', and were drawn to visit the Lakes in order to see those landscape qualities which her books depict (*L*: 306). Such appreciation was in no small part to do with the fact that New England was the first region of the United States to be transformed by the industrial revolution. As Jane Crowell Morse points out, New Englanders were 'enthusiastic conservationists' (1982: xi), because of the rapid change to their own old ways. Not only did Potter recognize that her books were helping to generate overseas interest in a landscape and way of life which was increasingly under threat, she also set out to harness that interest in order to protect the region she loved.

One of Potter's first letters to the editor of the *Horn Book* was intended to garner American support for the purchase of an area of lakeshore which was at 'imminent risk of disfigurement by extensive building and town extension' (*A*: 9). Noting that the *Horn Book* had made reference to the fact that the 'writer and illustrator of the "**Peter Rabbit**" books lived in the district of the Westmorland Lakes in the north of England', she writes that '"**Beatrix Potter**" has very much at her heart an appeal to raise a fund to save a strip of foreshore woodland and meadow, near Windermere Ferry', and enquires if American readers might be interested in giving a guinea in support of this fund, in return for an autographed drawing (*A*: 9–10). Potter's approach was successful, and she accumulated just over one hundred pounds from her 'Friends in Boston USA', which made a significant contribution towards the purchase of Cockshott Point by the National Trust (*A*: 19; MacFarlane 2021: 160). Potter wrote that, whenever I cross the ferry and look at the pleasant green banks 'I will think of the good friends across a wider stretch of water – who still believe in old England and all she has stood for in the past' (*A*: 14).

Potter's preservationist impulses and the use of her own literary identity to harness support for the Lakes clearly locate her in a conservationist tradition which reaches back through Rawnsley and Ruskin to Wordsworth.

Like them she sought to prevent the 'Lake country from being vulgarized' and added her voice to those who wish to 'preserve some portions of wild land unspoilt for the general good' (A: 14). However, in one important respect Potter veered away from the attitudes of Wordsworth and Ruskin as expressed in their campaign against the railways. Having written about her joy at the protection of this area of the lakeshore, Potter goes on to describe her happiness at the fact that the newly purchased land 'will be thrown open to the public next summer', to the great pleasure of 'strangers from the Lancashire mill towns who like to picnic beside the lake' (A: 15). The very particular reference here to those visiting 'from the Lancashire mill towns' suggests a self-conscious distancing from Wordsworth and Ruskin, who had infamously spoken out against just such visitors.

In his first letter to the *Morning Post*, Wordsworth had argued that those who 'labour daily with their hands for bread in large towns' needed to be trained to a 'profitable intercourse with nature' by strolling through 'neighbouring fields' after attending church on Sundays, rather than by taking the train to Windermere (Wordsworth [1844] 2004: 139). The writer, Harriet Martineau, who lived in Ambleside and socialized with the Wordsworth family in the 1840s, said that she herself noted an 'exclusive temper' among the 'cultivated' residents of the Lakes, who believed that the 'mountains and vales' were 'a privilege appropriate to superior people like themselves', adding that Mrs. Wordsworth took up her husband's views and 'declared with unusual warmth that green fields with daises and buttercups, were as good for Lancashire operatives as our Lakes and valleys' (Martineau [1861] 2004: 458–9). In the 1870s John Ruskin picked up Wordsworth's mantle, writing of the 'stupid herds of modern tourists' who are to be 'emptied, like coals from a sack, at Windermere and Keswick', and predicting that this would result in the opening of 'taverns and skittle grounds' and create a 'steam merry-go-round of the lake country' ([1876] 1908: 140–1).

Though Potter was herself capable of making classist and judgemental comments about tourists (Kelly 2022: 132), and whilst she agreed with Ruskin in the matter of education and the importance of teaching those of all classes to 'love fields, birds, and flowers' ([1876] 1908: 142), she did not share Wordsworth or Ruskin's scepticism at the idea of Lancashire mill workers responding positively and thoughtfully to these elements. Indeed, her description of these Lancashire visitors picnicking by the Lake implies that they are not the noisy and unsympathetic masses of Ruskin's fevered imagination. Potter's rather different views in this respect were no doubt influenced in part by her Unitarian Lancashire mill-owning grandfather,

N is for National Trust

Edmund Potter, who set up a library and reading room for his factory workers (Lear 2007: 12), but also perhaps owe something to her awareness of having 'descended from generations of Lancashire yeoman [sic] and weavers' (A: 207).

As Potter's involvement with the management of the **Lake District** increased through further land purchases and closer involvement with the National Trust, we see her insistence on control and careful monitoring, combined with a pragmatism regarding some necessary changes. Though resistant towards certain developments, such as the knocking down of old vernacular cottages, the widening of a road through a narrow valley, electricity pylons, the building of 'nasty' Swiss-style 'sham-chalets' below Langdale Fell (Kelly 2022: 123) and the aeroplane factory at Windermere, Potter accepted as inevitable other elements of a changing world, including railways and buses. Writing to one prospective visitor, she noted that there is a 'motor bus' which runs up the hill from the ferry every hour, 'which the fairies do not like; but undeniably it is convenient for mortals' (A: 35).

Potter's belief, no doubt influenced by Rawnsley, was that land ownership was the only way to ensure a necessary protection for the **Lake District**, and she threw her weight behind the National Trust rather than proposals to create a National Park. Ideas for the latter were being discussed in the late 1920s, but Potter dismissed the 'National Park rubbish' and entered instead into a 'remarkable agreement' with the Trust, buying up the whole of the vast Monk Coniston estate, selling a portion to the Trust as soon as possible, with a view to bequeathing them the rest in due course (Kelly 2022: 139, 126). As Kelly suggests, it is clear from these actions that by this stage Potter believed that the National Trust was the 'only salvation' for the **Lake District** (2022: 136), and during the years of her stewardship she set down careful precedents for the future farming and management of this region, which continue to affect decisions about land-management in the region today.

Just as Potter's interventions helped determine the future of the **Lake District**, so the way in which her work and legacy is presented to the public is, in part, shaped by curatorial choices on the part of the National Trust. As such, it is likely to be affected by evolving Trust agendas and the wider cultural contexts which inform their decision making in the future. In 2020 the National Trust published an 'Interim Report on the Connections between Colonialism and Properties now in the Care of the National Trust, including Links with Historic Slavery'. The report, which sparked heated public commentary and media coverage (Fowler 2020: 17–42), states that the 'National Trust has made a commitment to research, interpret and share the histories of slavery and the legacies of colonialism at the places we care for'; it 'provides an overview of current research into the connections that our places have to slavery and colonialism [...], exploring some of the most significant links to the places and collections in our care and focusing on the sources of wealth that helped to fund them' (Huxtable, Fowler, Kefalas, and Slocombe 2020: 5). Neither Hill Top nor **Beatrix** Potter are mentioned in the 2020 report, a fact which may not seem altogether surprising at first glance, given that a key criterion for inclusion was 'a strong historical narrative' relating to factors such as wealth 'connected to the proceeds of slavery' (Huxtable, Fowler, Kefalas, and Slocombe 2020: 5). However, some of the eighty plus properties listed in the report have quite tentative narratives of this kind. One such example is Allan Bank, a house in Grasmere in which the Wordsworth family lived for two years, between 1809 and 1811. The report notes that William and Dorothy Wordsworth expressed views in opposition to slavery but also records that their brother, John, 'became Commander of the East India Company ship *Earl of Abergavenny* in 1801' and 'captained two successful voyages to China, in which the family invested' (Huxtable, Fowler, Kefalas, and Slocombe 2020: 89).

Given the rather slender link here between colonial activity and Allan Bank itself, it is perhaps rather more surprising that Hill Top is not listed at all in the report since the vast Potter family wealth on both the maternal and paternal sides derived from the cotton industry. As the report itself notes, this industry was deeply implicated in colonial trading in the nineteenth century with raw materials being purchased from the slave plantations in the American South. Potter's paternal grandfather, Edmund Potter, owned what was, at the time, the largest calico printing firm in the world and John Leech, her maternal grandfather, owned textile mills and a fleet of ships which traded internationally. Potter's first Lakeland property, Hill Top, was purchased with the proceeds from her early publication success and a bequest from an aunt; however, Potter's major subsequent purchases of land and property in the **Lake District** were made possible by two significant sources of income: the 'phenomenally lucrative children's books' but also her 'northern industrial inheritance' (Kelly 2022: 78), and the latter is irrevocably linked to wider colonial economic contexts. As in the case of the Wordsworth family, the ideological framework is complex, not least because Edmund Potter spoke out against the injustices of slavery and proposed that British cotton supplies should come from free workers in India rather than the slave plantations of America. Nonetheless, it seems likely that future curatorial narratives regarding the 'Heelis bequest' will need to navigate and acknowledge the ways in which the National Trust's ownership of large tracts of land in the **Lake District** is inextricably connected to aspects of nineteenth-century British colonial history.

O IS FOR OVER THE HILLS AND FAR AWAY

The phrase, 'Over the hills and far away', has frequently been taken to have autobiographical significance since its first appearance in Potter's published work, even featuring in the title of a recent Potter biography (Dennison 2016). At the end of *Pigling Bland*, the eponymous hero and Pig-wig (a beautiful black Berkshire pig) make their escape from a life of danger and unhappiness, and are depicted **dancing** into their new life together 'over the hills and far away' (*PB*: 81). Readers have seen this unusually uplifting textual ending as inspired by Potter's own 'escape into happily-ever-after' in the **Lake District** via her marriage to William Heelis (MacDonald 1986: 120), not least because preparations for this book took place in the months running up to the marriage and it was published shortly after the wedding in October 1913.

However, when sending a presentation copy of the book to a friend, Potter accompanied it with a note which attempts to pre-empt an autobiographical reading of the story's central narrative. She writes that the image of the

> two pigs arm in arm – looking at the sunrise – is not a portrait of me and Mr. Heelis, though it is a view of where we used to walk on Sunday afternoons. When I want to put William into a book, it will have to be a very tall thin **animal**.
>
> (*H*: 217)

Despite this overt denial, the comment not only reinforces an autobiographical significance in terms of geographical contexts but also indicates that a connection between the story of her own life and that of the two pigs did exist in Potter's own mind, since she issues her disclaimer before the text had come to be interpreted in this way by other readers.

What also seems clear is that the phrase 'over the hills and far away' had some strong personal significance for Potter, since she returns to it

O is for Over the hills and far away

several times here and in later texts. Within *Pigling Bland* the phrase is closely connected to the nursery rhyme in which the line is most commonly encountered and working through these references provides an insight into the complex ways in which Potter draws on and engages with her primary sources (in this case a popular nursery rhyme as well as the title of a song which is referenced in that rhyme) in order to develop her own imaginary worlds.

The nursery rhyme is first sung by Pigling Bland and his brother Alexander as they travel from their home at Pettitoes Farm. They trot away together singing:

> Tom, Tom, the piper's son,
> stole a pig and away he ran!
> But all the tune that he could play,
> was 'Over the hills and far away!'
>
> (*PB*: 26)

Its first appearance in the story thus functions somewhat ironically and humorously, since a rhyme about a pig being stolen is sung by the pigs themselves as they take themselves off to market. However, after Alexander has been returned to the farm by a policeman (having not been able to find his licence to travel), Pigling journeys on alone and has a first encounter with 'Over the Hills' not as a song title quoted in the rhyme but as a phrase with a meaning of its own. He comes across a sign which directs him to the Market Town one way, back to his home another, or to 'Over the Hills'. Though Pigling only glances 'wistfully' along the 'road towards the hills' and sets off obediently to the Market Town as instructed, the signpost causes him to reflect on the new and different kind of life, in which he would live independently with a 'little garden where he could grow potatoes' (*PB*: 31-2). Henceforth, 'over the hills and far away' comes to represent the possibility of an alternative life about which the pig fantasizes (*PB*: 35).

A little while later, Pigling arrives at Mr. Piperson's farm and here the *Tale* turns back to and plays with ideas derived from the nursery rhyme. The farmer's name gives an intimation of danger, apparent to the reader if not to Pigling, suggesting that his impulse, like the 'Piper's son' of the rhyme, is to steal pigs. At the farm Pigling encounters Pig-wig and it is the singing of the nursery rhyme which establishes a primary point of connection between the two pigs. Hearing Pig-wig's story also reinforces Pigling's repressed desire to escape 'over the hills' since Pig-wig reveals that she herself has been stolen by Mr. Piperson for 'Bacon' and 'Hams' (*PB*: 55).

The last lines of the *Tale* continue to make subtle references back to the nursery rhyme which inspired it, in ways which point to Potter's rich and playful imaginative engagement with her sources. A later verse in the rhyme states that all who hear Tom playing begin to **dance** and 'Even pigs on their hind legs would after him prance' (Opie and Opie 1997: 488) and, whilst these lines are not cited in Potter's *Tale*, they are in fact suggested by the final image in the book which portrays the pigs **dancing** on their hind legs (*PB*: 81). In the *Tale*, however, the pigs' fate is subverted since Pigling and Pig-wig are **dancing** away from, rather than towards, the 'Piper's son'/Mr. Piperson.

Though Potter's engagement with this nursery rhyme is fascinatingly multi-layered, the text's overt references to this source have led to other cultural influences being overlooked. The intertextual allusions to the nursery rhyme do not account for the unusually romantic and uplifting mood of Potter's story, especially in the latter half of the *Tale*, which is imbued with evocative images of light after darkness. Kutzer suggests that the 'burgeoning romance between the two pigs […] is worthy of anything in a Jane Austen novel' (2003: 149) and this aspect of the story, particularly in relation to their subsequent escape, also has strong fairy-tale overtones which are not present in either the nursery rhyme or the song to which it refers.

According to the nursery rhyme, 'Over the hills and far away' is the title of the only song which the piper's son can play. The song itself dates back to the late seventeenth century and variable versions can be found, but the eponymous refrain usually refers to a soldier's commitment to follow the king's orders and travel far away from their home. In its original context, 'over the hills and far away' thus functions rather wistfully, suggesting not a journey towards happiness but a duty to leave all you know and love behind. However, the song's central refrain was taken up and reworked in subsequent literary texts, including John Gay's *The Beggar's Opera* (1728). Here the meaning of the line is deployed in romantic terms to suggest an imagined life of happiness for a young couple, but the satirical framework and comic plot of the play (one half of the loving couple is a highwayman who has professed his love to different women) undercut the positive effect of the words such as we find at the end of *Pigling Bland*.

A more pertinent literary appearance of the 'over the hills and far away' refrain occurs in Tennyson's poem 'The Day-Dream' (1842), a poetic reworking of 'Sleeping Beauty'. Not only is the line used here to suggest a 'happy-ever-after' for the young lovers, but other aspects of both the

O is for Over the hills and far away

underpinning story and Tennyson's treatment of it seem to be echoed in Potter's *Tale*. The second half of *Pigling Bland*, with its focus on the rescue of a female character and a happy future life for the young couple, draws on the central motif of 'Sleeping Beauty', a fairy tale for which Potter had earlier produced several illustrations (Whalley and Hobbs *et al.* 1987: 62). Though Pigling initially awakens Pig-wig from a state of inertia and acceptance of her fate rather than sleep, she does then fall 'fast asleep on the hearth-rug' and has to be woken by Pigling (*PB*: 62–3). It is Tennyson's own poetic handling of the 'Sleeping Beauty' story, however, which contains more significant parallels with *Pigling Bland*. Crucially, Tennyson focuses on a part of the story which does not appear in the original Perrault fairy tale: the couple's journey to happiness following the rescue of the princess from the palace. In a section of the poem called 'The Departure', Tennyson depicts their movement away from the site of imprisonment into an imagined future 'over the hills and far away', and their journey is partly measured by the passing of time as indicated by the movement of the sun:

> And o'er the hills, and far away
> Beyond their utmost purple rim,
> Beyond the night across the day,
> Thro' all the world she follow'd him.
> [...]
> Beyond their utmost purple rim,
> And deep into the dying day
> The happy princess follow'd him.
>
> (Tennyson [1842] 1880: 120)

Notably, Potter's tale also focuses on the journey which is undertaken by the two pigs and, as in Tennyson, this is partly measured by temporal changes, though in *Pigling Bland* the journey is towards the sunrise rather than the sunset, thus emphasizing their move from darkness into light. The two pigs leave 'between dark and daylight' and the sun rises as they cross the moor, appearing as a 'dazzle of light over the tops of the hills' (*PB*: 65–7).

Not only does Tennyson's focus on the imagined journey of the fairy-tale lovers foreshadow the journey of Pigling and Pig-wig, both texts use the 'over the hills and far away' refrain to suggest a projected wish-fulfilment for the happy couples. However, the precise significance of this future life is conveyed in Tennyson's poem by these enigmatic lines:

And far across the hills they went
In that new world which is the old:
Across the hills, and far away[.]

(Tennyson [1842] 1880: 120)

As Donald Hair suggests, Tennyson 'describes the exaltation of hero and heroine in terms of a new and better life for them' but he argues that the phrase 'that new world which is the old' reminds us that this 'exaltation is largely an inner illumination which enables them to see old things in a new way' (60: 1981). In Potter's *Tale*, the place in which this future will be experienced is clearly identified as 'Westmorland' (*PB*: 68); however, the joy which is suggested through Pig-wig's **dance** first occurs when the pigs look towards this place and all that it imaginatively represents to them, not following their arrival at the desired geographical destination (which in fact sits outside the pages of the text). In other words, in Potter's story the phrase is used to suggest hope in an imagined future rather than a new life which has already been realized.

The use of 'over the hills and far away' in relation to both geographical and more-than-geographical meanings is one which recurs in *The Fairy Caravan*. Although the refrain only appears on a couple of occasions in the book itself, it was clearly central to Potter's imaginative handling of the project. The first chapter was originally published in the **Horn Book** under the title 'Over the Hills and Far Away' and Potter subsequently referred to this as 'the first chapter of "Over the Hills and Far Away"', indicating that the stories in the book were for her linked by this phrase (*A*: 15 and 17). Again, Tennyson's poem seems to feed into Potter's imaginative engagement with the idea but this time rather more overtly. When Potter came to write the preface to *The Fairy Caravan*, she could not get the phrase 'that New World which is the old' out of her head, but had by this point forgotten the source of the quotation (*A*: 25–6). However, the meaning of the line comes to take on a new significance in this context, when Potter is writing a book for readers in New England. Here those readers literally represent the 'New World' which loves and values the 'old world' depicted in her stories. She plays with possible reworkings of the line which point to this precise meaning in more explicit ways: 'friends in that New World which still is Old' or 'that New World which remembers the Old', but in the end leaves the quotation out of the preface, explaining to her publisher that she had meant that those from New England seem to have 'more understanding and appreciation of old English traditions than the bulk of English people' (*A*: 26).

O is for Over the hills and far away

In other respects though Potter's handling of the 'over the hills and far away' refrain in *The Fairy Caravan* echoes that in her earlier text. Tuppenny, like Pigling Bland, is running away from one life into a new one and his story also involves a 'long, long' physical journey which will be transformational (*FC*: 14). Moreover, the new landscapes in which Tuppenny takes up his new life are very explicitly those of the **Lake District** and, more particularly, real places within Potter's own immediate environs of Sawrey: Wilfin Beck, Pringle Wood and Codlin Croft. Thus here, via both Potter's discussion of the quotation for the Preface and Tuppenny's own journey, the idea of escaping 'over the hills and far away' would seem to be very explicitly connected to an actual geographical space.

However, such a reading is complicated by the fact that in *The Fairy Caravan*, the phrase 'over the hills and far away' is never actually used to suggest the place that has already been found. Tuppenny has already made his initial momentous journey over the hills when he first meets the **circus** troupe but, on arrival, Paddy Pig comments: 'Lucky you found us today; we will be over the hills and far away tomorrow' (*FC*: 21). The elusiveness of what is indicated by this phrase is further suggested by the last lines of *The Fairy Caravan* which look beyond the landscapes in which the story has been set:

> They harnessed up, they trailed away – over the hills and far away – on a sunny windy morning. But still in the broad green lonnin going up to the intake, I can trace my pony's **fairy** footsteps. [...] I can hear the rattle of the tilt-cart's wheels, and the music of the **Fairy** Caravan.
>
> (*FC*: 264)

The shift from a third- to a first-person narrator here directs us back to Potter's perspectives on the phrase and its meanings. She is herself, to all intents and purposes, already 'over the hills and far away' in the new life she carved out for herself in the **Lake District**, but the continued journeying of her imaginary characters suggests that for them and for her the phrase refers to something or somewhere which exists beyond a current known reality.

Whilst escape from the city and into the rural environment of the **Lake District** is certainly closely associated with the phrase 'over the hills and far away', Potter's handling of these words indicates that they refer also to an imaginary place. In a later description of her actual discovery of a multitude of tiny hooves on Troutbeck Tongue which, in part, inspired *The Fairy Caravan*, Potter imagines them to be the footmarks of a 'troupe of **fairy** riders' who rode down 'old King Gait into Hird Wood and Hallilands' then 'away into Fairyland and the blue distance of the hills' (*A*: 212). Here then the far-off hills, which sit beyond the limits of her own Lakeland landscape, represent more explicitly the imaginative world of fairyland itself.

There is also another, much earlier reference, to 'over the hills and far away' in Potter's writing which suggests a further layer of complexity to the ideas and associations connected to this phrase. In an 1886 **journal** entry, she refers to a painting by John Everett Millais which he called *Over the Hills and Far Away* (*J*: 192). It depicts a Scottish landscape in the valley of the Tay, not far from Dalguise, where the Potter family spent most of their summer holidays between 1871 and 1881. Though Potter's reference to the painting occurs in a **journal** entry of 1886, Millais completed the work a decade earlier when the Potter family were themselves holidaying in this same landscape. Though Potter makes only a passing reference to the painting in her **journal**, it seems likely that Millais' use of the title *Over the Hills and Far Away* for his representation of a landscape amidst which Potter herself had spent so many happy holidays as a child connected those childhood experiences with these words in her imagination.

Moreover, in Potter's private writings about Dalguise, this place too takes on a significance which is more than geographical. It also comes to represent a particular time of her life, a period of childhood happiness that could never be fully reclaimed or re-accessed, in which she was vividly alive to the imaginative potential of the world around her:

> I remember every stone, every tree, the scent of the heather, the music sweetest mortal ears can hear, the murmuring of the wind through the fir **trees** [...] I could not see it in the same way now, I would rather remember it with the sun sinking, showing behind the mountains, the purple shadows creeping down the ravines into the valley [...] Then, an hour or two later, the great harvest-moon rose over the hills, the **fairies** came out to **dance** on the smooth turf[.]
>
> (*J*: 85)

In this memory of childhood experience, 'over the hills' is not a 'far away' place but rather exists within the context of Dalguise itself; the moon rises over those hills and the fairies are present in that landscape. This passage was triggered by a suggestion that the Potter family might return to this Scottish holiday home and Potter expressed profound anxiety at this possibility because she could never experience the place as she did in childhood. These words are an elegy for a lost way of experiencing the world as much as a lost place – a time when everything was 'romantic in my imagination' and when the woods were 'peopled by the mysterious good folk' (J: 85).

The phrase 'over the hills and far away' is thus a multi-layered one for Potter and has a complex autobiographical significance. Though intimately connected to certain geographical spaces in her imagination, especially Scotland and the **Lake District**, it is also suggestive of a wistful desire for something which is always out of reach, a childhood imaginary in which a 'strange wild music' can be heard in the wind and **fairies** come together to **dance** in the light of the harvest moon (J: 85).

P IS FOR PETER RABBIT

In recalling the publication history of *Peter Rabbit*, **Beatrix** Potter noted that about 1900 'there began to be a fashion for little picture books' but nobody 'would publish poor *Peter*!' (*A*: 9, 57). *Peter Rabbit* was in fact turned down by 'at least six' publishers, including Warne, before appearing in print in 1902 (*A*: 208). Within a year, however, an incredible 50,000 copies had been sold and Potter wrote to Norman Warne, in some astonishment, to observe that the 'public must be very fond of rabbits!' – adding, 'what an appalling quantity of Peter' (*L*: 82). More than twenty years later, when reflecting on the book's ongoing success, she commented that she had 'never been able to understand what is the attraction of the book, but it continues to sell' (*A*: 9).

In being turned down by several publishers before going on to become the first of one of the best-selling series of children's books in history, the story of 'Peter Rabbit' bears a remarkable similarity to one of the most notable children's publishing stories of recent times: the extraordinarily successful 'Harry Potter' books by J. K. Rowling, the first of which was turned down by multiple publishers before going on to top the best-seller charts. In both cases, and despite an initial catalogue of rejections, momentum gathered very quickly following initial publication, suggesting that these texts chimed particularly well with young readers at their respective cultural moments. The children's literature scholar, Jack Zipes, has described the 'Harry Potter' series as a socio-cultural 'phenomenon' (Zipes 2002: 172), and the same term might well be applied to **Beatrix** Potter's 'Peter Rabbit' books. As with Rowling, a crucial factor in the commercial success of these texts is the way in which the fictional creations have transcended the pages of the books in which their stories were originally told, to become absorbed and reproduced in our culture via a dizzying array of toys, games, branded merchandise and spin-off texts across multiple mediums. Indeed, so significant is the cultural 'mediation and multiplication of *Peter Rabbit*', that this aspect of Potter's legacy has warranted its own detailed scholarly analysis (Mackey 2002: 175; 1998).

P is for Peter Rabbit

In later years Potter wrote that she had never fully understood 'the secret of Peter's perennial charm' but went on to offer, in a typically insightful way, a partial explanation for his ongoing popularity, suggesting that it is perhaps because 'he and his little friends keep on their way, busily absorbed with their own doings'; they were 'always independent' (*L*: 422). Having brought Peter into the public domain in her first published book, Potter would go on to develop his story throughout further *Tales* which she occasionally referred to, rather disparagingly, as her 'bunny books' (*L*: 292). These stories in fact function as a sort of Bildungsroman, a book (or in this case several books) in which we follow the development of a main character from childhood into adulthood. After Peter's initial experiences in Mr. McGregor's garden in *Peter Rabbit*, he appears again in *Benjamin Bunny* in 1904. The action here sits very close to the first story, as Peter is still trying to deal with his traumatic experience, and is still missing his blue jacket and shoes. By the time we get to the *Flopsy Bunnies* in 1909, much more time has passed, and Peter is now an adult with his own 'nursery garden' (*FB*: 11). He appears again as an adult in 1912, this time helping his cousin Benjamin Bunny rescue the latter's baby bunnies, who have been stolen by Tommy Brock. The motif established by these books, of Peter going about his business and continuing to live his life, was further reinforced some seventeen years later with *Peter Rabbit's Almanac for 1929*, one of Potter's spin-off publications. Here we see Peter still 'busily absorbed in his own doings' over the course of a year: gardening, posting a letter, trying to hold an umbrella up in a high wind, as well as gathering daffodils, apples, or twigs for the fire, depending on the **season**. Via these publications Potter sets up the idea of a character who lives on in real time and space, or at least within this parallel world in which **animals** dress and behave like humans, and this is a crucial factor in enabling Peter to transcend the confines of his original textual frame so that we are predisposed to see his story as ongoing.

Whilst these books extend the imaginary textual space which Peter inhabits, within a year of the publication of *Peter Rabbit*, Potter was working on other kinds of merchandise which would ensure the capacity of her characters to fully step outside and exist as marketable commodities beyond the pages of her books. She began to produce a template for a Peter Rabbit doll, cutting out patterns from calico (*L*: 83), and registered the design at the Patent Office in December 1903 before going on to look for a British manufacturer who could produce a toy which would meet her high standards (Lear 2007: 172). As Linda Lear notes, Potter's instinct for the commercial possibilities of 'derivative merchandise' was far in advance of her publisher's and impressively entrepreneurial (2007: 172). From this moment on, Potter would become an 'enthusiastic commodifier of her little animals' (Mackey 2002: 178), with the Peter Rabbit doll being merely the first of what she referred to as her 'side shows' (*L*: 219).

So ahead of her time was Potter in this respect, that she is described in a recent article published in *The Times* as one of the 'first to recognize that content – as we now call the stuff that makes up a book or a film – was only the beginning' (Wagner 2009). Though Potter's awareness of extra-textual commercial possibilities for her imaginary characters seems unusually modern, her primary concern when pursuing these avenues was in ensuring that the quality of her own artistic creations be maintained, whatever the medium of its reproduction; in discussing a proposal for Peter Rabbit wallpaper, she wrote that the 'idea of rooms with badly drawn rabbits is appalling' (Lear 2007: 174). Nonetheless Potter clearly enjoyed these entrepreneurial endeavours, often taking a very active role in the development of products which became an extension of her creative life.

Though this process was spearheaded by Potter herself, as Margaret Mackey observes, the scale and number of 'reworkings, toys, and other objects is now daunting' and it is possible to be 'overwhelmed' by the 'sheer volume of commodification of a small set of texts' (2002: 178). Moreover, there is a strange kind of fetishization at work in the endless reproductions of Peter and other selected Potter characters at the specialist shops which sell this material. In the **Lake District** alone there are currently four dedicated 'Peter Rabbit and Friends' shops selling related merchandise, at Bowness, Grasmere, Hawkshead and Keswick, and it would seem that – along with Kendal Mint Cake and a Wordsworth tea-towel – a 'Peter Rabbit' branded gift has become a coveted souvenir of these popular tourist centres.

In an analysis of the ways in which British children's literature has been reconfigured within Japanese culture, Catherine Butler suggests that there are times when characters from the source texts 'seem entirely removed from their original context', pointing to modes of advertising which 'utilize a character design or other form of iconic imagery simply on the basis of recognition value, positive associations and the ability to capture a viewer's attention, rather than relevance to the product being sold' (2023: 94–5). By way of example, Butler cites the adoption of 'Peter Rabbit' as the official emblem and logo of the 'financial giant', Mitsubishi UFJ Trust and Banking. Here the function of such a 'high-recognition' children's literature character is 'associative rather than semantic' so that, stripped of the context of Potter's story, Peter's image is 'free floating' (2023: 95). Though the 'Peter Rabbit and Friends' shops sell Potter's books along with branded merchandise, it is fair to say that the latter significantly overwhelms the former, so that in some sense Peter's image seems to function in a 'free floating' way here too, conveying vaguely 'positive associations' (in this case, partly relating to the **Lake District** itself), rather than a direct connection to the imaginative framework of the books.

Whilst the commodification of Peter (and his friends) outside any sort of narrative frame is one form of reproduction and multiplication, his story (or a version of that story) is also told via other mediums. Lear suggests that Potter clearly 'enjoyed thinking about how children might respond to the story or the character in another medium and was artistically challenged by the adaptive process' (2007: 174). However, it was Potter's insistence on the 'quality of the original art' being maintained (Lear 2007: 174) which led to an early rejection of the idea of screen adaptation. In 1936 Potter famously received a letter from 'Walt Disney asking for permission to make a film of *Peter Rabbit*' as part of their Academy Award winning *Silly Symphonies* series of short musical films, but Potter felt that enlarging her drawings for the screen would show up their 'imperfections' (Taylor 1986: 184). It is clear from her private reflections that Potter gave thought to the idea, but had concerns about the overall quality and effect. She wrote that 'they propose to use cartoons', adding that it seems 'a succession of figures can be joggled together to give an impression of motion', but commented that the pictures would not be satisfactory 'without the landscape backgrounds' and doubted that these would work 'on a larger scale and without colour' (A: 72). In this respect Potter was perhaps doing Disney a disservice since, though the early *Silly Symphonies* films were black and white, by the time he approached her about the project, they were being produced in technicolour.

By the 1960s and 1970s, there was a renewed interest in reproducing Potter's work in other formats. Between 1959 and 1963, HMV produced around thirty records under its Junior Record Club label, including audio dramatizations of several Potter stories. Produced on distinctive red vinyl records, the adaptations feature a full cast and accompanying music, with British-born actress, Vivien Leigh – best known for her role as Scarlett O'Hara in MGM's epic 1939 film, *Gone with the Wind* – taking on the role of narrator. Whilst these are quite high-quality productions, the separation of words from image is problematic in relation to books in which the combination of the two is so vital. A much more successful adaptation from this period is the 1971 film of the ballet production, the *Tales of Beatrix Potter*, in which several of Potter's stories are woven together and told through **dance** and song. It is notable that during discussions about the proposed Disney film, Potter commented that a film with child actors in 'masks' would work better than a cartoon reproduction (*A*: 72), and the 1971 adaptation, which features **dancers** wearing **animal** masks, is still perceived as one of the most successful translations of Potter's work onto stage and screen (Hahn 2015: 568).

Given the ongoing cultural interest in Potter's work, it was though inevitable that further screen adaptations would be produced. One of the most effective and popular of these is undoubtedly the animated television series, *The World of Peter Rabbit and Friends*, which was first aired in Britain on the BBC between 1992 and 1998. There are many reasons for the success of this series, but an important factor is no doubt its attention to what Mackey refers to as 'fidelity to the spirit, if not the letter, of the original' (2002: 181). Peter is given words which do not appear in the book but he uses historically appropriate language, with phrases such as 'Mama will never find out', and these are delivered in a child-like voice, and in ways which remain true to the essential character of Peter as depicted in the books. Perhaps most importantly though, each animated episode is prefaced by a short introductory film with the actress, Niamh Cusack (who also narrates the stories), playing **Beatrix** Potter. In the first episode, we see Cusack as Potter painting outside in a Lakeland landscape and then returning to Hill Top after a shower of rain. Back at the house, 'Potter' talks to her pet rabbit Peter as she sits down to write her story about 'Peter Rabbit' to little Noel, who is poorly again. As Cusack begins to read and write the first words of the letter, we shift into the animated retelling of Peter's story, so that the production is threaded through with a sense of authorial authenticity.

Standing in stark contrast to this popular late-twentieth-century adaptation of Potter's work is *Peter Rabbit* (2018), an adventure-comedy film released by Sony Pictures, and its 2021 sequel: *Peter Rabbit 2: The Runaway*, both directed by Will Gluck. The films use 3D live-action and CGI animation techniques, and also boast an impressive cast of actors providing voice overs, including the English actor and comedian, James Corden, as Peter, Margot Robbie as Flopsy, and Sam Neill as both Mr. McGregor and Tommy Brock. However, the replacement of Peter's distinctive blue jacket with a short blue denim jacket is just one clue as to the radical act of reimagining which has taken place here, in which the disobedient but timid rabbit of Potter's books is reconstructed as a sort of cocky, rascally, gang-leader. Indeed, these films are a clear indication of the extent to which Potter's original imaginative creation has slipped outside not only his original narrative framework but also beyond authorial character construction, to the point where few 'associative' qualities remain, other than the presence of a rabbit wearing a blue jacket and a story featuring a battle over garden produce.

Despite being financially very successful, Gluck's 2018 reimagining of 'Peter Rabbit' received almost universally poor reviews. Criticism congregated around the absence of any 'fidelity' to the 'spirit of the original' (Mackey 2002: 181), and reviewers seem to have felt that Potter's worst fears – of Peter and his friends being 'perverted to vulgarity' (*A*: 195) – had been realized. In a piece for *The New Yorker*, titled 'The puerile emptiness of "Peter Rabbit"', Rebecca Mead observes that the film not only 'dispenses with Potter's illustrations' but also with 'everything that makes Potter's books great', substituting this for what makes contemporary films for children 'mediocre' (2018). In Mead's reading, the 'fable-like simplicity' of Potter's story has been replaced with a 'knowing veneer of contemporaneity', as well as a 'violence and a puerile sense of humour [...] that is at odds with Potter's subtler wit' (2018). A particular focus of this and other reviews is the complete transformation of the character of Peter himself. Mead suggests that he has been remodelled as a 'murderous yob' and Alison Flood contends that Potter would have been 'appalled' by the film's 'bullying rabbit' (2018). In a one-star *Guardian* review, Peter Bradshaw argues that Peter has been turned into 'a sassy, low-grade British Bugs', who is 'cynical and tiresome' (2018). Like Mead and Flood, Bradshaw deplores the way in which Potter's 'great' fictional creation has been 'reinvented' as a 'PG' certificate 'badass comic', forever 'leading the other rabbits in raids on Mr McGregor's vegetable patch' (2018). What these reviews suggest is so fundamentally 'wrong' with the film is this issue of 're-invention', since it ignores both the possibilities and the power of the original character for a young audience. As Mead observes, it is 'safe to assume that, whatever Disney imagined doing with Potter's story, he would not have followed the path chosen by the makers of "Peter Rabbit"' (2018).

Following an initial appearance in the pages of a book, Peter Rabbit, along with a handful of other literary characters (including, notably, Frankenstein's monster and Peter Pan), has become culturally animated in ways which have led to him transcending not only those original textual confines but also almost all of the narrative contexts in which his story first appeared. However, the deeply negative responses to these recent screen adaptations suggest that in the case of Peter Rabbit there are strong cultural associations which resist such radical reimagining. Indeed, a crucial factor which allows Peter's image to be used in a 'free-floating' way on merchandise and in advertising is the culturally embedded idea of him having some (however vague) 'positive' associations, and these are fundamentally called into question, if not abandoned, by the recent films.

The twenty-first century has also though seen other reworkings of 'Peter Rabbit' which respond to current contexts and yet draw on original textual meanings and possibilities. Of particular note in this respect are recent spin-off books which explore the potential of Potter's **animal** characters and their landscapes in teaching ecological awareness. In 2022 alone, three books were published by Puffin (Penguin Random House) under 'The World of Peter Rabbit' trademark, which offer the young reader interactive reading and outdoor activity experiences. In *Tales from the Countryside* we are invited to join Peter as he discovers the changing **seasons**. The blurb indicates that the book is 'full of stories of Peter's adventures through each **season**, as well as activities to help celebrate the natural world'; such activities include planting a herb garden, cloud spotting and making a bird feeder (The World of Peter Rabbit 2022b: 10, 62, 136). Also published that same year was *Peter's Nature Walk: A Sound Book*. Here we find 'Peter Rabbit and his family' learning 'all about nature' and, from 'dawn to dusk, the rabbits discover fascinating facts about the great outdoors, including the different types of insects and **trees** and the importance of pollination and hibernation'; young readers are encouraged to press the sound symbol on each page to 'bring the sounds and wonder of nature to life' (The World of Peter Rabbit 2022a). There is also *The Big Outdoors: Sticker Activity Book*, in which the reader is invited to join Peter as he 'walks through the woods, plants flowers and visits the farmyard, learning all about the natural world as he goes' (The World of Peter Rabbit 2022c). In some ways, these books hark back to more didactic eighteenth-century models of nature writing for children. In *Peter's Nature Walk,* for example, Mrs. Rabbit leads the walk and teaches Peter the names of **trees**, about hibernation, and other important aspects of environmental understanding. However, this older model is combined with more contemporary approaches and new kinds of book-production technology which encourage child engagement through interactive activities, such as pressing buttons to hear a recorded sound, or peeling off stickers to add to a book image.

Both *Tales from the Countryside* and *Peter's Nature Walks* are illustrated by Neil Faulkner, a talented artist and watercolourist in his own right. His illustrations closely copy Potter's own depictions of Peter and her other anthropomorphized characters, but bring into sharper focus those many other natural elements (such as foxgloves, birds, butterflies and bluebells) which often provide more subtle background detail in Potter's original illustrations. This technique suits the educational approach of these books, in which a young reader is encouraged to actively learn about the flora and fauna of the natural world along with Peter. The marketing of these two books is, however, revealing in terms of Potter's legacies since the names of the illustrators and authors in each case do not appear on the book cover, spine or title page. Indeed, this information can only be found on the book's copyright page so that, at first glance, the books appear to be not just 'inspired by' but actually produced by **Beatrix** Potter. In this sense, Faulkner and the authors who provide the written text function almost as ghost writers and artists, an approach which helps to create an illusion of Peter's adventures continuing. Though clearly designed to harness Potter's ongoing global popularity for marketing purposes, this has the effect of extending the imaginative textual space of Potter's original books for contemporary young readers. These publications in one sense become new 'side shows' and, given the focus here on depicting Peter's ongoing adventures in relation to environmental contexts and **seasonal** change, pick up nearly a century later from where Potter left off with *Peter Rabbit's Almanac*.

Q IS FOR QUEERLY

In a **journal** entry for April 1883, a sixteen-year-old Potter observes that everything 'goes queerly, terrible storms in January, floods all winter and early spring, snowstorms March' (*J*: 38). Finely tuned and responsive though Potter was to the natural environment and the pattern of the **seasons** from an early age, an entry in her diary just two days later suggests that her sense of everything going 'queerly' went beyond strangeness in relation to weather patterns:

> I am up one day and down another. Have been a long way down today, and now my head feels empty and I am nothing in particular. Will things never settle? Is this being grown up? If I could have seen my mind as it is now, when I left Dalguise, I should not have known it.
>
> (*J*: 39)

A general sense of being 'unsettled' is not untypical of many young people as they pass through the transitional state between childhood and adulthood, but for a woman in the Victorian period, this transition brought additional anxieties about the self and the future. Emily Brontë depicts the plight of her heroine, Catherine (Cathy) Earnshaw in *Wuthering Heights* (1847), in similar terms. Like Potter, Cathy has a strong affinity with the natural environment and spends much of her childhood immersed in the outside world. As Cathy moves towards adulthood though, she is increasingly expected to curb this behaviour and conform to the expectations of Victorian society. Brontë explores the deeply negative impact of this process on her heroine and expresses some of her frustrations in a scene in which Cathy exclaims: 'I wish I were out of doors! I wish I were a girl again, half savage and hardy, and free [...] Why am I so changed? [...] I'm sure I should be myself were I once among the heather on those hills' (Brontë [1947] 1985: 163). Though Potter never articulates her own feelings in quite such melodramatic terms, a similar sense emerges in her autobiographical writings as to the ways in which gendered expectations increasingly begin to restrict her life.

Q is for Queerly

Once Potter becomes a young woman, we encounter not only glimpses of her frustration, but also evidence of rebellion and resistance to the behaviour which was required of her. One such instance occurs in a **journal** entry from March 1893, when the Potter family were taking an Easter break in Torquay. Now in her late twenties, Potter was expected to spend her holidays engaged in 'lady-like' occupations and accompany her mother and other ladies on 'suburban' carriage drives. She commits her exasperations to paper in her **journal**, writing: 'I was so disgusted' with the drive that I 'privately incited papa' to going to Kent's Hole next morning 'by way of a reviver', adding that they 'slunk out after breakfast' and got away through the bushes (*J*: 315). The language of rebellion and subterfuge indicates that Potter recognizes her behaviour to be transgressive. The outing involved a long fast walk – fast 'for fear of pursuit' – and in visiting the cave system Potter was able to explore some of her scientific interests, as the site was one of 'geological antiquity' (*J*: 315). Neither strenuous physical exercise nor intellectual pursuits were expected of a respectable upper-middle-class young woman and this is certainly not the sort of activity Helen Potter sanctioned for her daughter. However, the anecdote seems to indicate a recognition on Rupert Potter's part that his unusual, intelligent and artistically talented daughter needed (as Charlotte Brontë expresses it in *Jane Eyre*) to 'do more or learn more than custom has pronounced necessary' for her 'sex' (Brontë [1847] 1966: 140). Though biographers and critics have tended to depict Potter suffering under a more general familial oppression, describing her as being frustrated by 'her parents' (Lear 2007: 50) and her 'family' as 'unusually constrictive and controlling' (Kutzer 2003: 2), within the **journal** there is a definite emphasis on Helen Potter as the primary source of difficulty, with Rupert Potter seeming to provide his daughter with many intellectual and practical outlets which offered relief and escape from an otherwise intolerably circumscribed life. Indeed, at one point, when her father goes to stay in Brighton for a period to visit his seriously ill brother, Potter writes: 'Oh faith, faith, what should I do without you?' (*J*: 36).

The adverb 'queerly', as used by Potter in her 1883 entry, is of course derived from 'queer' and in Potter's day this signified something 'strange' or 'odd'. However, since the late twentieth century, 'queer' has come to be applied more specifically to sexual and gendered identities which do not correspond to socially accepted models and traditional heterosexual 'norms'. Though it would be anachronistic to suggest that Potter was using the term in this way herself, nonetheless it seems clear that her sense of strangeness and being unsettled does relate in part to the matter of gender identity. In other words, to anxieties relating to the expectations placed on women in respect to culturally accepted models of female identity which began to radically, and often negatively, impact on Potter's life from her late teenage years onwards.

In that spring of 1883, Potter also writes in her **journal** about what she describes as the 'queer affair' of Lady Florence Dixie (*J*: 37). Potter's use of the term 'queer' here is again intended to mean 'strange' but, in this instance, part of that 'queerness' does overtly relate to gender identity. Dixie (1855–1905) was a Scottish writer, **war** correspondent and feminist. She was also known as a tomboy who rode astride and wore her hair short in a boyish crop, refusing even to conform to the gendered fashion dictates of the day when being presented to Queen Victoria. Potter records in her diary that there had been reports of an attack on Dixie by two men disguised as women who 'struck at her with daggers, cutting her **clothes**' (*J*: 35). The incident causes Potter to reflect on what she has heard of this woman and she adds, in a tone of admiration, that Dixie must be a 'lively and extraordinary person, much more like a man, strong-headed but brave and sound hearted' (*J*: 35). Twice more Potter returns in her diary to this 'queer affair'. In April she records that there had been challenges to Dixie's account of the attack and this leads to a reflection on the way in which women's identities were subject to public scrutiny and castigation (*J*: 37). A few days later, she returns to the story again, this time asserting that she believed Dixie's account of the attack to be 'quite true', adding it was 'highly probable' that she should be attacked in the current political climate (*J*: 38). Whilst noting that Dixie had incurred the hatred of both the Fenians and the Land League, Potter's handling of the 'queer affair' points to an understanding that cultural hostility also related to Dixie's challenging of acceptable gendered behaviour and norms (as suggested by both the strategic and symbolic donning of 'female' apparel on the part of Dixie's attackers).

In the 1880s and 1890s Britain began to see challenges in the public domain to traditional gender expectations for women, with articles on the 'Woman Question' discussing issues relating to women's education, careers and financial independence (Ledger 2007: 154). These debates arose largely in response to the fact that census results had shown there were more women than men in the country, thus fundamentally questioning an ideological model which proclaimed marriage and motherhood as the only acceptable social role for women. Potter, however, had few opportunities to engage in such discussions or personally encounter those women who were beginning to challenge the dictates of the age but, the year after her disappointing holiday to Torquay, such an opportunity arose when Potter was invited to stay with her cousin, Caroline Hutton, in Gloucestershire. At this point Potter was just a few weeks away from her twenty-eighth birthday but had not been 'away independently' for several years (*J*: 319). It was a momentous visit, and Potter wrote a detailed account of her stay with the Huttons in her coded **journal**. From the outset, the encounter with her lively cousin Caroline was something of an eye-opener for Potter and she writes, it 'is well in this world to discover there can exist a young woman, clever, brilliantly attractive and perfectly well principled, although knowing her own mind' (*J*: 320).

Caroline travelled to London to collect her older cousin and the two young women talked animatedly on the train about 'universal subjects' becoming, Potter tells us, 'indiscreet before reaching Swindon' (*J*: 320). On the final stretch of the journey, Caroline jumped down from their carriage at the beginning of a hill, striding vigorously alongside it; Potter lingers over this spectacle of her female cousin walking in this way, apparently oblivious to the dictates imposed on women's physical movement: how she did 'walk up the hill', as 'upright as a bolt, with longish firm steps' and then jumping back in at the top without stopping the carriage (*J*: 320). Potter's admission, that I was not 'sorry to sit still and watch her walk', suggests that she found Caroline, and all that she represented, absolutely fascinating (*J*: 320).

The journey to Caroline's home set the tone for the visit. As well as engaging in intellectual discussions, which ranged about between 'metaphysics' and 'political economy' (*J*: 323), Caroline encouraged Potter's participation in those more active outdoor pursuits which had increasingly been denied to her. One morning they walked together in a steep wooded bank at the back of the house and 'got dirty to our heart's content' (*J*: 324). They hunted for fossils up on the Common together and on another occasion trekked down some fields which were so steep, Caroline had to pull her cousin up with a walking stick (*J*: 325).

During the visit the cousins also discussed issues relating to the 'Woman Question' and, for the first time, Potter reflects openly on these debates in her **journal**, noting that 'Latter day fate ordains that many women shall be unmarried and self-contained' (*J*: 321). One outcome of the debates about women living more independent lives was the emergence of the 'New Woman', a label which was in fact coined in the same year Potter visited Caroline. The 'New Woman' sought independence, equal educational opportunities to men and economic control over their own lives. Not only does the Gloucestershire visit give Potter the opportunity to discuss these wider debates but, in the figure of Caroline, who is 'completely self-possessed', 'fearless' and who espoused a complete rejection of marriage (*J*: 321), she encountered someone who herself seemed to embody the values of the 'New Woman'.

Unsurprisingly perhaps, though Potter found this experience stimulating and exciting, she drew back from Caroline's radical stance, stating in response to her cousin's views that 'I hold an old-fashioned notion that a happy marriage is the crown of a woman's life', adding that it is 'unwise' on the part of a 'nice-looking young lady to proclaim a pronounced dislike of babies' (*J*: 321). Indeed, Potter goes on to compare her cousin to Jane Austen's eponymous heroine, Emma (who also claims she will not marry), and, in so doing, positions herself imaginatively as Emma's own eventual suitor. Potter writes: 'I share the curiosity of Mr. Knightley in wondering what will become of "Emma"' adding that, it seemed 'unlikely' she would escape matrimony (*J*: 321). Ironically though, another aspect of her visit to the Hutton family home appears to have triggered in Potter a strong feeling as to the desirability of the married state, since here she witnessed at first hand a deeply loving and happy marriage on the part of Caroline's parents. This feeds into her reflections on the 'Woman Question' and she adds with painful honesty, 'I cannot help thinking I would sink the whole lump of independence to have anyone so deservedly fond of me' as Mr. Hutton is of his wife (*J*: 321).

Despite Potter's avowal of a happy marriage in these private reflections of the 1890s, her published work in fact presents very few instances of traditional heterosexual relationships. Even in those stories which present an **animal** character 'family', such as *Tom Kitten* and **Peter Rabbit**, the father figure is absent, leaving the mother not only to raise her children alone but also to live a single life, in some cases supporting themselves financially. Mrs. Rabbit is of course a widow, who earns a living by making knitted items and by selling 'herbs, and rosemary tea, and **rabbit-tobacco**' (*BB*: 11). Many of her stories though avoid the depiction of family units altogether and focus instead on single 'adult' **animal** characters who live alone, including Mr. Jeremy Fisher, Mrs. Tittlemouse and Mrs. Tiggy-winkle (despite the use of the married title in the case of the latter two female characters). It is notable that throughout Potter's *Tales* we tend to encounter a predominance of same-sex or mixed-sex adult friendships or friendship groups, rather than nuclear families: we see Ribby inviting her friend Duchess to dinner, Jeremy Fisher dining with an all-male group of friends, Mrs. Tittlemouse socializing with friends and Timmy Willie inviting Johnny Town-mouse to visit. A mixed-sex friendship group also sits at the heart of *The Fairy Caravan*, with its group of **circus animals** who provide a mutual support network for each other.

Whilst most depictions of friendship in Potter's fiction are positive, the instances of married life which we encounter are rarely unproblematic. Perhaps the most romantic of her *Tales* is *Pigling Bland*, but this is of course a courtship story, so that the projected future happiness '**Over the hills and far away**' is left – as it is in most fairy tales and romances – to be imagined beyond the pages of the story. Actual married couples in the *Tales* are not only rare but are also usually problematized in some way. The mouse-couple, Tom Thumb and Hunca Munca in *Two Bad Mice*, for example, hardly reinforce an image of domestic contentment and their behaviour becomes anarchic and **violent** once transferred to the domestic space of the doll's house. Nuclear families are in evidence in the *Flopsy Bunnies* and *Timmy Tiptoes*. However, in the former, Benjamin and Flopsy are 'cheerful' but 'very improvident' (*FB*: 8) and, in the latter, it is male friendship rather than domestic contentment which sits at the heart of the story, since Timmy is nursed back to health by Chippy Hackee and there seems a reluctance on the part of the two male characters to return to their respective domestic spheres. Most troubling of all is Potter's depiction of marriage in *Sister Anne*, in which Bluebeard's wife is shown to be deeply vulnerable and subject to marital abuse and **violence**.

Despite the paucity of positive representations of traditional heterosexual relationships in Potter's published work, her private writings suggest that she continued to crave both the security and potential happiness of married life. Moreover, she often constructs this narrative through the lens of romantic fiction, especially those stories which tell of love finally coming to those whom society has excluded from such happy-ever-after narratives. The year after the death of her fiancé, Norman Warne, Potter visited Bath and, in a letter to his sister, Millie, reads her own life in relation to Austen's fiction. The street names remind her of *Persuasion* (1817), a novel which tells the story of Anne Elliot, a 27-year-old woman, who leads a dull life attending to the whims of her family and who feels herself to be an 'old maid'. In the letter, Potter writes that this had always been her favourite Austen novel and tells Millie she 'read the end part of it again last July', the day after receiving Norman's proposal of marriage, adding, 'I thought my story had come right with patience & waiting like Anne Eliott's [sic] did' (*L*: 139). Just a month after Potter received that proposal, however, her dream of a romantic end to her own 'story' appeared to be over when Norman died suddenly and unexpectedly.

Shortly after her engagement to Norman Warne, Potter had given him a copy of an illustration she had drawn for 'Cinderella', which depicts a pumpkin coach being pulled by a team of rabbits (*Art*: 216). This story appears to have resonated strongly with Potter and when, many years later, she came to write her own version of 'Cinderella' (*c.*1930), her treatment of this fairy tale seems informed both by many years of happy marriage to William Heelis but also the story she had woven in her mind following her engagement to Norman. The tone of the last paragraph is joyous and the writing is steeped in the language of romance. In Potter's retelling, the servant of Perrault's tale is replaced by the Prince himself, so that the fitting of the shoe provides the opportunity for a direct interplay between Cinderella and her Prince:

> Prince Charming began to laugh. He lifted the slipper himself from the purple velvet cushion, and advanced towards Cinderella, bowing low. He took her smutty little hand and handed her to the chair; their laughing eyes met as he knelt before the foot stool [...] The Prince married her within a week – and they lived happily ever after.

(*H*: 374)

What is perhaps most striking about the passage is the emphasis on their shared laughter at defying the social expectations of the society in which they lived. This imagined fictional marriage, like Potter's envisaged marriage to Norman Warne and her actual marriage to William Heelis, offers the 'heroine' an opportunity to escape the constraints which society would otherwise impose upon them.

Nonetheless, and despite Potter's doubts about Caroline's position on the late-Victorian 'Woman Question', of the two cousins, it is ironically Potter who came closest to modelling the 'New Woman' in her own life – educating herself far beyond the normal expectations of her gender, engaging in scientific study, writing and having an academic paper presented to a scientific society, before developing various entrepreneurial projects and finally establishing herself as a successful writer. Between 1902 and 1913 Potter functioned as an unmarried published author and businesswoman in a world in which such an identity continued to be unusual and frowned upon, buying her own property and achieving financial independence. Even after her marriage at the age of forty-seven, she never wholly conformed to a traditional domestic role, using the marriage instead to secure a different kind of freedom, in which she publicly ratified the new identity she had been carving out as countrywoman and landowner. Though Potter would resist the suffrage movement and had deeply ambivalent views on feminism, her 'story', as told through her public and private writings, represents a strikingly successful challenge to Victorian gender expectations and a careful and hard-won model of independent womanhood.

R IS FOR RABBIT-TOBACCO

In *Benjamin Bunny*, we learn that **Peter's** mother 'earned her living by knitting rabbit wool' products as well as by selling 'herbs, and rosemary tea, and rabbit-tobacco (which is what we call lavender)' (*BB*: 11). Both the accompanying image (*BB*: 10) and the book's frontispiece illustration show Mrs. Rabbit along with bunches of lavender and a sign for 'Tea and Tobacco'. Benjamin's father is later depicted in the story 'smoking a pipe of rabbit-tobacco' (*BB*: 46–7) and his habit is returned to in *Mr. Tod*. Here he sits in the sunshine outside the burrow, 'stricken in years', smoking 'a pipe of rabbit-tobacco' and, at the end of the story, he is presented with a 'long new pipe and a fresh supply of rabbit-tobacco' (*T*: 11, 79).

These apparently innocuous instances of humorous and playful anthropomorphism, have, however, been recently implicated in critical readings of Potter's work which point to problematic cultural 'borrowing' and 'appropriation' of 'black cultural forms' by a 'white British author' (Zobel Marshall 2019: 89). Specifically, these arguments relate to Potter's engagement with the *Uncle Remus* stories which were published by Joel Chandler Harris (1848–1908), an American journalist, in the 1880s and 1890s. The stories are based on old folk tales which derive from an African American oral story-telling tradition. They are told in dialect and feature anthropomorphized **animal** characters, including the 'wily anti-hero and cunning trickster' (Whalley and Hobbs 1986: 66), Brer Rabbit, around whose adventures most of the stories are based. In the books published by Harris, the stories are identified with the cotton plantations of the American South and are narrated by 'Uncle Remus', an elderly former slave, usually to the young son of the plantation owner.

As Potter herself acknowledged in a note on one of her manuscripts, the source for the idea of 'rabbit-tobacco' is *Uncle Remus* (Laws 2021: 130), though – in line with more typical British use of tobacco – it is smoked in a pipe by Benjamin rather than chewed. In the first of Harris's books, *Uncle Remus: His Songs and His Sayings* (published in America in 1880 and in Britain in 1881), Uncle Remus tells the little boy that Brer Rabbit 'tuck a

R is for Rabbit-tobacco

big chaw terbarker' and clarifies that this is 'Rabbit terbarker', what 'Miss Sally puts 'mong de cloze in de trunk' (Harris 1881: 66). Along with 'rabbit-tobacco', the reader can trace other specific localized influences on Potter's work. In another *Uncle Remus* story we learn that Brer Rabbit married 'Miss Molly Cottontail' (Harris 1881: 131), a name Potter would subsequently adopt for one of **Peter's** sisters and which derives from the visual similarity between a rabbit's bobtail and the fluffy white cotton-balls harvested on the plantations. Potter's description of **Peter** 'going lippity – lippety' (*PR*: 48) also echoes a description of Brer Rabbit coming down the road 'lippity-clippity, clippity-lippity' (Harris 1881: 24). Potter's love of unfamiliar words and linguistic word-play is well known and can be traced in her writing in a variety of ways, for example in the incorporation of Cumbrian dialect words or phrases from nursery rhymes and riddles, as well as in the literary or vernacular sources for some of her characters' names (including **Xarifa** and Mr. Tod), and in the sudden appearance of an archaic or difficult word for her young readers, such as 'soporific' (*FB*: 7). The specific borrowings from *Uncle Remus* mentioned above suggest that it was in part the unfamiliar language and imagery in the stories which Potter found particularly appealing.

Copies of both *Songs and Sayings* and the second collection, *Nights with Uncle Remus* (first published in 1883), were owned by Potter's father and in an 1884 **journal** entry she writes that a family friend used to read the stories aloud 'till the tears ran down with laughing' (*J*: 107). Potter adds though that he read the dialect 'very badly' (*J*: 107), a comment which suggests that she was herself interested in trying to hear the sound of the words as they would have been spoken. Along with these localized borrowings of words and phrases, Potter also acknowledged a direct link between an *Uncle Remus* story and *Mr. Tod*. In a letter to Harold Warne she comments that the 'principal defect' of the latter is 'imitation of "Uncle Remus"', but writes that it is 'no draw-back for children, because they cannot read the negro dialect' (*L*: 189), an observation which again indicates that her own pleasure in these stories – which were not published until she was older and could engage with the dialect speech – derived from the language in which they were written. The influence of *Uncle Remus* was not only acknowledged privately by Potter herself but is no revelation in the world of Potter scholarship. Indeed, the importance of Harris's books in terms of Potter's own development as a writer has been discussed since serious academic analysis of Potter's work began to appear in the 1980s (MacDonald 1986; Whalley and Hobbs 1987).

We can, moreover, clearly situate the *Uncle Remus* books – along with a wider repertoire of sources – in relation to a crucial earlier stage in Potter's own creative development, in which she began to produce illustrations for some of those stories and books which she found imaginatively engaging. In the 1890s, she drew scenes from many texts including 'Little Red Riding Hood', 'Sleeping Beauty', 'Cinderella', 'Puss in Boots', *Alice in Wonderland*, *The Arabian Nights*, 'The Owl and the Pussy Cat' and Aesop's Fables, as well as *Songs and Sayings* and *Nights with Uncle Remus*, both of which had been published initially with illustrations by Frederick Church and James Moser. Usually, Potter chose to depict scenes which had not been illustrated in the original texts so that she could give her own imaginative response free rein and, in so doing, we also see her beginning to transform the original material.

We see this in her illustration for 'Brother Rabbit rescues Brother Terrapin' (*Nights with Uncle Remus*), the story which is the main influence on *Mr. Tod*. Here Potter adds numerous details not present in the published story, which emphasize the predatory and dangerous character of Brer Fox as well as his **violent** intentions towards the terrapin (see Figure 8). Potter's depiction of a *mis-en-scène*, which includes meat cleavers, a shotgun, a skull, feathers and the wing of a bird, adds a Gothic touch and a mood of fear that is not present in the original tale. Indeed, the latter focuses on Brer

Figure 8 Illustration for 'Brother Rabbit rescues Brother Terrapin' by Beatrix Potter (1895).

Rabbit's laughter at finding his friend Brer Terrapin caught in a sack and his subsequent revenge on Brer Fox.

What is also notable about Potter's depictions of Brer Rabbit in the 1890s is the fact that her rabbit drawings are much more anatomically correct than those produced by Church and Moser, whose central character resembles a hare more than a rabbit. Her handling of other **animal** characters in the stories, including a fox, wolf and a ram, is also far more realistic. Thus, even when illustrating the *Uncle Remus* stories themselves, Potter begins to transform the material via an attention to realism which does not exist in the original and which would come to be a vital aspect of her own subsequent **animal** character creations. Potter's first *Uncle Remus* drawing was in fact produced in the same year in which she sent her **Peter Rabbit** story in a picture letter to Noel Moore, and though her ink sketches of rabbits in the letter look very different to the Church and Moser illustrations of Brer Rabbit, they do resemble the sketches of rabbits which frame the central picture in her own first *Uncle Remus* illustration (*Art*: 232). In a sense then, one of the things Potter learned from the Harris books was what she wanted to do differently; much as she loved the reading experience of these stories, when she began to develop her own anthropomorphized rabbit character she did so in significantly new ways.

In 1996 a more sustained critical reading of Potter's engagement with *Uncle Remus* was put forward by John Goldthwaite, alongside his wider claim that the Harris stories played a more significant role in the development of the next generation of 'Golden Age' children's literature than has been acknowledged. Goldthwaite argues that the publication of the first *Uncle Remus* book constitutes the 'central event in the making of modern's children's story' and suggests that at this point no 'leap into such an advanced state of anthropomorphism' existed in print (1996: 251). Goldthwaite's subsequent reading of the influence of *Uncle Remus* on Potter is detailed but at times intriguingly contradictory. He critiques Potter for not overtly acknowledging the influence of this source in print but also points out that these stories were 'so famous as to make the usual kinds of acknowledgement by the next generation of storytellers superfluous' (1996: 256). Moreover, on the one hand, Goldthwaite criticizes Potter for what he sees as an attempt to cover her tracks regarding borrowings from *Uncle Remus*, but also argues that she deliberately left behind a 'trail' of clues which refer back to the Harris texts (1996: 315–16).

Nonetheless, Goldthwaite's reading introduced perspectives on Potter's work which have gone on to influence more recent critical responses, including one which generated widespread media discussion. *American*

Trickster: Trauma, Tradition and Brer Rabbit (2019) by Emily Zobel Marshall contains a short section on Potter's work, but this material reached a wider public after the author subsequently published an article based on the claims made in her book in *The Conversation* in 2023. It was titled 'Beatrix Potter's famous tales are rooted in stories told by enslaved Africans – but she was very quiet about their origins' and it is no doubt both this deliberately provocative title, as well as Potter's significant cultural status, which resulted in immediate and widespread media coverage, including articles in *The Guardian* and *Daily Mail*.

Zobel Marshall reiterates many of Goldthwaite's claims and goes on to argue that 'by shielding the reading public from her sources, Potter's actions feed into a damaging and recurring type of cultural appropriation of black cultural forms', so that through 'Potter's silence the hierarchy of racial power stays intact' (2019: 89). This reading of Potter's work relates to the development of postcolonial theory and practice, spearheaded by the work of foundational scholars such as Edward Said who, in *Culture and Imperialism* (1993), explored the effects of colonialism on cultures and societies. A central focus of postcolonial scholarship is to examine and understand the role played by cultural products such as literary texts in promoting or ratifying aspects of an imperial mindset. Such readings respond to what Said describes as the 'massive intellectual, moral, and imaginative overhaul and deconstruction of Western representation of the non-Western world' (Said 1993: xxi). In this context, incorporation of elements of a story directly shaped by Western colonial activity in work by a white British author could potentially be seen as implicated in an imperial agenda, unless the handling of this material is overtly used to condemn or critique that agenda.

Whilst a postcolonial reading might see the presence of any material which derives from African American sources in Potter's writing as evidence that her work is entangled in the wider cultural context of nineteenth-century colonial activity, comments about Potter's own lack of public references to this source are something of a red herring, since Potter did acknowledge her 'borrowings' from Remus privately and she did not 'publicly' reference her many and varied sources, with the unique exception of a dedication 'To Aesop in the shadows' in *Johnny Town-Mouse*. The critique of Potter in *American Trickster* is, however, predicated on an assumption of much more extensive acts of borrowing and influence in relation to *Uncle Remus*. Underpinning the argument about Potter's damaging acts of 'cultural appropriation' is the claim that Potter's most famous rabbit character is himself closely modelled on the trickster figure of Brer Rabbit. Zobel

Marshall describes **Peter Rabbit** himself as a 'trickster figure' and adds, 'We can safely conclude that, through her stories, Potter brought a subversive African trickster back to life in the heart of the Lake District' (2019: 7, 87). Such a claim is though problematized by a study of the traits which define Potter's most famous **animal** character creation. Unlike Brer Rabbit, who is self-assured, cunning and wily, **Peter** is depicted as naughty but also extremely vulnerable and easily frightened. He often appears in a state of extreme distress and his childhood escapes, along with his rescue of other creatures as an adult, are always the result of luck or the helpful intervention of other creatures, rather than trickery. He is terrified in Mr. McGregor's garden, and at the end of the *Tale* we see him recovering from his ordeal in bed, not gloating and triumphant. **Peter** does not therefore seem to conform to, or even resemble, the 'trickster' figure, which is defined by Zobel Marshall herself as an 'amoral […] destructive, violent' character who will do 'anything to ensure their survival' (2019: 1).

Not only does a comparison between the brash rabbit 'trickster' of the *Uncle Remus* stories and **Peter** question claims regarding Harris's influence on Potter, it also draws attention to the extent to which Potter developed a new and imaginatively different kind of anthropomorphized **animal** character, who is not in any fundamental sense 'borrowed'. Potter's interest in naturalism and realism, which we see coming through even in her own illustrations for *Uncle Remus*, plays a significant part in the development of her own central rabbit character, who never really loses his rabbit-like personality. As Ruth MacDonald argues, in Potter's work **animals** are never so 'relentlessly human' that they lose their **animal** traits, and rabbits, far from being trickster figures, ultimately retain their 'timid, thoughtless rabbit natures' (1986: 47).

Potter herself acknowledged that it was her story of *Mr. Tod* which owed the greatest debt to Harris. The specific source of influence is a story in which Brer Fox snatches Brer Terrapin and places him in a sack with a view to **eating** him. Goldthwaite points out that the *Uncle Remus* story features a 'kidnapping, a rescue, and a brawl, which at its most primitive level is the story of *Mr. Tod* as well' (1996: 306) and this is true, but it really is only at this most 'primitive level' that we can trace the influence of Harris, since Potter transforms the story in ways which fundamentally affect its meaning and the reading experience. As Joyce Irene Whalley and Anne Stevenson Hobbs point out, 'the rabbits here do not win by outsmarting either fox or badger', and in fact it is 'only a stroke of luck that distracts both predators' and 'permits the rescue of the rabbit babies' (1987: 47). Though the 'battle' scene as described by Potter contains echoes of Harris, the power relations involved are very different. In *Uncle Remus* the chaos is caused by Brer Rabbit's trickery; the latter had placed a hornet's nest in the sack in which Brer Terrapin had been trapped and Brer Fox knocks the tables over and breaks the crockery in trying to escape the hornets who are attacking him. In *Mr. Tod*, however, the two predatory creatures, Fox and Badger, do battle together and the scene of carnage which follows has nothing whatsoever to do with **Peter** or Benjamin's interventions. In Potter's world the weaker or more vulnerable cannot thwart the stronger by trickery, but sometimes the **violent** natures of more powerful creatures are turned against each other.

What we discover then, even in a story which Potter herself claimed was directly influenced by *Uncle Remus*, are the limits of that influence. Here, not only is the rabbit-as-trickster element completely absent, but Potter's handling of a story about kidnapping and threatened murder produces a fundamentally different tone and mood. Though Brer Rabbit finds the discovery of Brer Terrapin tied up in a bag extremely funny, in *Mr. Tod* the two parent rabbits are terrified both for themselves and for the fate of the baby bunnies who have been stolen by Tommy Brock. In fact, the mood of *Mr. Tod* seems to be more significantly informed by Potter's own imaginative reworking of the *Uncle Remus* story in her 1895 illustration, than by the original story itself. In *Mr. Tod*, Potter writes that in the fox's home there 'are many unpleasant things lying about, that had much better have been buried; rabbit bones and skulls, and chickens' legs and other horrors', adding it 'was a very shocking place' (*T*: 34), and whilst none of these elements appear in Harris's story, they do feature in Potter's earlier imaginative engagement with that story in her drawing (see Figure 8).

Potter's earlier *Tale*, the *Flopsy Bunnies*, also contains echoes of 'Brother Rabbit rescues Brother Terrapin', since it too features **animal** characters being stolen and placed in a sack, this time by Mr. McGregor. A rare moment of trickery does occur in this story when Benjamin and Flopsy rescue their baby rabbits from the sack and fill it with rotten vegetables and other items from the rubbish heap (*FB*: 36). This idea seems to be derived from Brer Rabbit's actions but in his case a form of real vengeance is meted out, as the hornets physically attack Brer Fox. The power dynamic remains very different in Potter's world and, having played this trick on the McGregors, the rabbits flee the scene of their wrath, but not before the youngest bunny is 'rather hurt' by being hit by a rotten marrow that has been thrown in anger by Mr. McGregor (*FB*: 52–3). Goldthwaite himself acknowledges that *Mr. Tod* and the *Flopsy Bunnies* are not an imitation of *Uncle Remus* 'but a new order of story altogether' (1996: 308) and crucially, in Potter's **animal** stories, the anthropomorphism is always predicated on a more realistic attention to actual **animal** behaviour and inter-species relations.

As the Beatrix Potter Society pointed out in their own public response to the 2023 media coverage about Potter's indebtedness to *Uncle Remus*, the influence of Harris's work has never been a secret and has been widely acknowledged in discussions of Potter's work (Parker 2023). Nonetheless, it is important to revisit texts in the light of cultural shifts and changing perspectives. One important aspect of postcolonial scholarship has been to consider the processes by which other nations are characterized as 'other' and as negatively different to a Western 'norm', and it is notable that there is little evidence of this at work in Potter's books. Moreover, though Harris's original stories have been seen to reinforce 'problematic racial stereotypes' via the 'trickster figure' of Brer Rabbit and the trope of the 'sycophantic and contented slave' (Zobel Marshall 2019: 5), both figures are absent from Potter's work and her own acts of 'borrowing' do not extend to the replication of these characters. Claims that Potter's work ensures that the 'racist stereotypes perpetuated by Harris's collections were further disseminated round the globe' (Zobel Marshall 2019: 7) would only be justified if she did indeed include (rather than reject) those stereotypes in her stories. Indeed, there is some evidence that Potter was critical of attempts by British white writers to speak for the colonial 'other', since she described an early and popular instance of this – *The Little Black Sambo* (1899) by Scottish writer, Helen Bannerman – as a 'horrid little book' (*L*: 454). Moreover, Potter's own private references to the *Uncle Remus* books suggest a delight in the language and storytelling of the African American culture from which the stories derive, and point to a willingness on her part to imaginatively 'engage with other societies, traditions and histories' (Said 1993: xxii).

The *Uncle Remus* stories were widely and extensively influential in both England and America, and it is difficult now to realize the extent of their popularity in the late nineteenth and early twentieth centuries. Mark Twain called them the 'oracle of the nation's nurseries' (1883: 422) and in 1895, Rudyard Kipling wrote to Harris to say that the tales 'ran like wild fire through an English Public school', adding that we 'found ourselves quoting whole pages of Uncle Remus' (Green 1965: 166). As Whalley and Hobbs have argued, the 'impact of these tales on the modern **animal** fantasy tradition and writers such as Potter, Rudyard Kipling, Kenneth Grahame, and A. A. Milne cannot be overestimated'; indeed, they claim that talking-animal books 'took their place in children's literature' as a result of the *Uncle*

Remus stories (1986: 67). Given the extent of this influence, it is indeed vital to reflect on the precise ways in which these stories influenced British children's literature in the next generation. Nonetheless, there is something rather problematic about the recent critical handling of **Beatrix** Potter in this respect, not least the way in which discussion of her writing rapidly shifts into a critique of the woman writer herself. Zobel Marshall, apparently influenced by Goldthwaite, writes that 'Potter is indeed a poaching trickster' (2019: 89) and Goldthwaite takes this several steps further, referring to Potter as 'naughty' and as 'Sis Beatrix the trickster', before imagining her (in a passage rather reminiscent of the CGI techniques used in the film, *Miss Potter*) winking at a fictional rabbit – in this case not **Peter**, but Brer Rabbit (1996: 316–17). In both cases, there is a troubling shift from textual evidence to speculative biographical commentary, in which Potter becomes implicated in a problematic cultural appropriation of the 'trickster' character by somehow embodying that figure herself.

None of the other writers discussed by these two critics in relation to the *Uncle Remus* tradition, many of whom do overtly perpetuate racist stereotypes, are subject to the sort of criticism levelled at Potter, and it is perhaps revealing that at the end of the article published in *The Conversation*, Zobel Marshall goes on to point out that the 'Beatrix Potter and Peter Rabbit brands are highly lucrative' and Potter is a 'national treasure' (2023). It would appear then that claims about Potter's 'appropriation of black cultural forms' are being read in relation to, and are perhaps shaped by, the extent of her success. It is almost as if Potter is more significantly implicated in the widespread cultural influence of *Uncle Remus*, not because of the extent of that influence on her own work, but as a result of her status as a children's author in global contexts. In other words, she is more culpable than others because of the significant and ongoing impact of her work. Given the subsequent global popularity of Potter's *Tales*, we should though perhaps pose other questions here: about the ways in which her books encourage a permeability of language and culture across geographical and temporal contexts in ways which do not perpetuate problematic stereotypes or reinforce historic cultural divisions. In a sense, the very significant and unusual global success of her stories works against narratives of otherness and difference, and her 'borrowings' from diverse sources point to Potter's own instinctive resistance to cultural boundaries, as well as a recognition on her part that unfamiliar linguistic and cultural references can become important points of connection for young readers from very different backgrounds and contexts.

S IS FOR SEASONS

From her earliest private writings to her last letters, Potter recorded and described seasonal changes via observations of flowers, **trees**, crops, weather patterns and other natural phenomena. In one of the earliest spring entries in her **journal**, from April 1882, she notes that the leaves are almost all out and the chestnuts are 'beginning to flower' (*J*: 15), and in a letter written during her last January, she observes that a 'few snowdrops are peeping through the wet dark earth, showing white buds' (*A*: 194). Just as Potter depicts the repetition of cyclical seasonal patterns as reassuring, so she often relates seasonal disturbances to a wider sense that everything is going '**queerly**' (*J*: 38). In some instances, this relates to a deeply personal sense of unrest and, at other times, to wider factors, such as a Europe under imminent threat of **war**. Sitting between reflections on this latter threat and a description of her various **illnesses** is an observation that the seasons have also been 'all wrong', with March 'warm and lovely' and the bluebells coming out early, then rain all summer (*A*: 88).

Potter's close attention to the way the natural world changes day-by-day and month-by-month is no doubt in part influenced by the sort of reading she would have been exposed to as a very young child. By the late eighteenth century a number of influential nursery books had been published for children. Though rather didactic in tone, these texts were also notable for focusing a child's attention on the natural world around them. Much criticized by Romantic poets, William Wordsworth and Samuel Taylor Coleridge, books by female authors such as Sarah Trimmer and Anna Barbauld often engaged children with the natural world via lessons as to what to look out for during the changing seasons. Whilst Potter later recalled having 'hated' Trimmer's *The History of the Robins* (*A*: 208), there is no clear evidence as to her response to Barbauld's work. However, as Linda Lear points out, she could 'hardly have avoided Anna Barbauld', who was not only an extremely influential children's author, but also a prominent Unitarian figure, and Potter's grandparents on both sides were linked by their Unitarianism and affiliation with Non-Conformist circles (Lear 2007: 34, 14). Indeed, Barbauld has been identified as a likely source of influence on various aspects of Potter's work, including the small-sized books which would be suitable for a child's hands (Lear 2007: 34; Page and Smith 2021: 45), and in relation to her development of the talking-animals genre (Cosslett 2006: 152–3).

Barbauld is also though a crucial figure in the development of a body of nature-writing for children, which stretches from the late eighteenth century to the present, and includes work by Potter, as well as that of other well-known women writers, such as Enid Blyton (1897–1968). The latter not only regularly wove natural history references into her popular series-fiction stories, but also published texts such as her *Round the Year* books for spring, summer, autumn and winter (1934) and *Enid Blyton's Nature Lover's Book* (1944), in which a group of children engage in seasonal 'nature walks'. Potter herself is, however, a particularly important figure in the early-twentieth-century development of this sort of environmentally aware writing for children since, though her young readers encounter similar details about the natural world to those who read Barbauld, in Potter's work such learning has been stripped of both the didactic tone and Christian message of the earlier texts. Via Potter's books, a young reader not only develops an understanding of the natural world without the intervention of a teacherly figure, but also encounters environmental information framed in secular rather than religious terms.

All of Potter's *Tales* are set at specific and easily recognizable seasonal moments, with temporal settings established through accurately rendered natural landscapes. The abundance of foxgloves in *Jemima Puddle-Duck* suggests that the action of the story occurs in late spring, whereas the garden abundant with cabbage roses and pansies in *Tom Kitten* indicates high summer. **Peter Rabbit** clearly has a late summer setting, since Flopsy, Mopsy and Cotton-tail are collecting blackberries from the hedges. Both *Timmy Tiptoes* and *Squirrel Nutkin* are early autumnal tales, with nuts being harvested by the squirrels. There are many other subtle seasonal clues, such as the depiction of the **trees** in *Squirrel Nutkin*, which show a hint of **yellow** and brown here and there amidst the green, as well as the presence of scarlet rose-hips, and **fungi** growing next to a tree stump (*SN*: 34, 26). *The Tailor of Gloucester* is of course a winter tale, as signalled by the snow which covers the streets and gets into Simpkin's collar when he goes out shopping, but also via fireside scenes and references to seasonal **illnesses** (to which Potter herself was very susceptible). Even a very young child is thus able to gain

S is for Seasons

awareness of natural seasonal processes via Potter's detailed attention to the precise temporal contexts in which each story takes place.

As well as engaging with such details within the *Tales*, Potter also published a book in which the seasonal pattern of a calendar year is depicted chronologically through the lives of her **animal** characters. *Peter Rabbit's Almanac for 1929* moves Potter's characters outside the frame of their original stories so that we see their lives continuing in an extended fictional space. Single images are used to tell the story of the changing seasons, from the snowdrops and cold winds of March to the gathering of daffodils in April, the hay-gathering in August and the collecting of firewood in the snow in December. The accompanying month-by-month calendar for 1929 lists the dates in relation to the pattern of the church calendar, with the Sundays in March listed as the third, fourth and fifth Sundays in Lent, then fourth and fifth leading to Palm Sunday, Good Friday and Easter Saturday. However, the accompanying images make no allusion to these liturgical markers and instead focus on seasonal changes as represented by botanical, agricultural and meteorological signifiers. The images do also point to cultural markers, but these are secular rather than religious, relating to those older rural agricultural festivals which are informed by environmental cycles, such as a summer **dance** to celebrate the gathering of the harvest.

A similar handling of the seasons occurs in a poem which Potter wrote for her story, *Wag-by-Wall*, but which was not included in the final posthumous publication. The poem opens 'Spring comes to the uplands' and moves from spring through summer, autumn and winter (*H*: 329). Again, the seasons are understood here by changes in flora (the 'unfolding' of leaves) and fauna (the calling of the cuckoo and the return of the swallows) but also in the way in which these changes shape human life, with the onset of autumn marked with 'fiddles and **dancing**' and the 'kern supper', an ancient celebration to mark the end of reaping. The poem thus reminds us how, since ancient times, human lives have been bound up with the pattern of the seasons (*H*: 329).

The Fairy Caravan was published in the same year as *Peter Rabbit's Almanac* and though it has tended to be neglected by Potter scholars, this is an important text in relation to any ecocritical reading of Potter's work, since here the natural environment emerges as a vital living presence. In the book's 'Preface', Potter wrote that through 'many changing seasons these tales have walked and talked with me' (*FC*: xi) and there is a sense in which the passing of time which accompanied the gathering of the stories is woven into both the language and the structure of the book. Regular references to seasonal changes and the cyclical patterns of nature provide the book's most dominant narrative thread, with the journey made by the **circus animals** being both geographical and seasonal. As in her 'Spring comes to the uplands' poem, the natural world is closely associated with an older pagan understanding of the seasons but also here with ancient magical folklore.

The natural changes associated with the seasons are recorded in considerable detail in *The Fairy Caravan* and in ways which recall Barbauld's deeply influential, *Hymns in Prose for Children* (1781). Though Barbauld deploys a devotional framework and uses direct address to a child, *Hymns* nonetheless promotes an active and close engagement with the natural world. The child's lessons are learned outside, through detailed observation of nature:

> Come, let us go forth into the fields, let us see how the flowers spring, let us listen to the warbling of the birds, and sport ourselves upon the new grass. The winter is over and gone, the buds come out upon the trees [...] and the green leaves sprout. The hedges are bordered with tufts of primroses, and yellow cowslips, that hang down their heads; and the blue violet lies hid beneath the shade.
>
> (Barbauld [1781] 1864: 5–6)

Not only does *Hymns* promote an understanding of the natural environment through observation of seasonal changes, it also subtly anthropomorphizes plants as well as **animals**, in a way that helps a young reader encounter them as sentient lifeforms. These are also techniques deployed extensively by Potter in many similar passages of 'nature-writing' which appear in *The Fairy Caravan*:

> Spring advanced. The caravan wandered along green ways. Primroses were peeping out at the edge of the coppice; the oaks showed a tinge of gold; the wild cherry **trees** were snow-white with blossom. Beech **trees** and sycamores were bursting into leaf; only the ash **trees** remained bare as midwinter. The ash is the last to don her green gown, and the first to lose her **yellow** leaves; a short-lived summer lady.
>
> (*FC*: 60)

The similarity between the approach taken in the two extracts is interesting, not least because it points to a legacy of female-authored British children's ecological writing which has tended to be neglected in favour of a

Wordsworthian line of influence. Potter and Barbauld's work is also vital, though, in its shared commitment to engaging young readers with the beauty and processes of the natural world from an early stage.

As in the passage above, Potter regularly uses both **trees** and flowers to depict seasonal changes. The former have a particularly important function in this respect since, unlike most flowers which come and go, **trees** remain as a constant presence within our landscapes, and our main native deciduous species go through radical visual changes as leaves bud, then open, change colour and fall, leaving the branches bare. **Trees** thus connect us to and inform us about the shifting patterns of the year; as Roger Deakin suggests, they are 'our barometers of the weather and the changing seasons' (2007: xi). In *The Fairy Caravan* Potter describes individual **trees** as having a **fairy** that lives at their heart and via this trope the story conveys the idea of natural processes such as seasonal changes, as imbued with a kind of ancient magic, with each 'guardian **fairy**' getting 'a new green gown' (*FC*: 256) every spring.

Environmental understanding is developed in the passage through this **fairy** trope as Potter explores how changing seasons affect the way each **tree fairy** behaves. All leave their homes to **dance** together on moonlit nights but in autumn the **fairies** withdraw to the heart of their **tree** and sleep till spring (*FC*: 257). The only exceptions are the pine and fir **fairies** who keep awake and **dance** in the snow because their **trees** do not lose their 'needle-like evergreen leaves' (*FC*: 257). Even more precise seasonal details are provided in the story, since the oak **fairy dances** with the pine **fairies** beneath the 'hunter's moon' because the oak keeps its leaves till much later; the last of the 'russet oak leaves' are only borne off by a 'November gale', at which point the oak **fairy** settles herself to sleep (*FC*: 257).

Through Potter's handling of seasons, a young reader therefore develops an understanding of the cyclical patterns of nature and some of the natural processes which affect life on earth. The importance of this sort of education (or rather its absence) was drawn attention to in recent years by the controversial revisions to the *Oxford Junior Dictionary* which removed nature words and seasonal markers such as 'acorn', 'bluebell' and 'conker' on the grounds that they were no longer in such regular use as to merit inclusion. Robert Macfarlane and Jackie Morris's *The Lost Words: A Spell Book* (2017) was a direct response to this cultural shift and an attempt to ensure that contemporary young readers had opportunities to encounter these words in a lyrical and visually appealing way within the pages of a book. Indeed, the Preface suggests that the 'words were becoming lost' partly because they were 'no longer alive' in children's 'stories' (Macfarlane 2017).

In terms of keeping these words 'alive' in this way, it is notable that within Potter's books for children a vocabulary of the natural world is regularly embedded within the warp and weft of the stories. Young readers learn that acorns can be collected in the autumn, that they provide sustenance for small **animals**, and grow into mighty oak **trees**. Indeed, in *The Fairy Caravan*, time is measured both seasonally and arboreally, and one story is introduced with the line: 'Long, long ago, long before the acorn ripened, that has grown into yonder oak' (*FC*: 106). In this same book, a young reader does not merely encounter bluebells (another 'lost word') coming out in spring, but reads about these flowers in evocative, alliterative and poetical prose: 'How blue the bluebells were! a sea of soft pale blue; **tree** behind **tree**; and beneath the **trees**, wave upon wave, a blue sea of bluebells' (*FC*: 160). Potter's work is therefore an important resource for young readers in the twenty-first century and in a context in which the language and understanding of the natural environment is being lost or at least diminished. As we move farther and farther away from the pre-industrialized world depicted in Potter's books, in which humans were in closer contact with seasonal patterns, a body of literature which reconnects us to the language and experience of the seasons is vital. It seems that Potter herself understood the value of her books in this respect, since in 1928 she reflected, 'If I have done anything – even a little – to help small children on the road to enjoy honest simple pleasures [...] I have done a bit of good' (*A*: 14).

In a **journal** entry from 1894 Potter described Autumn as 'the pleasantest season of the year' (*J*: 363). Such a declared preference was probably inspired by the mycological interests which had begun to dominate Potter's life at this point and the ready availability of **fungi** in the autumn, but it is also connected to her strongly chromatic engagement with the world, since she writes of the beautiful 'autumn colours' which are 'bright in the woods' (*J*: 363). Nonetheless, across Potter's body of writing as a whole, it is to the beauty of spring that she turns again and again. As a child, but even more so as an adult, she found consolation and hope in the return of spring, and this is a motif Potter would come back to repeatedly in the latter years of her life, beset as they were by **illness** and **war**. Many of her late letters make references to the precise and beautiful details of an English spring, both documenting them for her various American correspondents but also perhaps reminding herself of the significance of this annual resurrection. In May 1940, she writes of the bluebells, the hawthorn blossom – 'like snow on the green hedges' – and the cuckoo calling, adding that this is a 'world of beauty that will survive, whatever happens to us' (*A*: 105), and in one of her last letters she refers to the return of spring, adding 'how the sad world longs for it!' (*A*: 202). Spring in this context is not simply the literal arrival of the year's seasonal renewal but also a metaphor for better times, a world rejuvenated and brought back to life, after so many dark years of **war**. In this context, the annual cycle of seasonal patterns, of life emerging from death and renewal after destruction, took on wider symbolic meaning, and the impulse behind her comment seems to echo that in the famous lines from Percy Bysshe Shelley's 'Ode to the West Wind': if 'Winter comes, can Spring be far behind?' (Shelley 1904: 642).

T IS FOR TREES

On the first page of her first published book, Potter introduces us not only to the family of rabbits whose adventures feature in the story, but also to their home. We discover that **Peter**, his sisters and their mother live 'in a sandbank, underneath the root of a very big fir-tree' (*PR*: 7). An accompanying illustration shows a non-anthropomorphized family of young rabbits peeping out of, or burrowing into, the tree's roots and thus a young reader learns that trees provide habitats for **animals** such as rabbits. Through later developments in the story, this is reinforced in more emotive ways since the fir-tree is depicted as a place of refuge for **Peter**. Having escaped from Mr. McGregor's garden, he 'never stopped running or looked behind him till he got home to the big fir-tree' (*PR*: 63), and the accompanying illustration shows **Peter** diving into the area of safety between the roots. The remainder of the story presents the interior space, under the tree's roots, as a place of domestic comfort and security in which **Peter** recovers from his ordeal. Though the sort of understanding of the natural world developed via an encounter with these words and images is subtle, it nonetheless constitutes a form of what we would now call 'nature literacy' or 'ecoliteracy', and recent work on the importance of this kind of learning has suggested that nature-literate children 'have the ability to engage with nature, both cognitively and emotionally, and feel empowered to take some form of positive action to benefit nature' (Grace, Griffiths & Hughes 2021: 17). What is so important about Potter's work is the way in which her stories themselves encourage both a cognitive and emotional engagement in even very young readers.

Trees make a further significant appearance in *Squirrel Nutkin*, providing a home for Nutkin and his fellow red squirrels, who live 'in a wood at the edge of a lake' (*SN*: 7), and Old Brown, who lives in a 'hollow oak-tree' on an island in the middle of the lake (*SN*: 8). The island also provides an important source of food for the squirrels since it is covered with not only 'trees' but also 'nut bushes' (*SN*: 8). Potter returns to the ways in which trees support squirrel-life in *Timmy Tiptoes*, in which Timmy and his wife Goody live in a 'nest thatched with leaves in the top of a tall tree' (*TT*: 7). As in **Peter Rabbit**, there is a strong sense of safety suggested by the squirrels' tree-home, here partly because the height of the tree protects them from bears and other creatures who roam the woods below. Timmy and his wife collect nuts to store up for winter, placing some in 'hollow stumps' (*TT*: 12) and dropping the rest into a hole high in a tree 'that had belonged to a woodpecker' (*TT*: 15). Although Timmy ends up being pushed rather **violently** into this tree by the other squirrels – who believe he has been stealing their nuts – once inside, the interior space of the tree becomes a place of refuge. Timmy is looked after by Chippy Hackee, a chipmunk, and is tucked up in a bed of moss inside the tree whilst he recovers. The final image of the book depicts the Tiptoes' family tree house with a little door and a cradle-swing in which the baby squirrels are being rocked by Goody, thus reinforcing the link between squirrel tree habitats and human domestic spaces, so that a young reader can project their own understanding of home onto the tree-house of the squirrels (*TT*: 55). In Potter's *Tales*, trees then are not merely a backdrop to the **animal** adventures, rather they are shown to provide a home for different species and a source of sustenance for these creatures, so that these stories subtly convey the importance of trees and woodland spaces for the **animals** with whom we share our world.

As so often in Potter, this powerful imaginative trope is informed by her own close observation of the natural environment. In an autobiographical piece called 'Memories of Camfield Place', she recalls staying at the home of her grandparents, where there was an 'enormous hollow elm' opposite the kitchen windows, which was a 'paradise for the birds' (*J*: 446). She describes climbing up to 'the holes looking for owls and starlings' and being awakened at four in the morning by the 'song of the birds in this elm' (*J*: 446). Memories of the hollow elm would conflate with her memory of the 'two great cedars on the lawn' – 'magnificent trees in their prime' (*J*: 445) – to form the basis for one of Potter's most important pieces of environmental writing about trees. In *The Fairy Caravan* **Xarifa** tells of 'Springtime in Birds' Place' and of how plants and **animals** have reclaimed a once-human space:

> Birds' Place had been the garden of an old, old manor house. No brick, no stone was standing […] Currant and gooseberry bushes had run wild in the thicket; they bore the sweetest little berries that the blackbirds loved. No one pruned the bushes, or netted them against the birds; no one except birds gathered the strawberries […] It was a paradise of birds.
>
> (*FC*: 62)

'Bird's Place' was in fact the name of a real manor house in Hertfordshire which had been pulled down in 1833. It was located near to the estate which was later owned by Potter's paternal grandfather. In Potter's story, the term comes to refer to the abandoned garden of the house which has now, more literally, become a 'Birds' Place'. The moving of the apostrophe makes this meaning clearer, suggesting somewhere which belongs to all birds. The space is protected from negative outside influence by a fence, so that inside 'Birds and butterflies and flowers lived undisturbed in that pleasant green wilderness' (*FC*: 62-3). At the centre of this ecosystem is a 'great cedar' tree: its 'head towered high above the self-sown saplings of the grove, its wide spreading lower branches lay along the mossy grass' which is 'carpeted with flowers, ground ivy, forget-me-nots' and 'blue periwinkle' (*FC*: 63). Among these lower branches, 'orange-tip butterflies' flit and 'red-tailed velvety bees' gather honey from the cowslip flowers, and starlings and nuthatches rear their broods in 'holes about the trunk', since 'the great cedar was large enough for all' (*FC*: 63). **Xarifa** recalls, 'Never, never anywhere have I seen so many flowers or listened to so many birds' (*FC*: 64). Potter presents her reader here with a powerful image of a complete and complex ecosystem thriving without negative human influence, but also with a vision of ecological abundance, with the tree providing a habitat for a wide range of **animal** species and plants.

In a second important story which is told by **Xarifa** in *The Fairy Caravan*, Potter also reminds her readers of the vital role played by trees within human lives and communities. In 'The Fairy in the Oak', Potter mourns the felling of an ancient oak in order to widen a road, but goes on to show how its wood is used to create a bridge 'across the rushing river' which provides a safe route for both humans and **animals** (*FC*: 263). Just as the living tree had existed for centuries, so this bridge will last for 'hundreds of years' because 'hard-grown oak lasts forever' (*FC*: 263). Again here, Potter not only focuses on the importance of trees but also links the lives of humans and the creatures with whom we share the world, in revealing the ways in which we are mutually dependent on trees and woodlands for our existence and survival.

This story also reveals Potter to be responsive to the spiritual, magical and other cultural meanings which have been connected to trees and woods since time immemorial. At the beginning of this story, **Xarifa** tells of how the ancient Britons believed the oak tree to be sacred and notes that the Saxons 'revered the Druids' trees' (*FC*: 254). She tells also of the way in which trees have functioned as cartographic signposts, helping us spatially define and map our world, since when William the Conqueror ordered a record of the country for the Domesday Book, ancient trees were used as landmarks. Within the story Potter thus points to some of the crucial ways in which, since ancient times, trees have helped us navigate and culturally construct the world around us.

A particularly important strand within a British arboreal cultural tradition, exemplified in Shakespeare's *A Midsummer Night's Dream* but also drawing on older pagan mythology and folklore, is that woods are magical places in which magical happenings and transformations can occur. This idea is suggested throughout *The Fairy Caravan* since, not only is the woodland inhabited by **fairy** creatures, it is also the place in which various strange but lovely community gatherings occur. A festive **dance**, in which many different **animal** species come together for a night of revelry, takes place around a 'a **fairy** spruce' (*FC*: 143), with the tree itself becoming transformed into a magical presence: 'Brighter and brighter it shone, until it seemed to bear a hundred **fairy** lights; not like the **yellow** gleam of candles, but a clear white iridescent light' (*FC*: 143). The later mysterious gathering of the '**dancing** shoes' occurs in a similarly irradiated space – 'a pool of light' which is 'silvery like moonlight' (*FC*: 182) and which is reached by walking into the 'middle of the great wood' (*FC*: 181). Repeatedly then within *The Fairy Caravan* both individual trees and woodland spaces are shown to be imbued with, or sites of, an ancient **fairy** magic.

It is notable that modern ecological writers, when discussing trees and woods, often touch on elements which are central to Potter's own arboreal writing. In the introduction to *Wildwood*, for example, Roger Deakin similarly shifts between the mythical or magical associations of trees and the more practical ways in which they shape our lives. He writes that:

> To enter a wood is to pass into a different world in which we are ourselves transformed. It is no accident that in the comedies of Shakespeare, people go into the greenwood to grow, learn and change [...] [I]n *Midsummer Night's Dream* the magical metamorphosis of the lovers takes place in a wood 'outside Athens' that is quite obviously an English wood, full of the faeries and Robin Goodfellows of our folklore.
>
> (Deakin 2007: x)

But Deakin also goes on to point to the practical function of wood, which we use to build shelters, keep us warm and cook our food. For Potter, both elements are vital to a rich understanding of trees and their meanings, and her own early-twentieth-century writing can be seen as deeply ecological in the way in which it weaves these elements together for a young reader.

Alongside the dominant British cultural influences on our handling of woodland spaces is an equally powerful European tradition, which depicts woods as frightening and dangerous spaces. Indeed, as Elizabeth Parker suggests, woods often function in a distinctly binaristic way: either a setting 'of wonder and enchantment' or a 'dangerous and terrifying wilderness' (2020: 1). This latter tradition has permeated children's literature from the fairy tale onwards and even within the Edwardian Golden Age of children's literature, dominated as it is by an arcadian vision of the English countryside, we find evidence of this trope. A notable example is Kenneth Grahame's *The Wind in the Willows*, in which Mole loses his way and has a terrifying experience in the 'wild wood'. Here the woodland space is depicted as 'other' and outside the idyllic English countryside represented by the riverbank. The wood functions as a place of danger, with faces appearing from every hole and fixing on Mole 'glances of malice and hatred: all hard-eyed and evil and sharp' (Grahame [1908] 1994: 43). The story makes clear that this is not an isolated experience, rather Mole has finally discovered the 'dread thing which other little dwellers in field and hedgerow had encountered' there: the 'Terror of the Wild Wood!' (Grahame [1908] 1994: 45).

Despite Potter's 'lifelong love of fairy tales' (Kutzer 2003: 166) and the fact that she regularly turns to motifs and themes from these stories in her work, she almost always rejects or at least qualifies a Gothic reading of woodland spaces. In a scene reminiscent of Mole's experiences, Potter's eponymous character, Pigling Bland, gets lost and ends up in a wood where it 'grew dark, the wind whistled, the trees creaked and groaned' (*PB*: 35). Like Mole, the pig is afraid, but here this is a very transient experience and his fear is shown to be unfounded. After an 'hour's wandering' (*PB*: 35) Pigling Bland gets out of the woods and the story suggests that the real source of danger is not to be found in this natural space but in proximity to human society, with its constant threat of the 'market' as well as 'bacon and eggs' (*PB*: 37).

Another rare instance of woods being experienced as a place of fear occurs in *The Fairy Caravan*. This story explores cultural anxieties about woodland spaces more fully, with the **animals** shown to be concerned about spending the night there. Moreover, when Paddy Pig gets lost in Pringle Wood he describes alarming occurrences, including 'things with red noses' which 'pulled my tail and pinched me, and peeped at me round trees' (*FC*: 167). His experiences are though soon explained as hallucinatory visions caused by the 'toadstool tartlets' which Paddy had eaten in the woods. However, Potter adds a humorous twist to the story since, if we look very closely at the colour plate depicting Pony Billy trotting through the woods, we see not only fairies living amongst the bluebells but also, at the foot of the tree on the left-hand side of the image, a mysterious tiny creature with a red nose (*FC*: 'The Fairy Hill of Oaks'). Despite this subtle validation of Paddy's account, the story does not ultimately affirm the existence of any real danger in the woods such as we find in fairy tales, and the overall emphasis is on the woods as magical spaces in which we hear a 'faint *tingle ringle* from the bluebells on the **fairy hill of oaks**' and 'laughing from the thousands of bluebells in the wood' (*FC*: 160–1).

The fairy-tale trope of danger lurking in woodland spaces is also touched on in *Jemima Puddle-Duck* and, though there is in fact real danger here for the title character, Potter plays with and subverts our expectations. She does not locate the danger in the heavily wooded and shadowy space of myth, rather the encounter with the fox occurs in an open space in the middle of the wood, 'where the trees and brushwood had been cleared' (*JPD*: 19). In accompanying illustrations, the meeting between fox and duck is shown to occur in a bright space, liberally adorned with pink foxgloves, and the predatory fox is reading a newspaper almost like a gentleman in his garden (*JPD*: 23). Potter further undercuts the idea that the story should be read as a warning about strangers or wandering alone since we are explicitly told that Jemima is a 'simpleton' (*JPD*: 39). Another instance in which the meaning of woodland spaces is played with and subverted occurs in **Peter Rabbit**, since here **Peter** escapes not *from* but *into* the woods. Having finally got away from Mr. McGregor he finds himself 'safe at last in the wood outside the garden' (*PR*: 59), in what Kutzer describes as a reversal of the 'usual fairy-tale motif of danger lurking in the forests' (2003: 45).

Potter's impulse to reject the cultural trope of woods as a space of fear and danger is perhaps most evident in her retelling of 'Little Red Riding Hood' (*c*.1912), the fairy tale which, perhaps more than any other, has been responsible for the widespread cultural promulgation of this myth. Though Potter follows Perrault in ending the story with both Red and her grandmother being **eaten** by the wolf, she subtly rewrites the meaning of the wood. In Perrault's version the young girl explicitly meets the wolf as 'she was going into a wood' (Perrault 2009: 158), and this primary woodland encounter comes subsequently to be emphasized in illustrations and other artistic representations of the story, which frequently depict Red and the wolf surrounded by trees in a dark and mysterious-looking woodland space. By way of contrast, Potter writes that the girl's path leads her 'under the flickering leafy shadows of the birch trees', where the 'bog myrtle smelled sweet in the warm sunny glades, and the west wind blew softly through the wood', bringing with it the 'cheerful sound' of the woodcutters who sing at their work of 'the woodland merry' and provide safety for Red (*H*: 360). Though the woodcutters are also present in Perrault and do prevent the wolf from immediately attacking the girl, Potter's extended woodcutter section helps to transform the wood itself into an arcadian space of beauty where humans and nature work together in harmony. In Potter's version, it is only when the young girl reaches 'the end of the wood', and is 'hard upon the open meadow' (*H*: 361), that danger lurks in the form of the wolf.

Though Potter's retelling of 'Little Red Riding Hood' appears to make only a very minor change to the story, it is a crucial one given the role this fairy tale has played in developing a cultural emphasis on woods as a zone of fear and danger. As Parker argues, the 'stories we tell about Nature – and specifically the stories we tell about the woods' are vital in informing our responses to these spaces. Just as a darker reading of woodlands can reinforce a sense of 'alienation from the natural world' (2020: 4), so those stories which depict them as spaces of natural beauty, in which humans coexist in harmony with the natural environment, can have a powerful role to play in encouraging a positive sense of connection. Increasingly ecocritics have pointed to the importance of the 'language' and 'symbolism' we use in 'our fictional portrayals of nature' (Parker 2020: 4), in shaping the way we respond to the natural world. What is so particularly crucial about Potter's writing in this respect is that she offers an alternative formative interpretation of a natural space which has tended to be depicted in a more negative light in stories encountered by children. Along with establishing an environmental understanding of trees and woodlands as **animal** habitats, she also – perhaps even more powerfully – resists depicting them as places of danger and presents them instead as scenes of natural beauty, community and joy.

U IS FOR UNCANNY

Though Potter resists the negative cultural associations of woodland spaces, we do find in her work an interest in the mysterious potential of place. There is a tendency to perceive Potter's textual handling of the **Lake District** as 'homely and reassuring' (Thompson 2010: 259) and as representing an idyllic English pastoral space. Indeed, her books are often aligned with the cultural celebration of an agro-pastoral bucolic vision of England, in which the fields are always green and the foxgloves in flower. Potter's writing, however, frequently reveals a darker subtext at work within rural spaces. There is a refusal to idealize or excise matters relating to death or **violence** as well as, at times, a deliberate turning to rather more unsettling experiences of place.

An interest in the stranger and uncanny qualities of the English **Lake District** is apparent in Potter's written engagement with the region from an early stage. In a **journal** entry from her first visit in 1882, Potter refers to a local popular tradition which tells of an old passage between Hawkshead Hall and Furness Abbey being 'frequented by a white lady' (*J*: 21) and three years later, when the family were staying at Lingholm in Keswick, she turns to a different kind of regional horror. In her **journal** account of this popular Lakeland tourist destination, Potter's focus is not so much on the area's natural beauty but on its social problems. She describes the town as a 'terrible place for drink', particularly every fourth Saturday when the miners are paid and go to the gin shop (*J*: 155). The teenage Potter goes on to record the drownings in Derwentwater which were an occasional consequence of this indulgence in gin, even recounting in graphic detail the recovery of the drowned bodies. She observes that one boy 'brought up a body at the first drag' and describes it coming up 'like a cork, caught by the flaps of the coat', going on to note – with some evident fascination – that the bodies are 'always upright, on their head or feet' (*J*: 155). Potter's description of the bodies here is suggestive of the German concept of 'Unheimlich': that which 'ought to have remained [...] secret and hidden but has come to light', an idea which Sigmund Freud uses as a starting point for his exploration of what generates a sense of the 'uncanny' in his famous essay on the subject (Freud [1914] 2017: 721).

Potter's experience of seeing the bodies recovered from the water engenders a powerful sense of unseen horrors lying beneath the surface. She writes, it is 'most horrible having those things under the water, we hardly like to go up the lake' (*J*: 155). In her **journal** she lingers over this idea of these disturbing 'things' hidden in the depths of the lake, adding that 'down below the water lilies, among the greedy pike, there is a man, the highest and lowest in the scale of creation' (*J*: 155). Along with the rather moralistic Victorian tone about the evils of drink, the passage is rich with Gothic overtones and suggests an early awareness on Potter's part that, beneath its beautiful surface, the **Lake District** had distinctly 'uncanny' potential.

Though reframed for a young audience, this idea of 'what lies beneath' re-emerges in *Mr. Jeremy Fisher*, published just over a decade after Potter witnessed the recovery of the drowned men from Derwentwater. Jeremy is only safe when he remains within his domestic space or (though more tenuously so) when separated from the water by his lily-pad boat. As soon as Jeremy dangles his foot into the water, disturbing its surface and transgressing beneath, the frame shifts and Potter's accompanying images take us down into the terrifying world within the pond itself. First, she depicts a huge water beetle swimming up beneath the lily pad which tweaks the frog's dangling foot. Then the rats, who inhabit the rushes at the side and of whom Jeremy is afraid, appear in the water. Finally, in an accumulation of horrors, we are presented by the truly terrifying and 'frightful' shadowy outline of a giant fish emerging from the depths, mouth agape (see Figure 9), which seizes the frog 'with a snap' and carries him away in its jaws 'down to the bottom of the pond' (*JF*: 40).

It is an image and an idea which seems to have been inspired by Potter's earlier private imaginative reflections on the bodies and the pike which live 'down below the waterlilies' (*J*: 155), since in previous incarnations of this story of a frog going fishing, the experience is far less terrifying. In an 1893 picture letter to Eric Moore and in Potter's subsequent reworking of these drawings for a small commercial publication in 1894, 'A Frog he would a-fishing go', the frog is laughed at by the fish and, though his fingers are at one point nipped, this only occurs after he has landed a fish in his boat (*H*: 179–82). The subsequent development of the story, with its terrifying image of something rising up from the depths and dragging Jeremy down, draws directly on language used in the 1895 **journal** entry describing the bodies in Derwentwater, with the account of Jeremy, popping 'up to the surface of

U is for Uncanny

Figure 9 Illustration from *The Tale of Mr. Jeremy Fisher*.

the water, like a cork' (*JF*: 44) picking up on the same simile used to describe the way the drowned bodies come to the surface. These revisions, which seem to be informed by Potter's own rather Gothic experiences in the **Lake District**, transform the original incarnation of the fishing frog story into one with a much darker and 'uncanny' overall feel.

Potter also draws on personal encounters with place in *Sister Anne*, and though Potter scholars have often been dismissive of this text's 'disconcerting, even estranging, effects' (Lovell-Smith 2013: 10), it has recently been described as a 'gothic horror story' and a 'fully developed atmospheric novella set in a detailed feudal era, centuries past' (Hermansson 2009: 130). However, the unsettling atmosphere of the story is achieved not only via Potter's handling of the unfamiliar historical context but also through the use of a precise geographical setting, since Potter transplants her 'Bluebeard' story to the Sands of Morecambe Bay. Her use of place here displays attributes of what has been termed 'coastal Gothic' – dark narratives which are inspired by edgelands, those 'marginal or wild places' which cannot be 'reconciled to the metropolitan centre or to the imperatives of "progress"', and are often marked by 'geographical and/or meteorological extremity' (Armitt and Brewster 2023: 94). Potter certainly makes the most of both the geographical and meteorological 'extremity' of the Sands in her story, a place she records in her **journal** having first seen in person in 1887 in the bleakest of weathers, with 'storms of sleet and snow' (*J*: 203). Potter's combined descriptions of place and weather play a significant part in establishing the Gothic atmosphere in *Sister Anne*. Bluebeard's castle stands on the edge of the unstable and dangerous landscape of the Sands: 'Muddy **yellow** water swirled under the arches with the ebbing tide' (*SA*: 28), its 'battlements gleamed white against black thunder-clouds; or lowered, darkly, menacing, over the Sands before rain' (*SA*: 8) and, as Sister Anne first approaches the castle, she sees it emerging from the bay 'in rain and gathering gloom' (*SA*: 23). As Jimmy Packham suggests:

> the coast is a space frequently defined by its 'inbetweenness,' an unstable amalgam of land and sea, whose tidal comings and goings have helped consolidate its reputation as a liminal space and limit, culturally and environmentally [...] [T]he coast has a long history as a key locale in gothic writing, [...] a site of gothic experience par excellence.
>
> (2019: 206)

In contrast to the vague and often unspecified locations of Perrault's original fairy tale, Potter draws on the potential of just such a liminal landscape to contribute to a sense of unease. She evokes its strange otherly qualities and the danger it represents from the outset:

> Towards the sea and the south the castle rock rose sheer, with wind-blown sand at its foot – sand that edged the coast for leagues in benty hillocks. Salt water lapped against the sand ridges at high tide; but at most hours of the day and night the bay was covered with mud. It stretched for miles and miles, glittering like gold at sunset, shining like silver at moonrise, treacherous with shifting quicksands when the tide came up. Rows of stakes half buried in slime marked fords across fresh-water channels, to guide those venturesome travellers who chose to cross the Sands instead of following the coast road round the bay.
>
> (*SA*: 7–8)

Effective though Potter's handling of this setting is, her story also features a location which we might more typically associate with the traditional Gothic genre: Bluebeard's castle, with its battlements, labyrinthine corridors and terrible secrets. Potter used Lancaster Castle as her model for this imaginary setting (*A*: 53) and in the story this fortress stands on a 'hill beyond the Sands' (*SA*: 7). One of the most important functions of the Sands in *Sister Anne* is therefore to create a powerful sense of separation between the castle, which will become the wife's prison, and the place of safety, her home on the other side of the Sands. Bluebeard marries his new wife Fatima at the 'fisherman's chapel' and they cross the Sands to the castle immediately 'before the tide came up' (*SA*: 14) so that, once removed to the castle, Fatima's only method of communicating with her family is to tie a note to the leg of one of the pigeons she takes with her.

For all the uncanny potential of the Sands themselves, Potter's handling of Gothic settings in the story ultimately works to separate out the meaning and function of the patriarchal castle from the natural landscape amidst which it stands, in a way that is reminiscent of the fiction of the great eighteenth-century Gothic novelist, Ann Radcliffe. As Anne Mellor argues, though Radcliffe uses 'landscapes of dark nights, mountainous peaks and chasms, raging torrents and fierce storms, to establish an environment in which human cruelty and physical violence can flourish', her novels suggest that 'sublime horror originates not from nature but rather from man' (1993: 92). So, though the sublime experience of terror, as developed by the eighteenth-century philosopher, Edmund Burke, is usually located within the natural world, in Radcliffe's fiction 'the horror of the Burkean sublime' is displaced 'from nature into the home, which is repeatedly described as the "prison" of women' (1993: 94). This same pattern is developed by Potter in *Sister Anne* since, as the story makes clear, the primary source of fear is Bluebeard himself and the most dangerous place for the women is inside the walls of his castle.

Moreover, as in Radcliffe, natural landscapes come to have a more positive, emotionally restorative effect on the women. As the story progresses, Anne encourages her sister to escape from the interior of the castle and go out and walk on the battlements. She tells her it is 'unwholesome to wander in that sickly gloom' and points to the 'gleam of sun' across the bay which becomes visible once the 'mist has drawn away with the tide' (*SA*: 85). Moreover, the story shows that Anne not only respects the power of the natural world, but also takes time to learn and understand it; she 'studied the landscape and the tide, and reckoned the age of the moon', since those 'who dwelt beside the treacherous Sands had need to learn its changes' (*SA*: 86). Though Bluebeard tries to impose his will on this place and desires an heir who will inherit his 'lordship of the Sands' (*SA*: 8), Anne's relationship with this strange landscape, and by extension with the natural world more generally, is one of respect and understanding.

Potter's personal engagement with the uncanny potential of place is evident in her writing to the end of her life and is fundamentally linked to her perception that there is something magical, or **fairy**-like within the natural landscape itself. In 'The Lonely Hills' she returns in her imagination to an area of the **Lake District** to which she had been drawn from an early stage, and reflects on the qualities of this landscape which she found so very appealing:

> Troutbeck Tongue is uncanny; a place of silences and whispering echoes. It is a mighty table-land between two streams. They rise together, north of the Tongue, in one maze of bogs and pools. They flow on either hand; the Hagg Beck in the Eastern valley; the Troutbeck River on the west. They meet and re-unite below the southern crags, making the table-land almost an island, an island haunted by the sounds that creep on running waters which encompass it.
>
> (*A*: 212)

It is within this haunted and haunting place that Potter 'loved to wander' and where she listened 'to the voices of the Little Folk' (*A*: 212). Along with its magical qualities, here the place names and physical traces of our ancestors function to evoke the past within the present: 'Woundale and the Standing Stones; Sadghyll and the hut circles; the cairns built by the stone men; the Roman road; Hallilands and Swaindale, named by the Norsemen; and the walls of the Norman deer park stretching for miles' (*A*: 212). The passage suggests that Potter's understanding of the place as 'uncanny' is partly to do with this eerie experience of seeing or sensing that which is normally hidden. However, such an experience of place is shown to be entirely positive and, in this exploration of the 'uncanny', there is a strong sense of its opposite, the homely or 'Heimlich', which is suggestive of things which belong and are 'not strange' but 'familiar' and 'intimate' (Freud [1914] 2017: 719).

There is no evidence here of the psychological disturbance which Freud attributes to the 'uncanny' and Potter writes in a way that points to a sense of comfort achieved through this co-existence with spectral voices and ancient lives. In *The Ecological Thought*, Timothy Morton argues that all forms of life are connected in a vast 'entangling mesh' and observes that no 'being, construct, or object can exist independently from the ecological entanglement' (2010: 53). He goes on to add that there 'is something sinister about discovering the mesh'; it is as if 'there is something else – someone else, even – but the more we look the less sure we are. It's uncanny' (Morton 2010: 53). Indeed, Morton claims that the 'more ecological awareness we have, the more we experience the uncanny' (2010: 54) and this offers an interesting way of thinking about Potter's own handling of the 'uncanny' in the passage, which is rooted in a powerful sense of the interconnections that exist within this particular landscape. Here, what Morton calls the 'mesh' is evident not only in Potter's awareness of the past lives, voices and sounds which continue to haunt the space, but also in her moving assertion that she is never 'lonely here' – joined and connected as she is with the 'gentle sheep', the 'wild flowers' and the 'singing waters', as well as with the voices of the 'Little Folk' (*A*: 212). Potter's use of the term 'uncanny' in this context resonates strongly with recent ideas about deep ecology, in that it points to a profound and vital sense of interconnection with the complex, and often invisible, entanglements which make up our world.

V IS FOR VIOLENCE

The word 'violence' appears very infrequently in Potter's writing and when it does so, it is rarely used to mean a deliberate exercise of physical force against a person or property. An unusual instance of such usage appears in a **journal** entry of 1883, in which she describes the 'incredible' levels of lawlessness and 'violence' in Ireland as comparable to the 'violence of the Middle Ages' (*J*: 42). More typically though Potter uses 'violence', as well as 'violent' and 'violently', merely to point to the strength or power of actions, emotions or experiences. In her **journal**, for example, she records being amused by the 'violence' of dislike towards a Holman Hunt exhibition (*J*: 196) and uses the adjective 'violent' to convey extreme **illnesses**, weather or emotions: she develops a 'violent cold' (*J*: 407), there are 'violent showers' (*J*: 334) and her grandmother is in a state of 'violent indignation' (*J*: 205). A similar usage occurs in her books for children; here, for example, Johnny Town-mouse starts 'violently' when he hears the 'fearful noise' of a cow (*JTM*: 47) and, in *The Fairy Caravan*, Paddy Pig sneezes 'so violently' his prosthetic trunk is blown off (*FC*: 69).

Though Potter rarely uses words such as 'violence' and 'violent' to convey a deliberate exercise of physical force, this should not lead us to assume that acts of violence of this kind do not feature in her writing. Indeed, Tess Cosslett suggests that contemporary parents are 'often shocked to discover the violence depicted' in classic **animal** stories for children such as ***Peter Rabbit***, and she argues that this violence is 'part of their realistic project' and a distinctive feature of the development of the 'children's animal story' in the eighteenth and nineteenth centuries (2006: 1). For a writer such as Potter, whose early imaginative treatment of **animals** is predicated on a scientific outlook and later by her experiences as a farmer, the violence inherent in **animal** behaviour as well as in human behaviour towards **animals** is never sidestepped but rather accepted as a fact of life.

Perhaps the most regular type of violence, or at least threatened violence, in Potter's work occurs in relation to the trope of **eating**, since most of the *Tales* involve a plot in which one or more of her characters attempt to avoid being eaten. Moreover, the stories often draw attention to the processes and mechanisms of food consumption. Kara Keeling and Scott Pollard argue that 'cooking disguises the inherent violence of the act of eating', by transforming 'a once-living organism into a much less recognizable version of its original form via butchering' and 'culinary preparation' (2020: 44). They go on to suggest that pie-making 'serves as a particularly effective means of disguising meat consumption', with the final dish, covered in pastry, effectively hiding the 'muscle, or organ' of the original **animal** (Keeling and Pollard 2020: 44). However, though the butchery involved in the process of turning **Peter's** father into a pie happens 'off-stage', the bald statement that your father 'was put in a pie by Mrs. McGregor', accompanied as it is by an image of the pie being brought to the table by a smiling farmer's wife, is quite shocking and functions to enhance the reader's anxiety for **Peter** as he tries desperately to escape the garden and the same fate (*PR*: 10–11). The horror of the scene is moreover emphasized by the anticipatory gastronomic relish of those seated around the table; the dog sniffs greedily at the pie and our attention is drawn to the cutlery which will be used to consume the rabbit (*PR*: 10).

In the case of **Peter** and Potter's other main **animal** characters, the fate of being eaten is avoided – though often narrowly – but the stories include regular reminders of the violence inherent in the process of **eating**. In *Mr. Tod*, for example, Tommy Brock's preparations for butchery are sharply in evidence as both the 'carving knife' and a 'pie-dish' are laid out in readiness for the turning of the baby bunnies into food (*T*: 35). This violence is even more explicit in *Samuel Whiskers*, where we learn that the cats and rats **eat** each other's children. When Tom Kitten is caught, he is tied up brutally with string in very 'tight knots' by Anna Maria as the rats plan to make 'kitten dumpling roly-poly pudding' (*SW*: 46) for their dinner. Here the violence of the process is emphasized not only by the image of the kitten tied up and in distress (*SW*: 55), but also by the fact that Potter depicts the rats wrapping the kitten up in pastry without any transformation from living **animal** to butchered meat having taken place, so that the reader is forced to contemplate the idea of Tom himself as food.

The children's author, Roald Dahl (1916–90), who was famously drawn to Potter's work as a child, seems to have been strongly influenced by these elements of her writing in the development of his own books, which contain stories of humans using glue to catch birds in order to put them in a pie, as well as giants and witches who eat human children. Indeed, in an essay first published in 1976, Dahl wrote that children 'like stories that contain a threat' and 'love being spooked' ([1976] 2009: 55), and in many of his own books, that 'threat' often revolves around the possibility of being eaten. Later writers have also pointed to the impact of these aspects of Potter's work on their own early imaginary development. In a recent article published in *The Guardian*, several contemporary horror writers identified childhood reading as the source of inspiration for their work and South African horror author, Sarah Lotz, cites **Beatrix** Potter 'and the utter horror that is The Tale of Samuel Whiskers' as a significant influence (Flood 2014). Lotz claims that the 'image of Tom Kitten being rolled into a roly-poly pudding by a pair of giant rats [...] gave me claustrophobia and nightmares for a full year when I was five or so', but suggests that 'there was also something fascinating and thrilling about feeling like that – it was the most powerful reaction I'd had to a story thus far, and since then I've wanted to replicate it' (Flood 2014). An intense recollection of horror at this particular story is also picked up by another contemporary novelist, Maggie O'Farrell, but she recalls refusing to have a copy of *Samuel Whiskers* in her bedroom as a child since she found it too frightening. O'Farrell describes finding Potter's stories 'sinister and scary' and compares **Peter Rabbit** to *Titus Andronicus*, Shakespeare's most violent and disturbing play, which features the murder of two boys who are 'then cooked and served up to their mother in a pie' (Kelly 2021). Both this comparison as well as the fascination and horror induced by reading Potter's work suggest that there is something archetypal in Potter's handling of violence, which accesses deep-seated fears and harks back to an older tradition of storytelling.

Though contemporary readers are increasing disconnected from those fairy tales which were once the staple of the nursery library and which influenced Potter herself, we can certainly trace here the origins of some of the motifs of violence to be found in her writing. The tales to which Potter was exposed include Perrault's 'Bluebeard', in which a new wife discovers a room containing the corpses of his former wives, and 'Hansel and Gretel' by the Brothers Grimm, in which a pair of abandoned child siblings fall into the hands of a witch who intends to fatten the male child up before **eating** him. Though Potter said of her own retelling of 'Bluebeard', that it was not 'food for babes' (*A*: 47), it is nonetheless the violent imaginary world of the fairy tale and these archetypal stories of power and cruelty, which inform and underpin much of her own writing for children.

As in fairy tales, acts of violence in Potter's work are closely linked to power relations, with violence wielded by those in power. In some instances this power is physical, such as that of larger predatory creatures over smaller ones, and in others it has a socio-economic basis, as in the case of the rich over the poor. Potter's work therefore often uses the trope of violence to explore such dynamics, showing how violence is deployed as a means of maintaining and securing power. Kutzer's reading of Potter's *Tales* focuses on the way in which they offer a coded commentary on the socio-political contexts in which they were written, and she argues that in *Squirrel Nutkin*, Old Brown treats 'Nutkin the way the upper classes often treated the working classes: he ignores the annoying underling, but when pushed too far he resorts to violence to contain the threat of the uprising' (2003: 27). Though Potter's books make clear that violence can be used as a form of control, what makes her treatment of this theme so subversive is the way in which she presents narratives of escape and survival for those who are vulnerable and disempowered.

Though many of Potter's shorter stories repeat this pattern, it receives a more extended treatment in *Sister Anne*. Here this formula is explored via a cast of entirely human characters and in this story the power relations and the violence used to maintain them are also shown to be gendered. Rose Lovell-Smith suggests that Potter's version of 'Bluebeard' is 'about violence within marriage, the widespread practice of wife-beating, and in particular, about the recurring pattern of domestic violence' (2013: 16). Whilst the story does overtly address the specific horrors of marital violence, it also points to a wider culture of male violence against women. Those wielding power in the story – Bluebeard, his servant Wolfram and his company of armed thugs – are all men. Not only are his wife and, to some extent, even Sister Anne herself subject to Bluebeard's violent actions, but we also learn of the fate of other women: the dead wives, a nurse to the first wife's child who was shot by a crossbow, and the female servant Elspeth, who lives in a state of terror. The connection between gender and violence is suggested by the main plot of the story but also in various symbolic ways, such as through references to **clothes** and **eating**. Bluebeard has a vast appetite which can only be surfeited with large quantities of **animal** flesh. He is a relentless consumer of meat and he demands beef and mutton each time he arrives back at the castle. Moreover, the connection between his different types of appetite is made explicit in his language. At one point he makes reference to 'Red-haired carrots', which is an allusion to the red-haired heiress who has been identified as next wife (*SA*: 75). Bluebeard's **clothes** also speak of the violence which defines him. Whilst the women's medieval costumes inhibit their movements and render them more vulnerable, Bluebeard's apparel functions as both armour and weaponry, from the spurs on his boots to his leather gloves, which are 'plated with steel scales on the back of the knuckles' (*SA*: 92).

What makes Potter's handling of the story so powerful though and encourages a feminist reading is the fact that Bluebeard's acts of violence are repeatedly thwarted by Sister Anne, who uses her own intelligence and wit to best him. In one of the most violent scenes in the book, Bluebeard kicks Fatima and drags her to her feet by the hair. Though Sister Anne cannot hope to overpower him physically she uses quick thinking to turn Bluebeard's own violence and property against him, throwing a stool in his path while he is attacking her sister, so that he falls and cuts his head on the table's edge (*SA*: 118). Here and elsewhere, when violence is threatened or enacted towards those who are more vulnerable, Potter's stories present narratives of escape: Fatima from her violent husband, **Peter** from Mr. McGregor's garden, the young bunnies from Tommy Brock, Squirrel Nutkin from Old Brown (albeit having had to first sacrifice his tail) and so on. As in the world of the fairy tale, Potter's stories present an imaginative space in which power relations are both scrutinized and usually thwarted, with the stories coming down forcibly on the side of the powerless.

That this functions as a central and important motif in Potter's writing is drawn attention to by the very different way in which she handles matters when violence breaks out between equals. In *Mr. Tod*, the title character and the badger, both predatory **animals** and evenly matched, do battle together. Since unequal power dynamics are not a factor here, Potter does not present a narrative of escape and instead allows the violent encounter between the two **animals** to take place: there was a 'terrific battle all over the kitchen' and 'everything' is broken 'except the mantelpiece and the kitchen fender' (*T*: 69–71). An accompanying image shows the fox and badger locked in a ferocious fight amidst a scene of chaos (*T*: 72). Their battle continues outside with 'distant sounds of fighting' echoing in the wood (*T*: 77) and even extends beyond the pages of the book, with the outcome of their violent encounter never revealed to us, since **Peter** and Benjamin do not wait to find out the 'end of the battle between Tommy Brock and Mr. Tod' (*T*: 80). Instead, the story's resolution focuses on the safe rescue of the stolen baby rabbits and the fact that the terrifying violence which would have been enacted on the powerless has been avoided.

V is for Violence

A much more problematic power dynamic within Potter's imaginative world is that of humans towards **animals** and the natural environment. Though ultimately **Peter** escapes his fate, *Peter Rabbit* foregrounds the human threat to **animals** both through the backstory about **Peter's** father but also via the visual representation of a giant human figure and the small rabbit. In one of the most physically threatening images from the *Tale*, when **Peter** is about to be squashed by Mr. McGregor's large hobnailed boot, **Peter's animal** nature is brought to the fore (*PR*: 45). He is depicted unclothed, and on all fours, in a way that draws attention to the idea of human violence towards **animals**. It is also **animal**/human relations which inspire Potter's most disturbing and graphic descriptions of violence. In 'The Mole Catcher's Burying' acts of human violence are made explicit not only via the vast number of moles killed by the mole catcher (he 'numbered his slain by thousands') but also by the terrible violence of these murders: their 'warm black velvet coats were ripped' and their 'raw red bodies dangled in the wind' (*H*: 380). Though the moles rise up in the story and wreak a kind of revenge on the mole catcher by digging his grave, not only is the violence of human actions made horribly explicit here, but no fairy-tale escape is possible.

Another powerful description of human violence and destruction occurs in 'The Fairy in the Oak' and, whilst the ending of this story offers a narrative of reconciliation between nature and culture, the ancient **fairy** magic of the woods is shown to be no match for the actions of humans who can wield both tools and technology to powerful effect. Here the violence seems inescapable because it is scientifically planned and calculated. The men arrive first with tape measures and a 'theodolite' (an instrument which allows for the precise measurement of angles) to do mathematical calculations, so that the eventual felling of the **tree** seems to be an inevitable outcome (*FC*: 258). Ancient magical forces are shown to be ineffectual against this sort of power and the **fairy** can only stand and watch as the men hack and saw, and drill and blast the rocks with a 'noise like thunder' (*FC*: 259–60). Though the impulse in this story is very different to that of 'The Mole Catcher's Burying', since the latter offers a narrative of vengeance whilst here the story moves towards reconciliation, it is notable that in neither case is the nonhuman world able to resist or prevent the violent actions of humans. The rejection of a narrative of escape in these two contexts has particular relevance to current discussions about human/nonhuman relations in what has been termed the Anthropocene, the epoch of the earth's history in which human activity is considered to be the dominant influence on the environment, climate and ecology of the earth. In Potter's early-twentieth-century imaginative world, humans are already shown to function as the ultimate threat to other species and to the natural environment. It is therefore perhaps no surprise that, within this context, the deliberate wielding of power by humans leads to acts of violence which are both brutal and inescapable.

W IS FOR WAR

Following **Beatrix** Potter's death in December 1943, her widower, William Heelis, sent a note to those from whom he had received letters of sympathy in which he observed: 'It is sad to think that her last years were so interfered with by this awful "war", but she was always cheerful and brave to the end' (A: 206). Potter's life in the Lakes as Mrs Heelis had in fact been bookended by the two world wars. The First World War broke out in the summer of 1914, just nine months into her married life and, as this letter suggests, the Second World War had a significant impact on the final four years of her life.

The First World War (1914–18), coming as it did, so soon after the newfound happiness of her marriage to William Heelis in October 1913 and in the early stages of her new role as a farmer in the **Lake District**, had a profound effect on Potter. From her private writings at this time, we get a vivid and poignant glimpse of the impact of war on small rural communities. Potter spent the war years engaged in farm work in Sawrey and she frequently addresses developments in the conflict in terms of the impact on running a farm, not least the shortage of farm hands. Though many of the references to war in her letters are of a practical nature, a sense of the emotional impact of war also comes through. Adopting the tone of one of her little books, Potter writes to Millie Warne in September 1914 to say, the 'war is very horrid' (Lear 2007: 269) and she makes frequent allusions in her letters during the war years to these 'sad times' (L: 222).

Following the publication of *Pigling Bland* in 1913, Potter had turned her attention more fully to marriage and farming. She left the story which was to follow it, *Kitty-in-Boots*, unfinished, so that December 1914 was the first Christmas for several years in which Warne had no *Tale* from Potter to market. This lack of new material by Potter was affected by many factors, but one was undoubtedly the additional burden of running a farm during a war. In early 1918, however, at the request of Warne, she began to experiment with two possible *Tales*, both of which are subtly inflected by the experiences of war. The first of these was *The Oakmen*, based on a story Potter had written for her niece-by-marriage, Nancy Nicholson, a couple of years earlier. Though this tale of 'little men' who live in the larch wood has strong fairy-tale overtones, the handling of the destruction of their home by **tree**-fellers seems redolent of the terrible disruption of lives caused by war – a point brought home more forcibly by Potter's reference to the noise of the wood being destroyed as 'worse than Zeppelins' (*H*: 242). In the end though Potter abandoned this story and turned instead to her second idea, a reworking of an Aesop fable, which would become *Johnny Town-Mouse*. Poignantly Potter received her advance copies from Warne just days before the Armistice was signed on 11 November and the little book came out in time for that first post-war Christmas of 1918, when the country was still coming to terms with its devastating losses.

Johnny Town-Mouse is a retelling of Aesop's 'The Town Mouse and the Country Mouse' and Potter dedicated her little book to 'Aesop in the shadows', but what is less well recognized is the way in which the war also functions as a shadowy influence on the story. Like *The Oakmen*, this is a tale which seems imbued with the recent experience of the war and, in particular, the terrible experience of watching young men leaving their homes to fight in the trenches. Some of William Heelis's nephews had signed up immediately in 1914, as had those of her publisher Harold Warne. In a letter to Warne in May 1915, Potter expresses her hope that his 'nephews are all alive & unhurt – or not so badly', reflecting that 'Sometimes it is a relief to have them safe in hospital' (*L*: 221). In this same letter she also talks about the distressing exodus of young men from her own village, writing: 'Last summer's recruits are having their leave about here, the last we shall see of many a fine lad. It is a weary job' (*L*: 221). A sense of yearning for what these young men were losing seeps into *Johnny Town-Mouse*.

Like the original fable, the tale works to affirm the idea of 'each to their own'; however, within Potter's handling of the story there is a decided investment in what is offered by the English countryside. This is suggested by the lingering and loving depictions of English pasture, hedgerows, fruit and flowers, which were based on the landscapes around Potter's home in the **Lake District** and are set against the rather stark and unappealing interiors and exteriors of the town scenes, not to mention the very real dangers of the house-cat from whom the mice have to take 'refuge in the coal-cellar' (*JTM*: 35).

Potter worked on the illustrations for the story during the last few months of the war, finishing the last during the summer of 1918. Nowhere in Potter's *Tales* is the yearning for a home amidst the English countryside so strongly reaffirmed as in the beautiful watercolours for this particular *Tale*, produced at a time of awareness that many young men would never be able to return home. This longing for home comes through particularly strongly in an illustration of Timmy Willie arriving gratefully back in the countryside he knows and loves with a brown sack over his shoulder, an image which is subtly evocative of young soldiers returning back to their Cumbrian villages with a kit bag on their back (see Figure 10).

Timmie Willie's sad reflections while far from home could, in their pared down simplicity, be those of a young soldier in the trenches: 'Timmie Willie longed to be back at home in his peaceful nest in a sunny bank'; the 'food disagreed with him' and 'the noise prevented him from sleeping' (*JTM*: 31). He reminisces about his home with its garden of flowers, where there is 'no noise except the birds and the bees, and the lambs in the meadows' (*JTM*: 32), in lines which have a faint echo of Rupert Brooke's elegiac early war poetry, with its powerful nostalgic evocation of the landscapes of rural England.

Figure 10 Illustration from *The Tale of Johnny Town-Mouse*.

As always though in Potter's work, the handling of contemporary sociopolitical contexts is complex and this is certainly no propagandist tale, despite the happy images of homecoming to the English countryside. Indeed, it is notable that when Potter first began thinking about a new story for Warne in February of 1918, some three and a half years into the war, she turns to a fable which works against the idea of cultural difference as a source of conflict. Whilst reaffirming the value and qualities of rural England, the story ultimately presents a message of harmony and of different sides getting on. When Johnny visits Timmy Willie, he is received 'with open arms' and the main moral of the story is that one 'place suits one person, another place suits another person' (*JTM*: 44, 57). One of the last images in the book is a picture showing the two very different creatures, sharing a meal together and apparently deep in conversation. It is a message which must have had a particularly powerful resonance for children reading the story for the first time during Christmas 1918, many of whom would have lost older siblings or parents as a result of the conflict.

Two decades later, Potter, now in her early seventies, became aware that another terrible war was looming and once again began to prepare for the impact of wartime privations. This was though a very different kind of war, with Hitler's policies of rearmament already becoming a subject of widespread fear within Europe following his appointment as Chancellor in 1933. By December 1934, Potter's letters reflect on the situation in Europe with concern; she expresses her fear that British troops could not forestall a German advance and describes herself as 'alarmed' by recent developments (*L*: 371, 372). By the end of 1938 her response was more strident; she describes Hitler as a 'brutal raving lunatic' (*L*: 392) and observes that it 'is fatal to give way to bullies in the first instance' (*A*: 89). Potter's underlying anxiety at the prospect of a Second World War also though comes through in the same letter, as she reflects on the proximity of likely enemy targets and the fact that the 'shipyards & docks' of Barrow are 'only 15 miles away' (*A*: 89). Always the pragmatist, Potter began to prepare for the increasing likelihood of war, considering what stocks to lay in and putting by a supply of dog biscuits for her two beloved, but gastronomically fussy, Pekingese dogs, Chuleh and Tzusee.

The run-up to war was made additionally fraught by the fact that Potter, following a period of prolonged **illness**, was due to undergo a subtotal hysterectomy – at this date a serious gynaecological operation – in the spring of 1939. She went into this with low expectations of survival, writing just before the operation of how glad she was to have 'seen the snowdrops again' and observing that, though the 'whole world seems to be rushing to Armageddon', not even 'Hitler can damage the fells' (*L*: 398). The comfort offered by the enduring qualities of the **Lake District**'s natural landscapes was clearly at the forefront of her mind as she contemplated both her own mortality and the prospect of war. In another letter of this period she writes, 'What a pretty country it is at the Lakes is it not? Hitler cannot spoil the fells; the rocks and fern and lakes and waterfalls will outlast us all' (*A*: 95).

To her own surprise Potter came through the operation and returned home, but just a few months later, at the beginning of September, Britain declared war on Germany. The daily impact and emotional strain of this war are made clear from the letters written in the remaining four years of her life, letters in which references to the war are rarely absent. She reports local incidents, such as an escaped German soldier and bombs being dropped in nearby fields, as well as the fact that, in the spring of 1941, a batch of **Peter Rabbit** books was destroyed when a bomb exploded at the binders.

By the time the Second World War came along, it was nearly a decade since Potter had published her last *Tale*; however, she had continued to write for children both in private letters and, increasingly, for an American audience. In May 1942 she published a moving essay in the **Horn Book** called 'The Lonely Hills'. It opens with Potter describing having heard a Danish girl playing an 'old spinet' and this reminds her of the fate of Denmark, 'poor Denmark, poor Europe, silent behind a blank curtain of fear' (*A*: 210). Though the essay does not deal any more explicitly than this with the conflict which was raging throughout Europe, the writing is from beginning to end tinged with the sadness of war. As Judith Page and Elise Smith suggest, one textual response to her anxieties about 'crisis, threat, and change' in the essay is a celebration and reconnection with traditional aspects of rural culture, including the English folk **dance** (2021: 52). Potter's powerfully elegiac description of the natural environment in the essay can also though be read as a response to the trauma of war. Perhaps the most moving section is that in which Potter reminisces about her walks up to Troutbeck Tongue, one of her favourite places in the **Lake District**. The reader is pulled back with her through memory to encounter the precise sights and sounds of this spot as she experienced them, but also further back in history, via topographical names and the traces of a Roman and Norman presence in the landscape. This recording of human history offers a powerful message in a time of war, in that it draws attention to the fact that this beautiful place has survived all previous invasions and conquests. Potter closes the essay with a quotation from Wordsworth's 1807 poem, 'The Solitary Reaper', which speaks of 'old unhappy far-off things and battles long ago', and uses this to affirm that 'the vastness of the fells' will cover the 'sorrows of yesterday and today and tomorrow' with a 'mantle of peace' (*A*: 213). This essay, published in the last full year of Potter's life, is both a deeply personal eulogy for a specific natural environment which she loved so much, with its 'gentle sheep, and wild flowers and singing waters' (*A*: 212), but also an affirmation of the value of such spaces for human happiness. The essay offers a quiet but compelling assurance to her young readers as to nature's capacity to endure and outlast the brutal destructive tendencies of humankind.

X IS FOR XARIFA

Several of the stories which make up *The Fairy Caravan* are narrated by a sleepy dormouse called Xarifa who is a member of the **circus** troupe. This character was named after a pet dormouse, who was described by Potter as the 'sweetest little **animal** I ever knew' (*J*: 202). When asked, many years later, how she had come up with the unusual name, Potter explained that the mouse was always sleepy 'so we used to say "Wake up, wake up, Xarifa!"' and 'that was how she got her curious name' (Taylor 1986: 47). This little anecdote points again not only to the influence of Potter's close encounters with real **animals** in the creation of her anthropomorphized characters, but also the extent to which her imagination was steeped in literary references and allusions derived from very wide reading. 'Wake up, wake up' is a play on the opening lines of a poem called 'The Bridal of Andalla', one of a group of 'Moorish Ballads' translated by Sir Walter Scott's son-in-law, John Gibson Lockhart (1794–1854), and published in *Ancient Spanish Ballads: Historical and Romantic* (1823). The poem tells the story of Xarifa, a betrayed woman who stitches as her lover rides into town, amidst pomp and ceremony, to marry another woman. Xarifa is repeatedly entreated to leave her sewing and go to the window to watch the spectacle in the poem's refrain: 'Rise up! Rise up! Xarifa! / Lay the golden cushion down' (Lockhart 1823: 105). The amendment from 'Rise up' to 'Wake up' shows Potter engaging playfully with her literary sources, and this private joke transfers over to *The Fairy Caravan* where a starling whistles: 'Wake up! wake up! Xarifa!' to the sleepy dormouse (*FC*: 25).

The granting of such a beautiful and exotic name to a small and insignificant creature is also amusing and similar, apparently ironic, acts of naming occur with other of Potter's mouse pets and characters. *Two Bad Mice* also features mouse characters who are modelled on Potter's pets and, in this case too, the original pet names stem from a literary source. Tom Thumb and Hunca Munca are named after characters in Henry Fielding's plays *Tom Thumb, A Tragedy* (1730) and *The Tragedy of Tragedies; or, The Life and Death of Tom Thumb the Great* (1731). Moreover, aspects of Tom

Thumb's mouse character in Potter's *Tale* are informed by the plays, since Fielding describes Tom as 'a little hero with a great soul, something violent in his temper, which is a little abated by his love for Huncamunca' (Lindsay 1993: 215). Potter's Tom Thumb also displays a rather **violent** temper; however, Hunca Munca does not so much 'abate' this tendency as join with him in smashing the doll's house. The reparations which the mice make for what they have done suggest, however, that both have a 'great soul'. Though the naming of mouse characters after Xarifa and Tom Thumb appears at first to be ironic, in fact the idea that these small creatures embody some sort of unexpected greatness is one which underpins Potter's imaginative treatment of several mouse characters.

Literary and cultural influences also shape Potter's construction of her mice figures in other ways. Potter's most famous tale about mice, *The Tailor of Gloucester*, was inspired by a story Potter heard from her Hutton cousins about an actual tailor who claimed to have been helped by fairies. As other critics have noted though, the story also owes a debt to the 'Elves and the Shoemaker' by the Brothers Grimm (Carpenter 1989: 285; Kutzer 2003: 20; MacDonald 1986: 56) and Potter suggested that the story was connected in her mind to other tales and folklore. In 1923, when a play of *The Tailor of Gloucester* was being developed, she wrote that 'mice working for humans, by night, *were* an honest unashamed imitation of Puck, Robin Goodfellow and the Scottish Brownie' – adding, 'There is nothing new under the sun' (*H*: 276). Crucially though, in all of these sources of influence, the good deeds are done by overtly magical figures (fairies, brownies, sprites or elves) and Potter's most significant innovation is to replace these mythological characters with mice. In so doing, she perhaps also had in mind Aesop's fable of 'The Lion and the Mouse', in which a lion first spares a mouse's life, only for the mouse to later return this act of kindness and save the lion's life by biting through the ropes by which hunters had bound him (*Aesop's Fables* 1874: 20). In Potter's story the same essential pattern is repeated: the Tailor frees the mice, thus saving them from being **eaten** by Simpkin the cat, and the mice return this kindness by finishing the Tailor's commission for the Mayor.

As in Aesop, Potter's story about one of the smallest and most vulnerable creatures coming to the help of one of the most powerful is a fable about kindness but also about power relations. Daphne Kutzer argues that Potter's *Tales* 'encode rebellion' and 'complaints against hierarchy, authority, and power', in much the same way that female Victorian novelists encoded such narratives within their domestic fiction (2003: 12). Mouse characters are particularly important to such coded readings since their apparent insignificance aligns them with those who are most vulnerable and oppressed in society. In *The Tailor of Gloucester*, the mice bring about a questioning of their lowly status through their skill but also by the fact that in the end both the Tailor and the Mayor depend upon them, giving the story what Humphrey Carpenter refers to as a 'sharp social edge' (1989: 285). The implicit reversal of hierarchies is reinforced by the illustrations in the book which emphasize the smallness of the mice, threading needles half as tall as themselves (*TG*: 33), but which also depict them parading around in the sorts of **clothes** usually worn by the most well-off in society (*TG*: 25, 10).

Though in Potter's imaginative world the reader is encouraged to identify with the weak rather than the dominant, as Kutzer points out, there is often 'a price to pay for rebellion' (2003: 30). However, this is more the case in relation to Potter's other **animal** characters, such as rabbits, kittens and squirrels, with mice taking on a rather different function and meaning in her work. Aesop's fable, 'A Fatal Courtship', follows on from 'The Lion and the Mouse' and, in the second story the mouse, 'emboldened' by the friendship offered to him by the lion after the rescue, asks for the hand in marriage of the lion's daughter (*Aesop's Fables* 1874: 23). The lion calls the young lioness over to meet her potential suitor, but she unfortunately crushes him by accident with one of her paws as he goes running to meet her and thus normal power relations are restored. However, in the imaginative space of Potter's fiction, her mouse characters often remain quietly victorious and thus offer a more sustained challenge to existing social hierarchies and the assumptions we make about the lowliest in society. Rose Lovell-Smith suggests that Potter's mouse characters, in working hard and entertaining themselves and each other with 'song and story', offer a reminder that the 'small and powerless, though commonly objects of predation and victimization, are not to be dismissed as nonentities' (2013: 8). Indeed, even when placed in minor cameo roles, Potter's mice demonstrate important qualities and establish their inherent worth. We see this in the actions of Mrs. Thomasina Tittlemouse in the *Flopsy Bunnies* who, like the baby rabbits, is forced to scavenge for food in the rubbish heap at the end of Mr. McGregor's garden. But the mouse is a 'resourceful person' and it is this quality which saves the Flopsy Bunnies from their fate. Benjamin and Flopsy cannot undo the string that ties the sack in which their children are trapped and in the end it is the mouse who nibbles a hole in the bottom of the sack, thus enabling the young rabbits to escape (*FB*: 35).

An A–Z of Beatrix Potter

The linking of mice with a certain kind of wisdom is also suggested by Potter's visual representations of a 'learned mouse' figure. Her drawing for the cover of *The Tailor of Gloucester*, which shows a bespectacled mouse reading a paper called 'The Tailor', is a reworking of an image which had already been in Potter's mind for around a decade at this point. In 1892 she drew a mouse wearing glasses, seated on a chair and reading the 'Day's News' (Whalley and Hobbs 1987: 57, fig. 106) and then returned to this idea in 1899 when producing a painting as a gift for her uncle, the chemist, Sir Henry Roscoe. It was Roscoe who had stood by Potter when she had been faced with the dismissive attitude of the Director of Kew Gardens regarding her mycological research, and it was Roscoe who had helped with the production of her scientific paper and its presentation to the Linnean Society. Two years later Roscoe co-authored a chemistry textbook and, to mark the occasion of its publication, Potter presented him with a beautiful painting of a bespectacled mouse sitting on the edge of a Bunsen burner and reading from a book. In the background, several mice are engaged in scientific activities, some holding test tubes and others a piece of cheese up to the flame (Noble 1992: 104, fig. 122).

Despite their propensity to kindness and wisdom, Potter's portrayal of mice also emphasizes the fact that they often live hidden lives and are invisible to most of society. In this respect Kutzer argues that there is a clear link between the mice who 'live a secret life within the walls of a house' and Potter herself, since she too 'lived for all intents and purposes, a secret life in the third-floor nursery', keeping much of her life (including many of her pets and some of her mycological experiments) secret from her parents (2003: 97, 100). Indeed, Tom Thumb and Hunca Munca's frustration at the domestic artifice of the doll's house in *Two Bad Mice* can be read in semi-autobiographical terms, with the mice acting out the **violent** impulses Potter herself may well have felt towards the sort of stultified life on offer within the main domestic spaces at Bolton Gardens.

The **violent** energy of this story is unusual though and for the most part Potter's mouse characters succeed because of their quiet wisdom and creative talent, at stitching or storytelling. Kutzer reads *The Tailor of Gloucester* as a coded tale of 'class hierarchy thwarted by hard work rather than outright rebellion' (2003: 21), but a more autobiographical reading is also possible here, since hard work would also be Potter's own means of escape. Indeed, the story (Potter's favourite) encodes such a reading, with the detailed and beautifully rendered paintings of the eighteenth-century **clothes**, illustrating

X is for Xarifa

but also mimicking the intricate work done in the stitching of these garments by the mice, so that the talent and hard work of the mice mirror Potter's own.

There is a photograph, dated 1885, which depicts a rather hollow-eyed **Beatrix** Potter, hair cropped because of recent **illness**, with her pet dormouse Xarifa seated on her hand (see Figure 11). It is a strange image, not least because both sets of eyes appear to be looking into camera in a way that creates a sense of connection between the two subjects. Also though, there is something extremely vulnerable about Potter in this image; she seems diminished by recent **illness**, and this suggests a link with the tiny creature in her hand. Potter repeatedly complains of extreme tiredness in her **journal**, a result of ongoing **illness**, and this too seems to reinforce a point of connection with the sleepy dormouse.

Potter's fictional Xarifa is her most fully developed nonhuman narrator and, though modelled on her pet, in a sense the fictional mouse has been endowed with Potter's own gifts of storytelling, underpinned by her deep

Figure 11 Photograph of Beatrix Potter with her pet mouse Xarifa (1885).

knowledge and understanding of the natural world. While Xarifa also seems to embody Potter's idea of the 'learned mouse', especially in relation to her knowledge of the natural environment, it is Potter's own learning which informs Xarifa's storytelling. Like Potter, Xarifa is in tune with the patterns of the **seasons**, she understands the life-cycle of **trees**, knows the names and habits of the '**myriads of fairy fungi**' to be found in the woods, and has knowledge of flowers, birds, butterflies and other forms of nonhuman life. Because Potter/Xarifa observe these things so closely, they are then able to construct stories which convey the magic and an understanding of these processes to others.

Though Xarifa speaks with Potter's own knowledge, the dormouse's wisdom is shown in the stories to be derived from her natural education and close connection with the environment. Xarifa was born in 'Birds' Place', the beautiful ecosystem which we learn about in *The Fairy Caravan*. It flourishes untouched by humans and has at its heart a great cedar **tree**. Xarifa's earliest memories suggest a sensory immersion in this environment. At night, she tells us, her mother 'closed up the opening of our nest with plaited leaves and grass' and 'in the deep black velvety darkness came the low slow note' of a nightingale, a sound which is 'weird and wonderful' to hear in the 'silence of the night' (*FC*: 64). Moreover, this sort of bodily and sensory immersion forms part of Xarifa's own ongoing seasonal life cycle. She does not travel with the **circus** in the winter but instead goes to live with the Oakmen in the woods and hibernates (*FC*: 30–1). The extent to which Xarifa is identified with the natural environment is suggested by an illustration for *The Fairy Caravan* which depicts the dormouse telling her stories to Tuppenny and other **animal** characters while seated on the ground, surrounded by wood sorrel, violets, unfurling ferns and spring blossom (*FC*: 'Xarifa's Fairy Tale').

Given the connection between Potter and Xarifa, as well as between Xarifa and the natural world, it is perhaps unsurprising to find that it is Xarifa's narrating voice which relays the most important ecological messages in Potter's work. Not only is it Xarifa who tells of Birds' Place and of the trauma experienced by the oak **fairy** when the ancient oak is felled, but it is Xarifa who answers questions about the natural world which are posed by Tuppenny but might well be those of a young reader. The mouse's authority here is reinforced at the beginning of 'A Walk amongst the Funguses' since we are told that, though she was much smaller than the guinea-pig, her 'presence of mind was superior' (*H*: 313). Not only is Xarifa shown to be deeply knowledgeable, telling Tuppenny of the names and habits of **fungi**, she also – and perhaps more importantly – teaches him to accept the limitations in our knowledge. She speaks out against his instinctive response of **violence** towards that which he does not understand, encouraging instead a respect towards the other forms of life with which we share the planet.

The connection between Potter and Xarifa is reinforced by the fact that at times we are offered further details of the natural environment through the book's omniscient narrator and these descriptions sound very like those of Xarifa herself. This narrator imparts **seasonal** information to us in a similarly figurative way: the snowdrops which had been 'a sheet of white – white as the linen sheets bleaching on the drying green' had passed, and now daffodils were out in their hundreds, not the tame ones but 'the little wild daffodillies that **dance** in the wind' (*FC*: 127). Nonetheless, when Potter wants to impart a particularly important piece of wisdom or a deeper understanding of the natural world, she does so through the gentle and wise voice of a sleepy little dormouse. The book's most important ecological messages are all the more compelling because they are conveyed by a nonhuman character who is herself closely connected to the natural world of which she speaks. When asked if flowers and plants can feel, Xarifa replies:

> I do not know how much or how little; but surely they enjoy the sunshine. See how they are smiling, and holding up their little heads [...] I think they take pleasure in the gentle rain and sun and wind; children of spring, returning from year to year; and longer-lived than us – especially the **trees**.
>
> (*FC*: 252)

Potter harnesses here the voice of one of the smallest and apparently most insignificant of creatures to impart a message about the limits of our knowledge of lifeforms different to our own, but also to suggest the importance of cultivating a kind of imaginative understanding. Through the voice of Xarifa, Potter's work not only promotes tolerance and care, but also subtly draws attention to our own position of relative unimportance in relation to the patterns, cycles and timespans of the living world.

Y IS FOR YELLOW

In February 1883 Potter wrote in her **journal**: 'Mr. Whistler is holding an Exhibition somewhere, termed an *Arrangement in white and yellow*. The furniture is painted yellow and the footman is dressed in white and yellow, someone said he looked like a poached egg' (*J*: 32). She goes on to note that the artist, James Whistler, sent yellow butterflies to 'the Princess of Wales and the fine ladies' to wear to the private view adding, in response to this: 'What a set of yellow butterflies! It's quite disgusting how people go on about these Pre-Raphaelite aesthetic painters' (*J*: 32).

Although Whistler had been linked with figures from the Pre-Raphaelite brotherhood earlier in his career, he was, by the 1880s, more firmly identified with a group of avant-garde figures who were known as the 'aesthetes'. Indeed, Whistler had come out in opposition to John Ruskin, an early champion of the Pre-Raphaelite movement, and Ruskin's ideal of 'Truth to Nature', prioritizing instead the 'senses' over any message in art (Evangelista and Ribeyrol 2023: 173). Potter's rejection of this approach to art is apparent in her response to Rupert Potter's comments on a William Holman Hunt painting. She observes, 'My father objects' to the fact that he 'can't understand it, but I had rather a picture I can't understand than with nothing to be understood' (*J*: 138). From an early stage then, Potter was interested in the meanings and stories which could be told through and by art, rather than the concept of art as a purely sensory experience.

Though the Whistler exhibition in question opened at the Fine Art Society on Bond Street, Whistler and the other members of the 'aesthetic' school were more closely associated with the Grosvener Gallery, which Potter visited many times. In July 1884, she admired some of the art on display but dismissed the work of the 'greenery yallery Grosvenor Gallery painters', who were there 'in full force, as contemptible as ever' (*J*: 100–1). The 'greenery yallery' reference here is a quotation from a song in Gilbert and Sullivan's very popular comic opera of 1881, *Patience*, which satirized the aesthetic movement's celebration of 'art for art's sake' and its attention to

Y Is for Yellow

ideals of beauty over and above moral or social themes in art. The song in question describes:

> A pallid and thin young man,
> A haggard and lank young man,
> A greenery-yallery, Grosvenor Gallery,
> Foot-in-the-grave young man!
>
> (Gilbert 1932: 230)

That Potter had been influenced by this popular satirical representation of the 'aesthetes' is apparent in her response to the appearance of a figure firmly affiliated with this group, Oscar Wilde, who turned out not to be the 'lanky' and 'melancholy man' of her expectations but 'fat and merry' (J: 100). The phrase 'greenery yallery' encompasses the perceived affectation of the group, but also refers more specifically to the greens and yellows which were popular with the aesthetes. Yellow emerged as a particularly favoured colour, leading to the period becoming known as the 'yellow Nineties', with art works and publications frequently drawing on this colour to signal avant-garde status. Perhaps the best-known example of this phenomenon is *The Yellow Book*, a periodical which first appeared in 1894 and has been seen to define the 'chromatic identity of this turbulent decade' (Evangelista and Ribeyrol 2023: 189).

Though Potter's private writings make clear that she had little time for the aesthetic movement, these references help to remind us that Potter came of age and began to develop her own art in London during the *fin de siècle*, a period which saw profound changes in the world of British art and culture. Written by a perceptive young woman with a passionate interest in art, her **journal** provides an unusual insight into the debates and cultural shifts of the period. Potter's father took her to numerous London exhibitions and galleries, and she documented her responses in some detail. Potter's acerbic commentary on Whistler is in fact not untypical of her art criticism within these private writings and, though her views on the painters closely associated with the Grosvenor are universally negative, her attitude towards other groups, movements and individual figures in the art world is rarely straightforward.

Whistler was notoriously pitted against John Ruskin on the question of the use of colour in art since Ruskin believed that artists should stick to the God-given colours of nature, whilst Whistler followed the aesthetic philosophy of 'colour for colour's sake'. In 1877, and in response to Whistler's painting 'Nocturne in Black and Gold', Ruskin had infamously described the artist as a 'coxcomb' who charged 'two hundred guineas for flinging a pot of paint in the public's face' (Gombrich 1996: 533). However, despite Potter's criticism of Whistler, her private comments on Ruskin suggest that she was also very ambivalent in her attitude towards this major Victorian art critic. When the seventeen-year-old Potter first saw Ruskin – then in his mid-sixties – in person in March 1884, she described him as 'one of the most ridiculous figures I have seen' and 'not particularly clean looking' (J: 73). Two months later Potter records that her father thought a study of laurel leaves by Ruskin to be 'simply dreadful' (J: 87) and in reference to the family acquiring a second-hand copy of Ruskin's *Modern Painters*, which Ruskin had dedicated to Dante Gabriel Rossetti, she observes that she did not 'think much of either chappy' (J: 57). Potter's instinctive dislike of Ruskin was no doubt partly to do with the close friendship which existed between her father and the painter, John Everett Millais. Though initially a protégé of Ruskin, Millais had married Ruskin's former wife, Effie Gray, in 1855 following the annulment of her marriage to John Ruskin on the grounds on non-consummation. Though the public scandal of this annulment occurred several years before Potter was born, her parents would have been aware of the failed marriage with Effie and no doubt sided with Millais in his subsequent personal dislike of Ruskin. A generation earlier Charlotte Brontë had written of the powerful impact of Ruskin's *Modern Painters* on her own response to art, claiming that 'I feel as if I had been walking blindfold – this book seems to give me eyes' (Shorter 1908: 442), but there is no acknowledgement of any influence of this kind on Potter's part, despite Ruskin's continued status within the art world.

The Ruskin and Whistler controversy was connected to a wider set of cultural debates which arose in the late nineteenth century as a result of the 'colour revolution', with developments in colour production and reproduction resulting in what has been described as the emergence of an 'age of colour' (Ribeyrol 2023: 17) and, though Potter's stance on particular schools of art was often ambivalent, she is in many ways a product of this revolution. What emerges in her private writing about art from the early 1880s onwards is a fascination with the function and effect of colour, as well as an interest in the new technologies which were enabling the effective reproduction of colour in a mass market context. Both elements would come to play a key role in the success of her little books.

A close attention to the handling of colour emerges in Potter's earliest piece of art criticism, dating from June 1882, when she was only fifteen.

A significant proportion of her comments made in response to work seen at the Royal Academy relate to the artists' use of colour, both in negative terms ('Flat, sentimental and unpleasant colour'; 'wood rather queer colour'; 'face too pink'; 'sky rather **violent** blue'; 'rather doubt colour of mountains') and more positive assessments, such as colour 'clear and beautiful' and 'very clear and rich' (*J*: 17–18). On a subsequent visit to see the Winter Exhibition of Old Masters at the Royal Academy, there is a similarly detailed attention to the use of colour and praise or criticism of the artwork on these grounds, regardless of the status of either the artwork or the artist. She writes that Gainsborough's colour is 'very fine, but almost unnatural', adding that he has used a great deal of 'crude green and yellow which throws out the pinks'; she is surprised that some of the Van Dyck's are not 'richer in colour' and that Romney's colour is 'so bright' (*J*: 29). Potter's favourite painting in this exhibition was by Titian and again the focus of her praise is the artist's use of colour: here the 'crude, unpleasant colour disappears, while simplicity remains', adding that the prevailing colour is 'dull green', relieved by the 'crimson pomegranate' (*J*: 30). At times she seems to be trying to capture in words exactly what she finds so effective about the use of colour in a particular work of art, describing the handling of colour in Raphael's *Virgin and Child* for example, as 'wonderful, clear, transparent and brilliant, yet soft and gentle' (*J*: 52). When read as a body of work, this early art criticism suggests that Potter had a profoundly chromatic imagination and was deeply interested in the way in which colour affects the viewer's imaginative engagement with what was being portrayed.

Though Potter later rejected some of her own early art commentary as 'childlike and simple' (*J*: 31) and though her art criticism does become more nuanced as the years go by, she never loses this sensitivity to the handling of colour. After attending a private viewing of a special exhibition of Millais' work four years later, she uses her **journal** to record a detailed analysis of his development as an artist, paying particularly close attention to *Ophelia* (1851–2), which she describes as 'probably one of the most marvellous pictures in the world' (*J*: 192). Potter felt that this painting exemplified the 'real essence of pre-Raphaelite art, as it is practised by Millais', in which everything is in focus at once, noting that though 'natural in the different planes of the picture', this produces a 'different impression from that which we receive from nature' (*J*: 192). She develops this idea further through attention to Millais' use of colour, writing that though the leaves on the rose bush are 'too green' they might 'appear as green in certain separate circumstances, it is the question of focus' (*J*: 192). In other words, even at this early stage, Potter is sensitive to the idea of colour as something which is *perceived* in certain ways rather than being innate and fixed. In this and other respects, her early engagement with Pre-Raphaelite artwork did have a lasting influence on her own art. Towards the end of her life Potter wrote that when 'I was young it was still the fashion to admire Pre Raphaelites' adding that their 'meticulous copying of flowers and plants' influenced me (*L*: 455), and after the death of Millais in 1896 Potter recorded that he had once really 'paid me a complement', telling her: 'plenty of people can *draw*' but you 'have observation' (*J*: 429). This careful observation of the natural world and attention to the precise ways in which colours are experienced would remain the staple of Potter's own artwork for the rest of her life.

Given Potter's fascination with colour, it is somewhat ironic that her first self-published edition of **Peter Rabbit** featured only uncoloured line-drawings and Warne had to persuade her to produce the book in colour. However, Potter's response to Warne's initial query, as to why she had chosen to use only black and white illustrations, indicates an awareness of both the use of colour in mass-market contexts and the importance of making coloured images in this context vibrant and interesting. She writes: 'I did not colour the whole book for two reasons – the great expense of good colour printing – and also the rather uninteresting colour of a good many of the subjects which are most of them rabbit-brown and green' (*L*: 55). Once a colour edition was finally agreed upon, Potter set to work to produce new drawings in which the dominant colours of 'rabbit-brown and green' are varied through the use of bright, often primary colours, for the **clothes** worn by the characters, in ways which suggest that she was attuned to those 'images which would make marketable art' (Paul 2002: 58). Her final illustrations also make the most of the, often vivid, colours which can be found in nature, from a robin's red breast to pink foxgloves and blue forget-me-nots. The fact that these colours could be reproduced so effectively for a mass market is itself a result of the late Victorian 'colour revolution', and Potter's agreement to produce the books in colour was informed by the new colourization technologies which were becoming available. Warne used the, still quite expensive, 'three colour process' for her *Tales* and **Peter Rabbit** would become one of the first picture books in which this printing process was used throughout.

Though Potter's fascination with colour is most obvious in the artwork produced for the little books, it is also apparent in her tendency to write in a chromatic language. Her prose contains frequent references to colour in relation to both man-made items, such as **clothes**, and the vibrant colours

Y Is for Yellow

of the natural world, such as the 'yellow and scarlet' oak apples gathered by Squirrel Nutkin (*SN*: 27), the 'sea of blue hyacinths' by which Benjamin Bunny pauses when following Tommy Brock (*T*: 18), and the 'Yellow pussy willow catkins' which adorn the hedge by which Pig Robinson sits to eat his picnic (*LPR*: 37). Perhaps the most striking example of Potter's use of chromatic language occurs in this latter *Tale*, a book which contains mainly black and white line drawings and only five colour plates. Despite the paucity of coloured images, *Little Pig Robinson* is profoundly chromatic, with repeated references which situate the story within a vividly colourful landscape. The two aunts, with whom the title character lived as a child, have a cottage called 'Piggery Porcombe' which is located at 'the top of a steep red Devonshire lane'; here the 'soil was red, the grass was green; and far away below in the distance they could see red cliffs and a bit of bright blue sea' where ships with 'white sails sailed [...] into the harbour of Stymouth' (*LPR*: 23).

Stymouth is a semi-fictionalized version of 'Sidmouth on the south coast of Devonshire' where Potter had holidayed (*A*: 159). The area is known as the 'red coast' due to the distinctive colour of the cliffs and this red colour comes through strongly in the story through repeated references: the bay is sheltered by 'high red headlands' (*LPR*: 49) and the footpath to Piggery Porcombe is 'a red' track (*LPR*: 27); there is 'red ploughland' (*LPR*: 40), 'steaming moist red earth' (*LPR*: 37), and even the 'big sleek Devon cattle' are 'dark red like their native soil' (*LPR*: 47). Just as Potter's illustrations help to situate her **animal** characters within what are often very precise geographical locations, so her written text here, with its repeated references to the red stone and soil, situates Pig Robinson's story within a Devon coastal landscape. The fact that Potter weaves so many chromatic references into a story which lacks many colour images suggests that she recognized the important role played by colour in the construction and imaginative experience of her fictional worlds.

Although in her prose Potter often focuses on references to clear primary or secondary colours, the actual execution of the colour-schemes in her illustrations relied on her artistic understanding of the effect achieved by specific paint pigments and their various combinations. This more subtle understanding of colour would later be introduced to her young readers within one of her 'side show' publications, a set of painting books which began with *Peter Rabbit's Painting Book* (1911) and which encourage understanding of how the precise colouring in the books is achieved. **Peter Rabbit** is depicted telling a group of young rabbits that they will need five paints – 'Antwerp Blue, Crimson Lake, Gamboge, Sap Green and Burnt Sienna' – whilst a further note tells them, 'You can mix Blue with the Sienna to make dark Brown' (Taylor 1986: 123). Potter's careful attention to colour also extended to other items of merchandise developed, including the **animal** character 'dolls'. In 1904, Potter was still experimenting with her **Peter Rabbit** doll, and trying to get the colour of his **clothes** right. Here again, we see her awareness of how our perception of colour is influenced by context and surrounding colours, since she writes, 'I don't think the blue & red would have been too bright if the rabbit colour had been quieter' (*L*: 93).

Though a young Potter rejected what she saw as the posturing of the 'yellow butterflies' and Whistler's gallery dressed up in white and yellow, she was herself innately and powerfully sensitive to the impact and effect of colour both within the framed confines of a specific artwork and within the wider contexts in which her artistic creations were experienced and encountered. Like Whistler, Potter was in part a product of the late-Victorian 'colour revolution' and she recognized the vital importance of colour not only in the viewer's imaginative response to an image but also in terms of what we would now call branding. The specific blue of **Peter's** jacket and Potter's insistence on that particular blue being accurately reproduced in all contexts, even beyond the pages of the books in which he appears, is vital in terms of making him such an immediately recognizable and therefore marketable character. Her harnessing of the new colour print technologies, which would enable her colour illustrations to be accurately reproduced in a mass market context, also positions Potter in relation to this moment of change, which saw the beginning of the 'modern technicolour world we live in today' (Ribeyrol 2023: 17). Though within the pages of Potter's little books we often encounter images associated with an older, rural, pre-industrial England, the books themselves are, in many ways, products of modernity.

Z IS FOR ZOO

London Zoological Gardens (also known as Regent's Park Zoo and London Zoo) is the world's oldest scientific zoo. It opened to Fellows of the Zoological Society of London in 1828 and subsequently to the public in 1847. Here on the edge of Regent's Park and just a few miles north of **Beatrix** Potter's Kensington home were 'animals from every corner of the globe' (Charman 2016: 307). The Zoological Gardens, like the **circus**, provided Potter with formative **animal** encounters beyond those offered by the many pets which were kept in the nursery at Bolton Gardens, including access to non-native species. Her experiences at the zoo also feature as subject matter in some of her earliest writing for children, in the form of picture letters sent to child correspondents.

Letters written to Noel Moore in 1895 and 1896 refer to 'new' creatures arriving at the zoo and record the fate of others in a way that suggests both familiarity with the **animals** as well as an interest in their behaviour and welfare. Potter tells Noel about a new giraffe, a new monkey called Jenny and a 'savage' lion who makes 'a great noise' (*LC*: 30, 38). Her written observations are, as usual, accompanied by small pen and ink sketches which help to convey the experience of the visits to Noel, who was aged seven when Potter's first zoo-letter was sent to him. These sketches include self-portraits of Potter feeding buns to both the elephant and a camel (see Figure 12), interactions which suggest that she felt comfortable around even very large and relatively unfamiliar creatures.

Potter's zoo-inspired letters also reveal an early awareness on her part of one of the important functions of anthropomorphism since, though most of the zoo **animals** are presented in a natural way, at one point she turns to anthropomorphization in order to elicit sympathy for a sick creature. In a letter of April 1896, she accompanies the sad news that the big elephant has died with a sketch of the elephant wearing a dressing gown and sitting upright in a chair, with tears rolling down its cheek (*LC*: 38). The anthropomorphized image here functions to help a young reader make

Figure 12 Self-portrait sketches from letter (1895).

an imaginative connection between human and **animal** suffering without recourse to didacticism. In the sketch, three human figures approach, two are rolling giant boxes of pills and one is carrying a bottle of medicine nearly as large as himself, suggesting also the significant levels of human effort engaged in trying to cure the poorly elephant, and thus the importance of caring for our fellow creatures (*LC*: 39).

As with Potter's close study of her pets, these zoo experiences also inform her understanding of **animal** behaviour – not only the quirks and tendencies of different species but also links between humans and **animals**. Sixty years earlier, Charles Darwin had been a regular visitor to the Zoological Gardens and became fascinated by the similarities in the behaviour of an orangutan called Jenny to that of a human child, experiences he would later write about in *The Descent of Man* (1871). Potter, visiting in the 1890s, makes similar observations about a new monkey (also called Jenny), who has 'black hair & a face like a very ugly old woman', and who displays human traits, putting on a pair of gloves and taking a bunch of **keys** to try and 'unlock its cage door' (*LC*: 30). Whilst Darwin's studies at the zoo would feed into the development of his theory of evolution, Potter's own observations can be seen to influence her extremely successful handling of the talking-animals genre and what has been noted as her tendency to 'blur the animal/human distinction' (Cosslett 2006: 151).

The Zoological Gardens, along with the menagerie of pets kept by the Potter siblings, also provided Potter with opportunities to study **animals** for the purposes of developing anatomically accurate drawings, and once she began to work on the illustrated *Tales* for Warne, the zoo proved to be a valuable study resource. Potter checked her owl drawings for end paper designs against the owls at the zoo and relied on the opportunity to study magpies there when it came to drawing Dr. Maggotty in the *Pie and the Patty-Pan* (*L*: 73, 116). Her sketchbook reveals a careful scientific approach to drawing even this minor **animal** character. There are sketches of a magpie from a variety of angles along with detailed notes as to the bird's appearance and precise colouring: its 'Brown black eye' and 'nose a little hookier than jackdaw', its tail 'more than half' the bird's overall length, and parts of its feathers 'very blue' while others are 'green' (*H*: 170). This detailed observation of the bird derived from her zoo studies clearly informs the beautiful illustration of Dr. Maggotty in the book, which – as he is not presented clothed – could almost be an ornithological drawing from a bird guidebook (*PP*: 45).

The zoo also proved to be an important study resource when Potter began to reach out to her expanding global readership with a story featuring non-native British **animals**. *Timmy Tiptoes* is a response to Potter's awareness of her growing popularity around the world and here she set out to tell, for the first time, a story about **animals** which were not native to Britain's shores – such as grey squirrels, chipmunks and bears. In preparing the illustrations for this book Potter once again turned to London Zoo – this time to study and draw the 'American Black bear' which makes an appearance towards the end of the story (*L*: 256). Here too, her close study of the **animal** at the zoo is suggested by a note added to the manuscript which observes that this bear has 'a smooth coat, like a sealskin coat' (*H*: 208).

More important than these localized examples of the ways in which experiences at the zoo inform Potter's work though are the insights this gives us into what growing up in London in the late nineteenth century meant to a young and intellectually voracious Potter. When we think about the places which inform her work, we tend to prioritize the **Lake District** and, to a lesser extent, Scotland, as having had the most significant impact on her development as a children's writer, but it is important to recognize the ways in which a childhood and early adulthood spent in Kensington also helped to shape Potter's intellectual and imaginative development. The tendency to dismiss the influence of London has largely been the result of Potter's own comments in a biographical note supplied later in life for the *Horn Book*, in which she famously asserted:

> My brother and I were born in London because my father was a lawyer there. But our descent – our interests and our joy was in the north country. It is immaterial to give the address of my unloved birthplace.

It was hit by shrapnel in the last **war**; now I am rather pleased to hear it is no more!

(*A*: 213)

In the light of Potter's own apparent rejection of the autobiographical significance of London, Potter scholars have tended to play down its shaping influence. However, though London may have been a place where Potter never entirely felt at home and which she often actively disliked, its environs did influence her in important ways.

Psychogeography has come recently to have a very specific application in relation to experiences of urban walking and, in particular, to certain kinds of politicized acts of walking which change our relationship with the environment. This application draws on a history of urban pedestrianism which identifies Thomas De Quincey, who walked London's labyrinthine streets in the company of streetwalkers, as an important forerunner. De Quincey's experiences are very far removed from Potter's own daylight excursions around London, which were usually undertaken in a carriage or, sometimes, via the London Underground and in the company of a chaperone. However, in its more fundamental meaning, the concept of psychogeography can help us to think about Potter and her relationship with London in different ways. Merlin Coverley cites the early definition of psychogeography by French philosopher and filmmaker, Guy Debord, as 'the study of the precise laws and specific effects of the geographical environment […] on the emotions and behaviour of individuals', adding that this functions as a means of 'calibrating the behavioural impact of place' (2018: 14). Such an idea is certainly relevant here, in focusing our attention on the ways in which Potter's engagement with the geographical environment of London, and more specifically the environs of Kensington, helped to 'calibrate' her intellectual and imaginative life.

Britain's imperial position in the late nineteenth century meant that scientists, entrepreneurs and intellectually curious members of the nouveau-riche were in a position to gather **animals**, plants and cultural artefacts from Britain's vast empire and put together extraordinary collections for the purposes of study. The problematic nature of such acts of colonial acquisition is of course now recognized, but these publicly available collections had an important impact on the rise of amateur scientific study in the late-Victorian period. Potter's childhood home in the wealthy Royal Borough of Kensington and Chelsea was situated in close proximity to a number of gardens, galleries and museums which housed major global natural and cultural history collections, and for Potter – denied as she was the more advanced University education open to men – these sites would become crucial. While her brother Bertram was sent off to boarding school at the age of eleven and then (albeit abortively) to Oxford University, the young **Beatrix** was left at home to continue the sort of education which was delivered to upper-middle-class girls via a governess. She extended her education, however, through auto-didactic strategies which were in part inspired and facilitated by the opportunities offered by her residence within this culturally rich area of London.

As her **journal** and early letters indicate, Potter spent a great deal of her time visiting not only the zoo, Kew Gardens and many of London's art galleries, but also other places which provided opportunities for study and which were located a comparatively short distance from her home, including the British Library, South Kensington Museum (now the Victoria & Albert Museum) and the Natural History Museum. The latter was to be a 'cathedral to nature' and the South Kensington Museum, which Potter's own grandfather, Edmund Potter, had helped to found, was described by its first director as a 'schoolroom for everyone'. Though such claims smack of late-Victorian hubris, in a sense both did become advanced schoolrooms for Potter or, perhaps more accurately, a kind of open university. It is certainly abundantly clear from her private writings that she visited these sites not as a tourist but as someone intent on learning from the extraordinary collections housed there. For a young woman with a deeply enquiring mind but also subject to late-Victorian expectations about woman's education, these open access collections offered unique opportunities for self-guided learning.

A **journal** entry for January 1896 not only shows clearly that Potter did utilize the museums in this way but also reveals her private frustrations that these places, which were intended to encourage learning, did not facilitate this more effectively. She records studying insect labels at the Natural History Museum but, being in 'want of advice' and not in a good temper, worked herself into 'indignation about that august Institution' which has 'reached such a pitch of propriety that one cannot ask the simplest question' (J: 415). Despite these experiences, Potter persisted in her wide-ranging and eclectic studies, and her access to these spaces undoubtedly helped her to develop the scientific and scholarly understanding which underpins virtually all her undertakings, including her later writing for children.

Potter's experience of working at these sites in fact began to improve after she became a published author. When she turned to the costume archive at the South Kensington Museum to study eighteenth-century embroidered **clothes** in preparation for her drawings in *The Tailor of Gloucester*, she wrote to Norman Warne to say 'I have been looking at them for a long time in an inconvenient dark corner of goldsmith's court', but the 'clerk says I could have any article put on a table in one of the offices; which will be most convenient' (*L*: 73). The clerk in question was a museum trainee who later recalled having been called to the office of the Head Curator and told: 'You see the young lady just entering the door. She is Miss Potter who writes children's books. I want you to make her your special care'; the trainee was then introduced to Potter as 'your own special attendant' and a room put aside for her private use (*H*: 118). The anecdote suggests that museum staff treated a well-known and popular children's author, who was studying the collection for professional reasons, very differently to the young woman undertaking studies in an amateur capacity and who was made to feel unable to 'ask the simplest question' (*J*: 415).

Despite Potter's later allusions to her 'unloved' home, there is some evidence that the environs of Kensington also played a more important role in shaping her early imaginative life than has tended to be acknowledged. In a letter written in 1921, nearly a decade after Potter had cut ties with the landscapes of her childhood almost completely, she writes in a surprisingly moving way of her memories of this place:

> I can remember 'Old Kensington'; when the Hammersmith road was deep in summer dust & winter mud, under the high brick wall of Kensington Gardens [...] I have seen Jack in the Green and the sweeps & milk maids **dancing** on May day somewhere near Kensington Square; where there was a slum on the north side of the cabbage gardens that stretched down to Fulham; where Miss Thackeray's Dolly Vanborough and I walked with our nursemaids. We were matter of fact little people. We believed in **fairies** and the sweeps.
>
> (*L*: 272)

The allusion to Dolly Vanborough, the central character in Anne Thackeray's popular novel, *Old Kensington* (1873), is significant since this book offers a loving evocation of the Kensington of Potter's own early childhood, where the lanes were 'white with blossom in spring or golden with the yellow London sunsets that blazed beyond the cabbage-fields' and where, in Kensington Gardens, 'elms spread their shade, and birds chirruped and children played behind them' (Thackeray 1873: 3). Potter's passage evokes a similar and apparently shared nostalgia for this place, on the outskirts of the metropolis, where the old rural traditions and rituals still held sway, including the annual dressing up of someone in foliage to play the part of 'Jack in the Green' in the May Day procession.

Potter's passage presents a similarly nostalgic vision of Kensington to that depicted in Thackeray's novel, but her own handling of place weaves together the everyday with the magical in a typically Potteresque way, asserting that as a child of this place she believed in both **fairies** and sweeps. Along with the Scottish nanny, who told her stories of **fairies** in the nursery at Bolton Gardens, the wider cultural context of this London of Potter's childhood was itself inflected by the late-Victorian cult of the **fairy** which had emerged in art and literature. As Nicola Bown suggests, '**Fairies** were everywhere in nineteenth-century culture: in the nursery, certainly, but also in the parlour or drawing room, on the stage and on the walls of annual exhibitions' and were, she argues, a response to the forces of progress, modernity and the rise of the age of machines (Bown 2001: 1). Whilst Potter's own imaginative engagement with the idea of **fairies** tended to be rather different from that more generally found in Victorian art and literature, it is important to recognize that her earliest encounters with **fairy** tropes and stories occurred primarily in London rather than in the holiday landscapes of her childhood, via the nursery, through exposure to Victorian art work, and as a result of early reading. Indeed, Charles Kingsley's *The Water-Babies* (1863), which Potter recalls enjoying as a child (Lear 2007: 30), is set in London and features a chimney sweep who falls into a river and is transformed into a magical 'water-baby', thus bringing together the realist and magical elements which Potter perceives as constituting integral elements of her childhood imagination.

Ironically then, 'z', rather than being about endings, takes us back to the question of beginnings and to the impact of the 'geographical environment' of Kensington on Potter's work. It was here that she first encountered many of the foundational elements which would engage her imagination, and which were already being rehearsed in late-Victorian art and literature. Alongside this, the proximity of the zoo and botanical gardens, as well as museums, libraries and galleries, provided Potter with relatively easy and regular access to art, science, culture and knowledge well beyond the confines of learning which would normally be experienced by a woman of her class in the late-Victorian period. Understandably perhaps, many accounts of Potter's development as an artist and a writer have focused on the **Lake District**, but we should not underestimate the formative importance of London – and in particular the environs of Kensington – on her early intellectual and imaginative development, and in shaping the writer and artist she would become.

WORKS CITED

Aesop's Fables (1874), ill. E. Griset, London, Paris and New York: Cassell Petter and Galpin.
Armitt, L. and S. Brewster (2023), *Gothic Travel through Haunted Landscapes: Climates of Fear*, London: Anthem Press.
Assael, B. (2005), *The Circus and Victorian Society*, Charlottesville: University of Virginia Press.
Auden, W. H. and L. MacNeice (1936), *Letters from Iceland*, London: Faber and Faber.
Bahram, M. and T. Netherway (2022), 'Fungi as Mediators Linking Organisms and Ecosystems', *FEMS Microbiology Reviews*, 46 (2): 1–16.
Bakhtin, M. ([1965] 1984), *Rabelais and His World*, Bloomington: Indiana University Press.
Barbauld, A. ([1781] 1864), *Hymns in Prose for Children*, London: Murray.
'Beatrix Potter's Gifts to the Nation' (1944), *The Times*, 17 February, 5–6.
Bernheimer, M. (1971), 'Mrs. Tiggy-Winkle, Jemima Puddle-Duck and Royal Ballet', *Los Angeles Times*, 13 June.
Bown, N. (2001), *Fairies in Nineteenth-Century Art and Literature*, Cambridge: Cambridge University Press.
Bradshaw, P. (2007), 'Review of *Miss Potter*', *The Guardian*, 5 January. Available online: https://www.theguardian.com/film/2007/jan/05/drama.romance (accessed 30 May 2024).
Bradshaw, P. (2018), 'Peter Rabbit Review – in a Hole with James Corden's Unfunny Bunny', *The Guardian*, 15 March. Available online: https://www.theguardian.com/film/2018/mar/15/peter-rabbit-review-james-corden-beatrix-potter (accessed 27 November 2024).
Brontë, C. ([1847] 1966), *Jane Eyre*, ed. Q. D. Leavis, London: Penguin.
Brontë, E. ([1847] 1985), *Wuthering Heights*, ed. D. Daiches, London: Penguin.
Buckley, N. and J. Buckley (2007), *Walking with Beatrix Potter*, London: Lincoln.
Buell, L. (2014), 'Environmental Writing for Children: A Selected Reconnaissance of Heritages, Emphases, Horizons', in G. Garrard (ed.), *The Oxford Handbook of Ecocriticism*, 408–22, Oxford: Oxford University Press.
Burney, F. (1842), *Diary and Letters of Madame D'Arblay*, ed. C. Barrett, vol 1, 1778–80, London: Henry Colburn.
Burney, F. (1889), *The Early Diary of Frances Burney, 1768–1778*, ed. A. R. Ellis, London: George Bell and Sons.
Butler, C. (2023), *British Children's Literature in Japanese Culture: Wonderlands and Looking-Glasses*, London: Bloomsbury.

Works Cited

Butler, J. (1990), *Gender Trouble: Feminism and the Subversion of Identity*, London: Routledge.

Carpenter, H. (1989), 'Excessively Impertinent Bunnies: The Subversive Element in Beatrix Potter', in G. Avery and J. Briggs (eds), *Children and Their Books: A Celebration of the Work of Iona and Peter Opie*, 271–98, Oxford: Oxford University Press.

Carter, A. (1979), *The Bloody Chamber*, London: Vintage.

Carter, A. (1984), *Nights at the Circus*, London: Vintage.

Chandler, K. (2005), 'Beatrix Potter's Fairy Rings and Fungi', *River Gazette*, December–January, 12.

Charman, I. (2016), *The Zoo: The Wild and Wonderful Tale of the Founding of London Zoo*, London: Penguin.

Coates, P. (2015), 'Creatures Enshrined: Wild Animals as Bearers of Heritage', *Past & Present*, 226 (10): 272–98.

Cohen, N. (2020), *The Real Beatrix Potter*, Yorkshire: White Owl.

Coleridge, S. T. (1997), *The Complete Poems*, ed. W. Keach, London: Penguin.

Cooper, G. C. (2007), *Beatrix Potter's Lake District*, London: Warne.

Copeland, M. W. (2004), 'The Wild and Wild Animal Characters in the Ecofeminist Novels of Beatrix Potter and Gene Stratton-Porter', in S. I. Dobrin and K. B. Kidd (eds), *Wild Things: Children's Culture and Ecocriticism*, 71–81, Detroit: Wayne State University Press.

Cosslett, T. (2006), *Talking Animals in British Children's Fiction, 1786–1914*, Aldershot: Ashgate.

Coverley, M. (2018), *Psychogeography*, Harpenden, Herts: Oldcastle Books.

Craik, M. (1871), *Little Sunshine's Holiday: A Picture from Life*, London: Sampson Low, Son, and Marston.

Crisp, C. (2010), 'Peter and the Wolf/Tales of Beatrix Potter, Royal Opera House London: Dancing Pigs Whet the Appetite – for Supper', *Financial Times*, 21 December. Available online: https://www.ft.com/content/d621b540-0d28-11e0-82ff-00144feabdc0 (accessed July 2024).

Dahl, R. ([1976] 2009), 'Writing Children's Books', *The Writer*, 16 September, 55.

Daniel, C. (2009), *Voracious Children: Who Eats Whom in Children's Literature*, Abingdon and New York: Routledge.

Davies, H. and C. Pemberton-Piggot (1988), *Beatrix Potter's Lakeland*, London and New York: Warne.

De Sélincourt, E. (1933), *Dorothy Wordsworth: A Biography*, Oxford: Clarendon Press.

Deakin, R. (2008), *Wildwood: A Journey through Trees*, London: Penguin.

DEFRA (2019), *Landscapes Review*. Available online: https://assets.publishing.service.gov.uk/government/uploads/system/uploads/attachment_data/file/833726/landscapes-review-final-report.pdf (accessed 30 May 2023).

Dennison, M. (2017), *'Over the Hills and Far Away': The Life of Beatrix Potter*, London: Head of Zeus.

Denyer, S. (2000), *Beatrix Potter: At Home in the Lake District*, London: Lincoln.

Dickens, C. ([1854] 1969), *Hard Times*, ed. D. Craig, London: Penguin.

Dobrin, A. (1977), *Peter Rabbit's Natural Foods Cookbook*, New York and London: Warne.

Works Cited

Ebert, R. (1971), 'Peter Rabbit and the Tales of Beatrix Potter', *Chicago Sun-Times*, 19 November. Available online: https://www.rogerebert.com/reviews/peter-rabbit-and-tales-of-beatrix-potter-1971 (accessed 20 July 2024).

'England Visitor Attractions Latest' (2023), *VisitBritain/VisitEngland*. Available online: https://www.visitbritain.org/annual-survey-visits-visitor-attractions-latest-results (accessed 30 May 2023).

Evangelista, S. and C. Ribeyrol (2023), 'Colour for Colour's Sake', in C. Ribeyrol, M. Winterbottom and M. Hewitson (eds), *Colour Revolution: Victorian Art, Fashion & Design*, 173–95, Oxford: Ashmolean Museum, University of Oxford.

Flood, A. (2014), 'Ramsey Campbell and Stephen King on Why Rupert Bear and Bambi Are Truly Terrifying', *The Guardian*, 31 October. Available online: https://www.theguardian.com/books/2014/oct/31/ramsey-campbell-stephen-king-horror-novel-rupert-bear-bambi (accessed 20 September 2024).

Flood, A. (2018), 'Beatrix Potter Would Not Have Liked Peter Rabbit Film', *The Guardian*, 9 March. Available online: https://www.theguardian.com/books/2018/mar/09/beatrix-potter-would-not-have-liked-peter-rabbit-film-biographer-james-corden (accessed 27 November 2024).

Fortey, R. (2021), 'Miss Potter, the Mycologist', in A. Bilclough (ed.), *Beatrix Potter: Drawn to Nature*, 88–91, London: V&A Publishing.

Fowler, C. (2020), *Green Unpleasant Land: Creative Responses to Rural England's Colonial Associations*, Leeds: Peepal Tree.

French, P. (2007), 'Review of *Miss Potter*', *The Guardian*, 7 January. Available online: https://www.theguardian.com/film/2007/jan/07/drama.documentary#:~:text=It%20is%20that%20the%20movie,the%20nature%20of%20her%20art (accessed 30 May 2023).

Freud, S. ([2014] 2017), 'The Uncanny', in J. Rivkin and M. Ryan (eds), *Literary Theory: An Anthology*, 717–43, Oxford: Blackwell.

Gilbert, S. and S. Gubar (1979), *The Madwoman in the Attic: The Women Writer and the Nineteenth-Century Literary Imagination*, Yale: Yale University Press.

Gilbert, W. S. (1932), *Complete Operas*, London: Random House.

Goldthwaite, J. (1996), *The Natural History of Make-Believe: A Guide to the Principal Works of Britain, Europe, and America*, Oxford: Oxford University Press.

Gombrich, E. H. (1996), *The Story of Art*, London: Phaidon.

Grace, M., J. Griffiths and C. Hughes (2021), 'Nature Literacy: Rethinking How We Teach about Nature in Secondary School Science', *School Science Review*, 102 (381): 15–20.

Grahame, K. ([1908] 1994), *The Wind in the Willows*, London: Penguin.

Green, R. L. (1965), *Kipling and the Children*, London: Elek.

Greene, G. ([1971] 1999), *A Sort of Life*, London: Vintage.

Gristwood, S. (2021), *The Story of Beatrix Potter: Her Enchanting Work and Surprising Life*, Swindon: National Trust Books.

Guest, K. (2017), 'Well Done Unesco for Honouring the Culture of the Lake District', *The Guardian*, 15 July. Available online: https://www.theguardian.com/books/booksblog/2017/jul/15/unesco-world-heritage-site-lake-district-culture-wordsworth-beatrix-potter-ransome#:~:text=Well%20done%20Unesco%20for%20honouring,District%20%7C%20William%20Wordsworth%20%7C%20The%20Guardian (accessed 30 May 2023).

Works Cited

Hahn, D. (2015), *The Oxford Companion to Children's Literature*, 2nd edn., Oxford: Oxford University Press.

Hair, D. (1981), *Domestic and Heroic in Tennyson's Poetry*, Toronto: University of Toronto Press.

Harper, S. (2011), *British Film Culture in the 1970s: The Boundaries of Pleasure*, Edinburgh: Edinburgh University Press.

Harris, J. C. (1881), *Uncle Remus: His Songs and His Sayings*, New York: D. Appleton.

Harris, J. C. (1883), *Nights with Uncle Remus*, Boston, MA, and New York: Houghton Mifflin.

Heelis, H. B. (1939), 'The Last Will and Testament of Helen Beatrix Heelis', 31 March. Available online: https://www.arnisonheelis.co.uk/news/beatrix-potter/ (accessed 30 November 2024).

Hermansson, C. (2009), *Bluebeard: A Reader's Guide to the English Tradition*, Jackson: University Press of Mississippi.

Hobbs, A. S. (1987), 'Flora and Fauna, Fungi and Fossils', in J. Taylor, J. I. Whalley, A. S. Hobbs and E. M. Battrick (eds), *Beatrix Potter 1866-1943: The Artist and Her World*, 71-94, London: Warne and The National Trust.

Hobbs, A. S. (1989), *Beatrix Potter's Art*, London: Warne.

Hobbs, A. S. (1992), 'Beatrix Potter's Scientific Art', in E. Jay, M. Noble and A. S. Hobbs (eds), *A Victorian Naturalist: Beatrix Potter's Drawings from the Armitt Collection*, 139-81, London: Warne.

Hobbs, A. S. and J. I. Whalley (1985), *Beatrix Potter: The V&A Collection*, London: The Victoria and Albert Museum and Frederick Warne.

Hobbs, A. S., J. I. Whalley and J. Taylor (1987), 'The Little Books', in J. Taylor, J. I. Whalley, A. S. Hobbs and E. M. Battrick (eds), *Beatrix Potter 1866-1943: The Artist and Her World*, 107-68, London: Warne and The National Trust.

Hollindale, P. (1999), *Aesop in the Shadows*, London: Beatrix Potter Society.

Humble, N. (2014), 'Liniment Cake, Beavers, Buttered Eggs: Children Cooking; Cooking [for] Children', in B. Carrington and J. Harding (eds), *Feast or Famine? Food and Children's Literature*, 52-68, Cambridge: Cambridge Scholars Publishing.

Huxtable, S.-A., C. Fowler, C. Kefalas and E. Slocombe, eds (2020), *Interim Report on the Connections between Colonialism and Properties Now in the Care of the National Trust, Including Links with Historic Slavery*, Swindon: National Trust.

Jamie, K. (2005), *Findings*, London: Sort of Books.

Kalnay, E. K. (2019), 'Beatrix Potter's Mycological Aesthetics', *The Oxford Literary Review*, 41 (2): 160-84.

Keeling, K. K. and S. T. Pollard (2020), *Tablelands: Food in Children's Literature*, Jackson: University Press of Mississippi.

Kelly, L. (2021), 'Beatrix Potter's Brutal Tales Terrified Me, Says Novelist', *The Sunday Times*, 21 October. Available online: https://www.thetimes.com/culture/books/article/beatrix-potters-brutal-tales-terrified-me-says-novelist-w2bxz356q (accessed 29 September 2024).

Works Cited

Kelly, M. (2022), *The Women Who Saved the English Countryside*, New Haven, CT: Yale University Press.

Kerslake, L. (2021), 'Environmental Imagination and Wonder in Beatrix Potter', in D. Villanueva-Romero, L. Kerslake and C. Flys-Junquera (eds), *Imaginative Ecologies: Inspiring Change through the Humanities*, 67–80, Leiden: Brill.

Knight, L. (2023), 'Beatrix Potter's Peter Rabbit Story Originated in African Folktales, Expert Argues', *The Guardian*, 19 May. Available online: https://www.theguardian.com/books/2023/may/19/origin-of-beatrix-potter-tales-african-folklore-brer-rabbit (accessed 20 July 2024).

Kutzer, M. D. (2003), *Beatrix Potter: Writing in Code*, New York and London: Routledge.

Lake District National Park Partnership (2015), *Nomination of the English Lake District for Inscription on the World Heritage List*. Available online: file:///C:/Users/User/Downloads/422rev-2171-Nomination%20Text-en.pdf (accessed 30 May 2023).

Lane, M. (1946), *The Tale of Beatrix Potter: A Biography*, London and New York: Warne.

Laws, E. (2021), 'A Natural Storyteller', in A. Bilclough (ed.), *Beatrix Potter: Drawn to Nature*, 94–131, London: V&A Publishing.

Lear, L. (2007), *Beatrix Potter: A Life in Nature*, London: Penguin.

Ledger, S. (2007), 'The New Woman and Feminist Fictions', in G. Marshall (ed.), *The Cambridge Companion to the Fin-de-Siècle*, 153–68, Cambridge: Cambridge University Press.

Lefebure, M. (1964), *The English Lake District*, London: Batsford.

Linder, L. (1966), 'The Code-Writing', in L. Linder (ed.), *The Journal of Beatrix Potter 1881–1897*, xvii–xxiii, London and New York: Warne.

Lindsay, D. W., ed. (1993), *The Beggar's Opera and Other Eighteenth-Century Plays*, London: Everyman.

Lockhart, J. G. (1823), *Ancient Spanish Ballads: Historical and Romantic*, Edinburgh: Blackwood.

Lorimer, J. (2007), 'Nonhuman Charisma', *Environment and Planning D: Society and Space*, 25 (5): 911–32.

Lovell-Smith, R. (2013), 'Of Mice and Men: Beatrix Potter's Bluebeard Story, *Sister Anne*', *Children's Literature Association Quarterly*, 38 (1): 4–25.

MacDonald, R. K. (1986), *Beatrix Potter*, Boston, MA: Twayne.

MacFarlane, L. H. (2021), 'Living Nature: Beatrix Potter in the Lake District', in A. Bilclough (ed.), *Beatrix Potter: Drawn to Nature*, 139–65, London: V&A Publishing.

Macfarlane, R. and J. Morris (2017), *The Lost Words: A Spell Book*, London: Hamish Hamilton.

Mackey, M. (1998), *The Case of Peter Rabbit: Changing Conditions of Literature for Children*, New York and London: Garland Publishing.

Mackey, M. (2002), 'The Mediation and Multiplication of Peter Rabbit', in M. Mackey (ed.), *Beatrix Potter's Peter Rabbit: A Children's Classic at 100*, 173–88, Lanham, MD, and London: The Children's Literature Association and The Scarecrow Press, Inc.

Works Cited

Martineau, H. ([1861] 2004), 'Lights of the English Lake District', in M. R. Hill (ed.), *An Independent Woman's Lake District Writings*, 423–70, New York: Humanity Books.

Mead, R. (2018), 'The Puerile Emptiness of "Peter Rabbit"', *The New Yorker*, 21 February. Available online: https://www.newyorker.com/culture/cultural-comment/the-puerile-emptiness-of-peter-rabbit (accessed 27 November 2024).

Mellor, A. K. (1993), *Romanticism and Gender*, London and New York: Routledge.

Mendelson, E., ed. (1996), *W. H. Auden: Prose*, vol 1, 1926–38, London: Faber and Faber.

Miss Potter (2006), [Film] Dir. Chris Noonan, UK: Momentum Pictures.

Monbiot, G. (2017), 'The Lake District's World Heritage Site Status Is a Betrayal of the Living World', *The Guardian*, 11 July. Available online: https://www.theguardian.com/commentisfree/2017/jul/11/lake-district-world-heritage-site-sheep (accessed 30 May 2023).

Monbiot, G. (2023), *Regenesis: Feeding the World without Devouring the Planet*, London: Penguin.

Morse, J. C. (1982), 'Introduction', in J. C. Morse (ed.), *Beatrix Potter's Americans: Selected Letters*, ix–xvi, Boston, MA: Horn Book Inc.

Morton, T. (2010), *The Ecological Thought*, Cambridge, MA: Harvard University Press.

Murphy, P. (2019), *Reconceiving Nature: Ecofeminism in Late Victorian Women's Poetry*, Columbia: University of Missouri.

Newson, K. (2021), 'Peter Rabbit: The Design Evolution of a Blue-Jacketed Rabbit', *Penguin Articles*, 19 September. Available online: https://www.penguin.co.uk/articles/2021/09/peter-rabbit-brand-evolution (accessed 20 July 2024).

Nicholson, N. (1963), *Portrait of the Lakes*, London: Hale.

Noble, M. (1992), 'Beatrix Potter and Charles McIntosh, Naturalists', in E. Jay, M. Noble and A. S. Hobbs (eds), *A Victorian Naturalist: Beatrix Potter's Drawings from the Armitt Collection*, 55–138, London: Warne.

'Obituary: Beatrix Potter' (1943), *The Guardian*, 23 December. Available online: https://www.newspapers.com/article/the-guardian-1943-obituary-for-beatrix-p/74820471/?locale=en-GB (accessed 20 September 2024).

Opie, I. and P. Opie (1997), *The Oxford Dictionary of Nursery Rhymes*, Oxford: Oxford University Press.

Packham, J. (2019), 'The Gothic Coast: Boundaries, Belonging, and Coastal Community in Contemporary British Fiction', *Critique: Studies in Contemporary Fiction*, 60 (2): 205–21.

Page, J. W. (2012), '"The Lonely Hills": Beatrix Potter, William Wordsworth, and the Lakeland Landscape', in R. Gravil (ed.), *Grasmere 2012: Selected Papers from the Wordsworth Summer Conference*, 87–103, Penrith, CA: Humanities E-Books.

Page, J. W. and E. L. Smith (2021), *Women, Literature, and the Arts of the Countryside in Early Twentieth-Century England*, Cambridge: Cambridge University Press.

Parker, C. (2023), 'Beatrix Potter Experts Challenge Claim She Stole from African Folklore', *The Sunday Times*, 26 May. Available online: https://www.thetimes.

com/article/beatrix-potter-experts-challenge-claim-she-stole-from-african-folklore-xs7s3j73j (accessed 16 October 2023).
Parker, E. (2020), *The Forest and the EcoGothic: The Deep Dark Woods in the Popular Imagination*, London: Palgrave.
Paston-Williams, S. (1991), *Beatrix Potter's Country Cooking*, London: Warne.
Paul, L. (2002), 'Beatrix Potter and John Everett Millais: Reproductive Technologies and Coolhunting', in M. Mackey (ed.), *Beatrix Potter's Peter Rabbit: A Children's Classic at 100*, 53–75, Lanham, MD, and London: The Children's Literature Association and The Scarecrow Press, Inc.
Perrault, C. (2009), *The Complete Fairy Tales*, trans. C. Betts, Oxford: Oxford University Press.
Peter Rabbit (2018), [Film] Dir. Will Gluck, USA: Sony.
Peter Rabbit 2: The Runaway (2021), [Film] Dir. Will Gluck, USA: Sony.
Raine, K. (1975), *The Land Unknown*, New York: George Braziller.
Ranlett, J. (1983), '"Checking Nature's Desecration": Late-Victorian Environmental Organization', *Victorian Studies*, 26 (2): 197–222.
Ribeyrol, C., M. Winterbottom and M. Hewitson, eds (2023), *Colour Revolution: Victorian Art, Fashion & Design*, 173–95, Oxford: Ashmolean Museum, University of Oxford.
Riley, J. (2006), 'The Art of "Miss Potter"', *Back Stage West* 13 (51). Available online: https://www.backstage.com/magazine/article/art-miss-potter-35637/ (accessed 26 May 2024).
Robison, R. (1984), 'The Journal of Beatrix Potter', *Prose Studies*, 7 (3): 232–9.
Ruskin, J. ([1876] 1908), 'The Extension of Railways in the Lake District: A Protest', in E. T. Cook and A. Wedderburn (eds), *The Works of John Ruskin*, vol 34, 137 43, London: George Allan.
Sabor, P. and L. E. Troide (2001), 'Introduction', in P. Sabor and L. E. Troide (eds), *Frances Burney: Journal and Letters*, xiii–xxii, London: Penguin.
Said, E. W. (1993), *Culture and Imperialism*, London: Vintage.
Shakespeare, W. (1954), *The Tempest*, ed. F. Kermode, London: Methuen.
Shelley, P. B. (1904), *The Complete Poetical Works of Shelley*, ed. T. Hutchinson, Oxford: Clarendon.
Shorter, C. (1908), *The Brontës: Life and Letters*, London: Hodder and Stoughton.
Slothower, J. and J. Susina (2009), 'Delicious Supplements: Literary Cookbooks as Additives to Children's Texts', in K. K. Keeling and S. T. Pollard (eds), *Critical Approaches to Food in Children's Literature*, 21–38, Abingdon and New York: Routledge.
Stone, W. and W. E. Cram (1902), *American Animals*, New York: Doubleday, Page.
Tales of Beatrix Potter (1971), [Film] Dir. Reginald Mills, UK: GW Films and EMI Elstree.
Taylor, J. (1986), *Beatrix Potter: Artist, Storyteller and Countrywoman*, London: Warne.
Taylor, J. E. and I. N. Gregory (2022), *Deep Mapping the Literary Lake District: A Geographical Text Analysis*, Lewisburg, PA: Bucknell University Press.
Tennyson, A. (1880), *The Works of Alfred Tennyson*, London: Kegan Paul.

Works Cited

Thackeray, A. (1873), *Old Kensington*, London: Smith, Elder.
The World of Peter Rabbit (2022a), *Peter's Nature Walk*, London: Puffin Books.
The World of Peter Rabbit (2022b), *Tales from the Countryside*, London: Puffin Books.
The World of Peter Rabbit (2022c), *The Big Outdoors: Sticker Activity Book*, London: Puffin Books.
The World of Peter Rabbit and Friends (1992–1998), [TV Programme], BBC.
Thompson, I. (2010), *The English Lakes: A History*, London and New York: Bloomsbury.
Twain, M. (1883), *Life on the Mississippi*, London: Chatto and Windus.
Urry, J. (1995), *Consuming Places*, London: Routledge.
Wagner, E. (2009), 'Peter Rabbit Blazed a Trail Still Well Trod', *The Times*, 23 December. Available online: https://www.thetimes.com/article/peter-rabbit-blazed-a-trail-still-well-trod-c9zdfx2c6nk (accessed 5 December 2024).
Wallace, G. (2013), 'Beatrix Potter (1866–1943) in Japan', in H. Cortazzi (ed.), *Britain and Japan: Biographical Portraits*, vol 8, 394–402, Leiden: Brill.
Walton, J. K. (2013), 'Setting the Scene', in J. K. Walton and J. Wood (eds), *The Making of a Cultural Landscape: The English Lake District as Tourist Destination, 1750-2010*, 31–48, Surrey: Ashgate.
Watling, R. (2000), 'Helen Beatrix Potter', *The Linnean*, 16 (1): 24–31.
Whalley, J. I. and A. S. Hobbs (1987), 'Fantasy, Rhymes, Fairy Tales and Fables', in J. Taylor, J. I. Whalley, A. S. Hobbs and E. M. Battrick (eds), *Beatrix Potter 1866–1943: The Artist and Her World*, 49–70, London: Warne and The National Trust.
Wordsworth, D. (2008), *The Grasmere and Alfoxden Journals*, ed. P. Woof, Oxford: Oxford University Press.
Wordsworth, W. (1953), *The Poetical Works of Wordsworth*, ed. T. Hutchinson, Oxford: Oxford University Press.
Wordsworth, W. (2004), *Guide to the Lakes*, ed. E. de Sélincourt, London: Frances Lincoln.
Yoshida, S. (2002), 'Peter Rabbit in Japan and My Approach to Beatrix Potter's World', in M. Mackey (ed.), *Beatrix Potter's Peter Rabbit: A Children's Classic at 100*, 189–95, Lanham, MD, and London: The Children's Literature Association and The Scarecrow Press, Inc.
Zobel Marshall, E. (2019), *American Trickster: Trauma, Tradition and Brer Rabbit*, New York and London: Rowman & Littlefield.
Zobel Marshall, E. (2023), 'Beatrix Potter's Famous Tales Are Rooted in Stories Told by Enslaved Africans – but She Was Very Quiet about Their Origins', *The Conversation*, 19 May. Available online: https://theconversation.com/beatrix-potters-famous-tales-are-rooted-in-stories-told-by-enslaved-africans-but-she-was-very-quiet-about-their-origins-202274 (accessed 20 August 2024).

INDEX

Aesop's Fables 138, 140, 174, 180, 181
aesthetes, the 186–7
American books and authors 62–4
American correspondents and readers 5, 6, 61–7, 107, 150, 195
animal/human relations 12–14, 63, 84, 93, 171, 194
   nonhuman charisma 8
Anthropocene 171–2
anthropomorphism
   Potter's treatment of 10–11, 12–13, 49–55, 139, 143, 193
Appley Dapply's Nursery Rhymes 100
Arnold, Matthew 68
Assael, Brenda 54, 56, 57, 59, 60
Auden, W. H. 2, 90
Austen, Jane 114, 132, 133

Bakhtin, Mikhail (*see also* carnivalesque) 59, 60
Bannerman, Helen 143
Barbauld, Anna 101, 145–6, 148–9
Beatrix Potter Society, The 143
Birch, Reginald B. 27
Blyton, Enid 40, 146
Bonham Carter, Helena 16
Bown, Nicola 199
Bradshaw, Peter 49, 124
British Mycological Society 96
Brontë, Charlotte 129, 188
Brontë, Emily 128
Brooke, Rupert 175
Buell, Lawrence 11, 50
Burke, Edmund 163
Burnett, Frances Hodgson 27
Burney, Fanny 78–82
Butler, Catherine 67
Butler, Judith 55

Camfield Place, Hertfordshire 5, 153
carnivalesque 36, 59–60

Carpenter, Humphrey 1–2, 25, 77, 81, 180, 181
Carroll, Lewis 1, 2, 27, 62
Carson, Rachel 5
Carter, Angela 55–6, 85
Cecily Parsley's Nursery Rhymes 65
Chandler, Kate 98
Christmas cards 37–8, 72
Christmas stories 14, 34, 35, 64, 173–4, 176
class, social
   in Potter's life 18, 56, 80, 108, 197, 199
   in Potter's writing 41, 56, 169, 182
coded writing 16–17, 23, 70, 75–8, 87, 131
Coleridge, Samuel Taylor 14, 92, 145
colonial history (British) 109–11, 140, 143, 196
Cookbooks (Potter-themed) 45–6
Copeland, Marion 51
Corden, James 124
Cosslett, Tess 11–12, 26, 44, 146, 166, 194
Country Life (magazine) 105
Coverley, Merlin 196
Craik, Dinah 41
Crisp, Clement 38
Cryptogamic Society of Scotland 96
cryptogams 96
Cusack, Niamh 124

Dahl, Roald 167–8
Daniel, Carolyn 40–1, 43
Darwin, Charles 4, 194
De Quincey, Thomas 93, 196
Deakin, Roger 149, 155
death
   Potter's own 5, 15, 22, 78, 103, 173
   in Potter's writing 8, 13, 47, 159
Debord, Guy (*see also* psychogeography) 196
DEFRA (*Landscapes Review*) 94
Dennison, Matthew 16, 112
Dickens, Charles 57–8
Disney, Walt 123, 124, 125

Index

Dixie, Lady Florence 130
Dobrin, Arnold 45
Doyle, Arthur Conan 29

ecofeminism 51–3
ecosystems 98, 102, 105, 154, 184
Eliot, T. S. 4
environmental writing for children
    Potter's development of 4–5, 10, 11–12,
        49–53, 146–51, 153–4, 157–8
    and women writers 101, 145–6, 148–9

Fairy Caravan, The (*see also* 'The Fairy in
    the Oak') 4, 10, 12, 22, 28, 34–5,
    50, 57–9, 61, 64–5, 71, 83, 101,
    116–17, 133, 147–50, 153–6,
    179, 184
'Fairy in the Oak, The' 50–3, 65, 154–5, 171–2
fairy tales 44, 64, 84–5, 157, 168
    'Bluebeard' (*see also Sister Anne*) 23–4,
        64, 84–7, 133, 161–4, 168–70
    'Cinderella' 134, 138
    'Elves and the Shoemaker, The' 180
    'Hansel and Gretel' 44, 168
    'Little Red Riding Hood' 99, 138, 157–8
    Potter's illustrations for 115, 138
    'Sleeping Beauty' 114–15, 138
fairyland 18, 48, 118
Faulkner, Neil 126–7
feminism; feminist (*see also* ecofeminism)
    51, 85, 130, 135, 170
Fielding, Henry 179–80
fin de siècle 4, 76, 187
First World War 4, 54, 173–6
Flood, Alison 125
Freud, Sigmund 35, 159–60, 164

Gaskell, William 18, 27
Gay, John 114
Gilbert, Sandra 18
Gilbert and Sullivan 186–7
global reception (*see also* translations of
    Potter's work)
    in America (*see* American
        correspondents and readers)
    in Japan 66–7, 97, 122
Gluck, Will 124–5
Goldthwaite, John 5, 64, 75, 139–40, 141,
    142–4
Gothic 12, 84, 86, 138, 156, 160–3
    coastal Gothic 161–2

Grahame, Kenneth 11, 40, 44, 143, 156
Greene, Grahame 2
Gregory, Ian 93–4
Grimm brothers (*see also* fairy tales) 44, 99,
    168, 180
Gubar, Susan 18

Hair, Donald 116
Harris, Joel Chandler (*see also* Uncle
    Remus) 64, 136–7, 139, 141–3
Heelis, William (husband) 15–16, 112, 134,
    173, 174
Herdwick sheep 22, 61, 91
Hildesheimer & Faulkner (publisher) 79
Hilter, Adolph (*see also* Second World War)
    176–7
Hobbs, Anne Stevenson 97, 99, 136, 137,
    141, 143
holidays (Potter family) 5, 18, 29, 41, 88–9,
    104, 131, 191
    holiday journals; travel writing 80–3,
        95, 102
    illness during 69, 70
    memories of 41, 118, 129
Hollindale, Peter 9
Holman Hunt, William 166, 186
Humble, Nicki 47
Hutton, Caroline (cousin) 29, 71, 73, 78,
    131–2, 134

Invalid Children's Aid Association (ICAA)
    37, 72

Jamie, Kathleen 7

Kalnay, Erica 97, 100, 102
Keeling, Kara 167
Kelly, Matthew 94, 103, 105, 108, 109, 110
Kew Gardens 95–6, 182, 197
Kingsley, Charles 62, 199
Kipling, Rudyard 143
Kutzer, M. Daphne 1, 2, 4, 20–1, 26, 32, 42,
    57–8, 68, 75, 84, 114, 129, 156–7,
    169, 180–1, 182

Lake District Defence Society 104
Lake District (locations)
    Ambleside 108
    Castle Cottage 5, 64, 87
    Coniston 36, 88, 103, 109
    Derwentwater 88, 89, 159–60

Index

Esthwaite 90, 103
Fawe Park 88
Furness Abbey 159
Grasmere 36, 110, 122
Hawkshead Hall 159
Hill Top 20–1, 89, 90, 93, 104, 110, 124
Keswick 108, 122, 159–60
Lingholm 88, 159
Low Wray 104
Newlands valley 89
Sawrey 12, 21, 65, 89, 90, 95, 104–5, 117, 173
Troutbeck Tongue 65, 117, 164, 177
Windermere 51, 64, 88, 93, 103, 104, 105–7, 108, 109
    Cockshott Point 105–7
    Wray Castle 88, 104
Lake District National Park 4, 89, 93, 94, 109
Lake District tourism
    Potter's impact on 89–91, 93–4, 97
Lake Poets, the 92–3
Lane, Margaret 11, 13, 15, 16, 84
Lear, Edward 2
Lear, Linda 15, 76, 91, 98, 121–2, 123, 145–6
Leech, Helen (maternal grandmother) 23
Leech, John (maternal grandfather) 110
Leigh, Vivien 123
Linder, Leslie 3, 17, 66, 70, 75–6, 77–8, 87
Linnean Society 95–6, 182
Lister, Anne 77
Lockhart, John Gibson 179
London (locations and places of interest)
    Bolton Gardens 75, 80, 182, 193, 199
    Grosvener Gallery 186
    Kensington 10, 80, 193, 195–200
    Kensington Gardens 10, 198
    Kew Gardens 95, 96, 182, 197
    Natural History Museum 95, 197
    South Kensington Museum (now the Victoria and Albert Museum) 24, 197–8
    Zoological Gardens (Regent's Park Zoo) 19, 55, 80, 193–5, 197, 199
'Lonely Hills, The' 35, 58, 164–5, 177–8
Lopaz, Barry 11
Lotz, Sarah 168
Lovell-Smith, Rose 85, 86, 161, 169, 181

MacDonald, Ruth K. 2, 105, 112, 141
Macfarlane, Robert 149

Mackey, Margaret 120, 122, 124, 125
Mahony, Bertha (later Miller) 61
Martineau, Harriet 108
Massee, George 96
McIntosh, Charles (Charlie) 96, 97, 98
McKay, David (publisher) 61
Mead, Rebecca 125
Mellor, Anne K. 163
Millais, John Everett 27, 118, 188, 189, 190
Milne, A. A. 143
Miss Potter (2006 film) 16–17, 49, 144
'Mole Catcher's Burying, The' 12–13, 171–2
Monbiot, George 46, 91
Moore, Anne Carroll 61–2, 64
Moore, Annie (née Carter) 18, 68
Moore, Eric 57, 160
Moore, Freda 24
Moore, Noel 68, 139, 193
Morecambe Bay 89, 161–4
Morris, Jackie 149
Morrison, Blake 1
Morse, Jane Crowell 3, 64, 65, 107
Morton, Timothy 102, 164–5
mycology; mycological studies 9, 76, 95–102, 150, 182

nature literacy (ecoliteracy) 152
Neill, Sam 124
'New Woman', The 131–2, 134–5
Nicholson, Nancy 173
Nicholson, Norman 90
nursery rhymes
    Potter's collections of (*see also Cecily Parsley's Nursery Rhymes* and *Appley Dapply's Nursery Rhymes*) 99–100
    in Potter's fiction 113–14, 137

Oakmen, The 173–4
O'Farrell, Maggie 168
'On the Germination of the Spores of Agaricineae' 76, 95–6, 182
'Over the Hills and Far Away' (*see also The Fairy Caravan*) 116

Packham, Jimmy 162
Page, Judith 36, 53, 93, 146
Paget, Sidney 29
Parker, Elizabeth 156, 158
Paston-Williams, Sara 45–6

211

Index

Perrault, Charles (*see also* fairy tales) 84, 85–6, 87
Peter Rabbit (2018 film) 124–5
Peter Rabbit 2: The Runaway (2021 film) 124
Peter Rabbit's Almanac for 1929 30, 121, 127, 147
pets 7–8, 19, 179, 183
Pollard, Scott 167
postcolonial theory and practice (*see also* Edward Said) 140, 143–4
Potter, Bertram (brother) 7, 17, 195, 197
Potter, Edmund (paternal grandfather) 108–9, 110, 154, 197
Potter, Helen (mother) 17, 68, 70–1, 129
Potter, Rupert (father) 5, 57, 129, 186, 187, 195
Pre-Raphaelites, the 186, 189–90
psychogeography 196

Radcliffe, Ann 163
Raine, Kathleen 90
Ransome, Arthur 63–4, 88, 91
Rawnsley, Canon Hardwicke 52, 104, 105, 107, 109
Robbie, Margot 124
Robison, Roselee 18, 75
'"Roots" of the Peter Rabbit Tales' 21, 48
Roscoe, Sir Henry (uncle) 182
Rossetti, Dante Gabriel 188
Rousseau, Jean-Jacques 26, 88
Routledge, Dame Patricia 16
Rowling, J. K. 1, 40, 120
Ruskin, John 23, 93, 103–4, 186, 187–8
    campaign against railways 105, 107–9

Said, Edward 140, 143
Scotland (locations)
    Dalguise House 18, 118, 128
    Dunkeld 55
    Lennel House 5
    Tay valley 118
Scott, Sir Walter 5, 106, 179
Second World War 173, 176–8
Shakespeare, William 5, 66, 97, 155, 168
Shelley, Percy Bysshe 151
'side-shows' 122, 127, 191
Sister Anne 23–4, 61, 84–7, 89, 133, 161–4, 169–70
Smith, Elise 36, 53, 93, 146
Story of Miss Moppet, The 32

Tailor of Gloucester, The 14, 24–6, 29, 64, 72, 83, 146, 180–1, 182–3, 198
Tale of Benjamin Bunny, The 20, 62, 71–2, 84, 121, 136, 191
Tale of the Flopsy Bunnies, The 42, 66, 121, 133, 142, 181
Tale of Ginger and Pickles, The 44, 89
Tale of Jemima Puddle-Duck, The 23, 44, 46, 66, 90, 146, 157
Tale of Johnny Town-Mouse, The 41, 71, 132, 140, 166, 174–6
Tale of Little Pig Robinson, The 12, 42, 44, 45, 61, 191
Tale of Mr. Jeremy Fisher, The 26, 44, 45, 90, 100, 132, 160–1
Tale of Mr. Tod, The 43, 44, 84, 136, 137, 138, 141–2, 167, 170
Tale of Mrs. Tiggy-Winkle, The 20, 49, 89, 105, 132
Tale of Mrs. Tittlemouse, The 11, 32–3, 41, 100, 132
Tale of Peter Rabbit, The 1, 11, 26, 29, 30, 38, 42, 48–9, 62, 65–6, 68, 83, 85, 97, 99, 120–2, 123, 132, 139, 141, 146, 152–3, 157, 167, 168, 171, 177, 190
Tale of the Pie and the Patty-Pan, The 45, 195
Tale of Pigling Bland, The 20–1, 33–4, 45, 89, 105, 112–16, 117, 133, 156, 173
Tale of Samuel Whiskers, The 11, 20–1, 44, 167–8
Tale of Squirrel Nutkin, The 32, 42, 89, 100, 146, 152, 169, 170, 191
Tale of Timmy Tiptoes, The 1, 65, 68, 133, 146, 152–3, 195
Tale of Tom Kitten, The 26–7, 89, 105, 132, 146
Tale of Two Bad Mice, The 41, 133, 179, 182
Tales of Beatrix Potter (ballet) 36–9, 123–4
talking-animal stories 11–12, 43–5, 46, 49–50, 146, 194
'Toad's Tea Party, The' 99
Taylor, Joanna 93–4
Taylor, Judy 3, 17, 22, 69
Tenniel, John 27, 68
Tennyson, Alfred Lord 114–16
Thackeray, Anne 198–9
Thompson, Ian 51, 89, 159
translations of Potter's work 61–2, 65–7

Index

Trimmer, Sarah 145
Twain, Mark 63, 143

Uncanny, the; Unheimlich (*see also*
    Sigmund Freud) 35, 86, 89, 96,
    159–61, 164–5
Uncle Remus books (*see also* Chandler, Joel
    Harris) 5, 64, 136–44
UNESCO
    'Cultural Landscape' 53, 91–4, 105
    English Lake District Nomination 91–3
    Lake District World Heritage
        inscription 91, 94
Unitarianism 146
Urry, John 94

Wag-by-Wall 13–14, 61, 64, 72, 147
Warne (publishing house) 1, 37, 61, 62,
    65–6, 72, 89, 120, 173–4, 190
Warne, Harold 137, 174
Warne, Louie 20
Warne, Millie 133, 173
Warne, Norman 16, 99–100, 120, 133–4, 198

Whalley, Joyce Irene 136, 137, 141, 143
Whistler, James McNeill 186, 187–8, 192
Wilde, Oscar 23, 187
'Woman Question', The 28, 130, 131–2, 134
Woolf, Virginia 4, 75
Wordsworth, Dorothy 73–4, 75, 77, 92, 110
Wordsworth, William 26–7, 68, 73, 88, 89,
    110, 145, 148–9, 178
    campaign against railways 50–1, 105,
        107–9
    legacy in the Lake District 91–4, 103–4,
        122
    Potter quoting 34, 50, 106, 177–8
World of Peter Rabbit and Friends, The
    (TV series) 124

Yellow Book, The 187
Yoshida, Shin-ichi 66–7

Zellweger, Renée 16, 17, 49
Zeppelins 174
Zipes, Jack 120
Zobel Marshall, Emily 136, 139–41, 143, 144